Crabbe's Arabesque

Crabbe's Arabesque

Social Drama in the
Poetry of George Crabbe

Ronald B. Hatch

MCGILL–QUEEN'S UNIVERSITY PRESS

Montreal and London 1976

© McGill–Queen's University Press 1976
International Standard Book Number 0–7735–0250–5
Legal Deposit fourth quarter 1976
Bibliothèque nationale du Québec

This book has been published with the help
of a grant from the Humanities Research
Council of Canada using funds provided by
the Canada Council

Design by Richard Hendel
Printed in Great Britain by
Robert Stockwell Ltd, London SE1

To S. E. READ

Contents

Chronology

1754
24 December, born at Aldborough (now Aldeburgh), Suffolk, the son of a collector of salt-duties whose salary is £10 a year.

c. 1762
Sent to school at Bungay on "the borders of Norfolk."

1766
Sent for two years to "a country boarding school" at Stowmarket, Suffolk.

1768
Apprenticed to Smith, a poor apothecary at Wickham Brook, where he is forced to help with farm work.

1771
Apprenticed for four years to Mr. Page, surgeon and apothecary at Woodbridge, under "very favourable conditions."

1772
Meets and shortly after becomes engaged to Miss Sarah Elmy, the "Mira" of the early poems. Publishes verse in *Wheble's Magazine*.

1775
Inebriety published anonymously at Ipswich. Returns penniless to Slaughden Quay to work with his father as a warehouseman. Then sets up as an apothecary-surgeon in Aldborough.

1776
Attends lectures on midwifery in London.

1777
Returns to his practice in Aldborough.

1780
Goes to London with £5 borrowed from Dudley North to become a man of letters.

1781
Appeals successfully to Edmund Burke for patronage. *The Library* published by Dodsley. Burke introduces him to Charles Fox and Sir Joshua Reynolds. Ordained deacon, with the title of curate to the Rev. Benet, of Aldborough.

1782
Ordained priest. Becomes domestic chaplain to the Duke of Rutland at Belvoir Castle.

1783
Dr. Johnson reads and praises *The Village* in MS, and alters the opening lines. *The Village* published. Marries Sarah Elmy after an 11-year engagement.

1785
The Newspaper published. Becomes curate at Stathern, near Belvoir. Meets Dr. Edmund Cartwright, inventor of the power loom.

1788
Presented with the livings of Muston (Leicestershire) and West Allington (Lincolnshire), the joint income being £270 a year.

c. 1790
Illness leads to taking of "opiates," which continues for the rest of his life.

1792
Moves to Suffolk, leaving his parishes in the charge of curates.

1795
"The Natural History of the Vale of Belvoir" published in J. Nichols's *The History and Antiquities of the County of Leicester.*

1796
Wife's mental illness begins (manic-depressive?) and continues until her death.

1801—1802
Writes and burns three novels

1805
Returns to Muston.

1807
Poems published. Includes "The Parish Register," "Sir Eustace Grey," "The Hall of Justice," and earlier poems.

1810
The Borough published.

1812
Tales in Verse published.

1813
Wife dies. Crabbe dangerously ill.

1814
Resigns Muston and Allington. Moves to Trowbridge, Wiltshire, as rector. Engaged briefly to Charlotte Ridout, considerably younger than himself.

1816
Finishes "The Insanity of Ambitious Love."

1817
Makes the first of several visits to London at the invitation of the poet Rogers. Meets Moore and Campbell.

1819
Tales of the Hall published.

1822
Visits Sir Walter Scott in Edinburgh.

1825
Appointed justice of the peace.

1828
Meets Wordsworth and Southey.

1832
Dies at Trowbridge, aged 77.

1834
The Poetical Works, in 8 vols., published. Vol. 1 consists of his son's *Life.* Vol. 8 contains *Posthumous Tales.*

Preface

In writing about the poet George Crabbe, I was conscious that many readers would probably smile politely and agree that Crabbe was a poet worth reading; indeed, should be more widely read. But I was aware also that most of these same people, if pressed, would have put in a caveat that they were unsure about the overall impact of Crabbe's poetry, that they felt unclear about the tone and direction of many of Crabbe's individual poems. Or as a puzzled admirer of Crabbe's poetry recently remarked to me: "Crabbe always seems to take away what he gives." This uncertainty about Crabbe's poetry is fairly widespread, I believe, and in part stems from the difficulty of coming to terms with a poet who generally works in the Augustan couplet of Pope, but whose cast of mind is very different from that of those who saw eighteenth-century Britain as "a new Augustan Reign." Even more crucial to an understanding of Crabbe than his verse form—as I have attempted to demonstrate in this study—is his manner of handling conflicting social, moral, and religious questions in terms of a drama where the ideas can rarely be subsumed into an integrated theory, but are introduced as independent entities, each with its own degree of truth. Nor should this be unexpected when it is recalled that Crabbe is heir to the tradition of Swift, Sterne, and Smollett, none of whom could be said to have advanced his views of man's condition in an orderly, linear manner. Born in 1754, and very much influenced by the works of the great Augustan masters, Crabbe had to develop for himself a poetic form that would hold together the contradictions so evident in the "Augustan synthesis."

Perhaps the most characteristic feature of Crabbe's poetry is his technique of including within a single poem a number of different and often contradictory attitudes to a social problem or human dilemma, without committing himself to one point of view. In many of the poems, Crabbe employs a number of "voices" to represent different opinions. To some extent this technique may have been a subterfuge to allow Crabbe to gain a hearing for new ideas among his conservative readers. But there are a host of other possible reasons as well, which I shall be treating in the course of the discussion. However, my chief aim is not to settle the reasons why Crabbe wrote the way he did (which in the end it is impossible to determine) but to point out the recurring patterns created by his opposing attitudes, and to suggest how these give his poems a richness and variety which is ultimately far more satisfying than simplistic answers.

Since my intention is to show Crabbe's development in the handling of dramatic structures in which conflicting questions clash or are reconciled, it seemed best to choose one of Crabbe's central preoccupations and follow it through in his poetry. To this end I have chosen to study in particular Crabbe's handling of social issues. My main concern is not with the issues *per se*, but with Crabbe's development as an artist in presenting them. Indeed, in his last poems, I undertake to show how the term "social critic" is no longer wide enough to encompass Crabbe's deepened perception of what constitutes the social. At one time I contemplated exploring the content of Crabbe's social criticism, but his own poetry quickly revealed that social criticism in literature cannot be divorced from artistic achievement. This is not to say that an investigation of the background of particular social problems, showing contemporary social and literary influences, is not helpful, nor that a comparison with Crabbe's contemporaries is not enlightening. Indeed, I have attempted both. Yet as Crabbe himself quickly discovered, if he were to give an accurate presentation of late eighteenth-century England, then he would have to find a means of literary presentation that would distort his vision as little as possible. It is, of course, this sense of the need to create a poetic form sufficient to the complexity of his vision that makes Crabbe an artist and not simply a versifier interested in social questions.

In his early poetry Crabbe employed the device of the single narrator to give *his* account of the rural poor of England as opposed to the false and artificial views of the pastoralists. Yet even in such early poems as *The Village* and "The Hall of Justice," Crabbe's sense of the disjunction between "what is" and "what ought to be" led him to introduce a second perspective to qualify his original account. As his understanding of man's relationship to society matured, and his mastery of narrative technique became more assured, he moved away from describing social questions from an omniscient point of view, and in poems such as *The Borough* began to employ a narrator whose views could be challenged by the events and people he described. In the final development of his style, *Tales of the Hall,* Crabbe found that he required not one narrator but many, so that his views about the subtle interaction of personality, morality, society, and religion could find an adequate expression. It is here, in *Tales of the Hall,* that we find the culminating expression of his profound and lifelong search for "the real."

In the end, however, Crabbe's importance as a commentator and analyst is related directly to his imaginative profundity and to his linguistic powers as a writer. Crabbe possesses both, but because he writes in the genre of the long narrative poem the patterning and the cumulative effect of his writing is not easy to develop in brief quotation. As Francis Jeffrey observed, "the pattern of Crabbe's Arabesque is so large, that there is no getting a fair specimen of it without taking in a good space." Moreover, the twentieth-century penchant for verbal acrobatics and "intensity" of feeling has made it difficult to value the long poem for its own special merits. And yet, time and again, it will be seen that Crabbe's drama of voices and opposing points of view creates an enveloping panorama of the human condition altogether remarkable for its depth and comprehension.

I wish to thank a number of people who kindly read the manuscript at various stages of completion. John Price, drawing on his extensive knowledge of the eighteenth century, was often able to point out sources for Crabbe's literary and intellectual development.

Both Howard Mills and Michael Black offered suggestions which improved the strength of my argument. I wish also to thank the Humanities Research Council's anonymous reader for encouragement and truly painstaking attention to detail. I owe special thanks to George Payerle for his Herculean help in reducing a large and cumbersome manuscript to a practicable length. His artist's sense of form added immensely to the book's shape. Veronica, my wife, has read the manuscript numerous times; her fine ear for prose rhythms has saved me from much cacophony and jargon.

Several institutions have given me generous financial support during the writing of this study. I am grateful to the Commonwealth Scholarship Program for the grant under which the initial research was completed. The Canada Council was also most helpful in granting a Leave Fellowship, which gave me the leisure and freedom to finish the writing. I am also grateful to the University of British Columbia for its research grant to cover the cost of typing the manuscript. And to the Humanities Research Council I am indebted for a grant in aid of publication. I should like to thank John Murray for permission to quote from his manuscript collection.

Earlier versions of portions of this study have appeared in *Eighteenth-Century Studies* and *Philological Quarterly*. Excerpts from *New Poems by George Crabbe*, edited by Arthur Pollard, are reprinted by permission of Liverpool University Press.

Chapter 1
Sad splendour

I

That the poetry of the late eighteenth century is both enigmatic in tone and difficult to classify, few readers in the period will deny. Recently, however, scholars have been adopting a more positive approach to the old complaint that many poets of this period found difficulty in creating a "voice" for their poetry. Northrop Frye, for instance, has suggested that one way of looking at the writing of this period is to see the work of art, not as "a product" with a single voice, but as a "process" which incorporates moods and voices of the ever-shifting present.[1] Similarly, Martin Price has argued of this period that "the very range of styles that are tried on makes one all the more aware of the nature of style itself."[2] One apparent reason why writers of the late eighteenth century experienced such difficulty in creating a voice was their growing awareness that both philosophy and science had revealed an undoubted if somewhat confused relation between the perceiver and the perceived. Blake's comment—"the eye altering, alters all /. . . And the flat Earth becomes a Ball"—declares that the most fundamental facts depend upon the mode of perception or the angle from which they are viewed. While the influence of the writings of Locke, Hume, and Montesquieu made it increasingly apparent to writers throughout the eighteenth century that the choice of perspective was crucial to their themes, it was by no means clear which should be chosen.

The poet George Crabbe is typical of many of the post-Augustan writers, such as Thomson, Shenstone, Goldsmith, and even Johnson, in that his work embodies alternate or antithetic visions of the world which result from a conflict between consciously-held ideas and those developed under the pressure of creative practice. That this is not an entirely unusual state of affairs confined solely to artists has been demonstrated in recent times by taxonomists in their important discovery that most people generally use two or more unrelated principles of organization to describe familiar phenomena.[3] In *The Village* (1783), for instance, Crabbe's attack on the pastoral representation of country life, with its ethically oriented universe, leads him to develop an empirical outlook which establishes man, not as a unique creation with an immortal soul, but as another species of fauna. As is well known, however, this view is complicated in the second half of the poem with the introduction of the figure of Robert Manners in the idealistic mode, countering the empirical, descriptive approach of the early part of the poem.

Crabbe's growing awareness of the problems implicit in the choice of an appropriate perspective can be seen in those early poems which were loosely grouped together by Sir Adolphus Ward as "juvenilia" in the three-volume Cambridge edition of Crabbe's *Works*. There is no space here for a full discussion of these poems, but they deserve a wider audience than they have so far received. Several are of high quality and deserve recognition in their own right. Taken together, these early poems offer a chronological account of how Crabbe achieved his characteristic and somewhat paradoxical approach to social questions. In "Midnight," written around 1779, Crabbe is already grappling with the problem of finding a "voice" for his view of the world. A partial imitation of the graveyard school, the poem permits Crabbe to use as his narrator a man of vision set aside from his fellow men. Acutely aware of his skimpy formal education and his lower-class origins, Crabbe recognizes that he cannot write in the same tradition as that of most previous poets. Respectfully the young poet asks the men of learning to forgive him for tampering with their subjects, but in the seeming humility of this address to the "Wise" lies a Socratic irony. Quite obviously Crabbe has no faith in their type of wisdom:

> Forgive me then, ye Wise, who seem awake,
> A Midnight Song, and let your Censure sleep.[4]

Since the Wise only "seem" to be awake, their "wisdom" can be a knowledge only of other times and other places. Crabbe implies that the situation has changed, and that acknowledged men of letters are no longer competent to deal with new conditions. The great poets of the past—Homer, Virgil, Milton—all dealt with grand and beautiful themes; Crabbe feels the modern age needs poets to describe man's disappointments in everyday life. As he says, theirs was a "blest Task, a gloomier task is mine" (111). Akenside for instance, Crabbe feels, "led the soul thro' Nature, and display'd / Imagination's Pleasures to its Eye" (109-10). While recognizing the value of Akenside's themes, Crabbe feels that his own experience of the bleak Suffolk coast, and his continual struggle to earn enough to feed and clothe himself, have ill-equipped him to write poetry in the same grand style.

Akenside, it will be recalled, had maintained that a true poet would concern himself only with the greatest themes:

> Who but rather turns
> To Heaven's broad fire his unconstrained view,
> Than to the glimmering of a waxen flame?
> Who that, from Alpine heights, his labouring eye
> Shoots round the wide horizon, to survey
> Nilus or Ganges rolling his bright wave
> Through mountains, plains, through empires black with
>   shade,
> And continents of sand; will turn his gaze
> To mark the windings of a scanty rill
> That murmurs at his feet?[5]

Yet Crabbe want to write about the very subjects Akenside thought poets should scorn; Crabbe wants to turn away from the grand and marvellous to detail the minute. As a consequence, he believes that he must begin a new style of poetry:

> He, tyed to some poor Spot, where e'en the rill
> That owns him Lord untasted steals away,
> Hallows a Clod, and spurns Immensity.   (126–28)

Not only are the themes and forms of the past insufficient to handle the new situations, they are obstacles to a clear presentation of the new problems.

In "Midnight," the youthful Crabbe had humbly requested his audience to permit his new perspective; by 1783, the time of *The Village*, Crabbe is adamant about the correctness of his view. Most of the previous poetry of the century about life in the country had strayed widely from the truth, he feels, because the poets themselves had been unacquainted with village life and had consequently looked to models from the past for their inspiration. By turning to authority or by relying on the "Muses" for their inspiration instead of referring to the empirical world for their evidence, the poets had distorted their descriptions. Crabbe notes:

> . . . the Muses sing of happy swains,
> Because the Muses never knew their pains.   (I. 21–22)

Since the Muses, or the traditional sources of poetic inspiration, have nothing to say about the contemporary world, Crabbe takes upon himself to "paint the Cot, / As Truth will paint it, and as Bards will not" (I. 53–54). In part Crabbe is claiming that complete verisimilitude to the ordinary facts of the world is antithetical to the more traditional concerns of poetry which had relied upon the Muses' divine inspiration. But also he is suggesting that communication between the divine and the human, where it has been attempted, has led to misleading interpretations about the material world. Crabbe, it should be noted, is not running the risk of Thamyris, the Thracian bard who was deprived of sight when he boasted himself the equal of the Muses, since Crabbe is not competing with the Muses. Whereas in Homer and Hesiod, the Muses, around the altar of Zeus, had glorified the deeds of gods and heroes, Crabbe wishes to take over a new province of poetry that the Muses had never claimed; he is not inspired to write of divine harmony, but will attempt to deal with evidence manifest to the five senses.

Crabbe in a curious way resembles Keats in that both had a strong desire for concrete perception. In reading Keats one feels that man is rediscovering his body; and in reading Crabbe one feels that man is rediscovering his social world. Of course the differences between Crabbe's approach and that of the Romantic poets are almost total. Whereas Crabbe at this time was attempting to discover *the* correct perspective from which man's condition could be viewed, the Romantic poets were interested in showing that any given perspective of the world, no matter how powerfully rooted, was a product of man's making. For Crabbe in *The Village* there exist "weighty griefs" and "real ills" which he scorns to hide "In tinsel trappings of poetic pride" (I. 48). In order to impress upon his readers that his descriptions of hardship were not merely poetic effusions, Crabbe felt it necessary, in later editions of *The Village*, to add a footnote to this passage explaining the circumstances of the peasant. The social evils described in the poem were to be read as documentaries, not poetic images. For Crabbe, a dangerous schism had grown up between the imaginative arts and the real world.

Crabbe, however, also recognized that the sort of verse he was beginning to find himself most at home with—the heroic couplet—gave his poetry a good many affinities to the eighteenth-century pastoral. This of course created problems for him in his desire to demolish the pastoral myth that a life of ease and pleasure existed in England. So, just as Raleigh answered Marlowe's "The Passionate Shepherd to his Love" by having the nymph reply to the shepherd in his own style, Crabbe ensures that his criticism of the classical pastoral is formulated in a classical manner:

> In fairer scenes, where peaceful pleasures spring,
> Tityrus, the pride of Mantuan swains, might sing:
> But charmed by him, or smitten with his views,
> Shall modern poets court the Mantuan muse?
> From Truth and Nature shall we widely stray,
> Where Fancy leads, or Virgil led the way?[6]

Written in the formal style, with classical allusions, these lines appealed greatly to the Augustan sensibility,[7] and led Johnson, to whom *The Village* was shown in manuscript, to interest himself in a rewording which Crabbe accepted.[8] But the point is that in spite of their classical appearance, they are a repudiation of the classical aesthetic as practised in the eighteenth century. Crabbe is claiming that Roman models will cause English poets to stray from the truth of English life. But it should also be noted that in claiming the Muses cannot give a better picture than that of the truthful documentary, Crabbe is consciously creating a parallel between his guiding model—empirical observation—and the inspiration of the nine Muses. Thus is he attempting to strike out a new path for poetry without appearing to overthrow traditional patterns. The poem's opening lines maintain the voice, while refuting the substance of the pastoral. As will be seen later, this satire at the beginning of the poem, before the introduction of the social documentary, allows Crabbe to alter the speaking voice at the poem's conclusion.

Also worthy of note is that Johnson's revision, the lines now usually preferred, partially obscure Crabbe's intention. Where Johnson declares that the poet would go astray if he followed Virgil and not his "Fancy," in the original, Crabbe had said that the poet would be mistaken if he followed either Virgil or his "Fancy." Obviously what Crabbe wanted was poetry which incorporated direct observation, and which did not attempt either "fanciful" or Virgilian commentary.

It is hardly necessary to observe that Crabbe was by no means the first to criticize the pastoral. The controversy between Philips and Pope at the beginning of the century is well known, as is Gay's burlesque in *The Shepherd's Week* and Richard Jago's in *The Scavengers*, satires of the pastoral based on the antipathy between character and situation, personality and environment.[9] Johnson also had added his powerful voice against the pastoral, in Ramblers 36 and 37, and in his critique of *Lycidas*, which no doubt partially accounts for his admiration of *The Village*. However, Crabbe's main argument is not with classical poetry *per se*, but with the inclusion of classical subject matter in descriptions of English country life. Crabbe no doubt realized as well as we do that the landscape of the traditional pastoral was meant to symbolize a state of innocence, and not to represent a physical environment. Yet the pastoral underwent some extremely curious changes in the eighteenth century, first when Pope altered the tradition by including "the best side only of a shepherd's life,"[10] and later when poets such as William Shenstone and his friend Richard Jago introduced classical shepherds into their poems of topographic description.[11] The result, a curious mixture of myth and geography, was neither symbolic nor naturalistic. It is this eighteenth-century development of the pastoral which Crabbe is denouncing.

Because *The Village* describes the villagers' harsh and unjust life it has been often assumed that Crabbe was making an appeal to the reader's sympathy. Yet this is to misunderstand the tradition in which Crabbe was writing, and to ignore the poem's tone. If he had simply asked his readers to pity the poor, he would not have been offering anything new, and he would not have been giving a faithful account of the "real picture." *The Village* was written in protest against a particularly obnoxious version of sentimentalized humanitarianism which was rife in the period 1740–90. Very often throughout the century when the poor were discussed the emphasis fell not on the condition of the poor, but on the feelings of the observer. This can be seen in Richard Steele's comment on the paupers of London: "Such miserable Objects affect the compassionate Beholder with dismal Ideas, discompose the Chearfulness of his Mind, and deprive him of the Pleasure that he might otherwise take in surveying the Grandeur of our Metropolis."[12] One sees immediately that Steele is interested as much in the effect of poverty on the mind of the beholder as he is in poverty itself.

Had Crabbe made a simple plea for the reader's sympathy towards the poor, instead of adopting a narrator who could satirize the pastoral and objectively describe the rural labourers, he would inevitably have fallen into a series of those stock epithets which one finds attributed to any member of the leisured class claiming to fulfil Shaftesbury's ideal of the man of taste, humanity, and culture. It was standard procedure to include in poems as widely different as Pomfret's *The Choice*, John Philips' *Cyder*, and James Thomson's

Winter an acknowledgement that the true gentleman and humanitarian remembered and pitied the poor. Even when Richard Savage
in *The Wanderer* (1729) wished to show his dislike for contemporary attitudes about the "lazy poor" by describing the vagrants
being harassed by the wealthy, he found it difficult to escape
sentimentality. In the following passage one can observe the slide
from honest indignation to self-satisfied charity:

> But soft! the Cripple our Approach descries,
> And to the Gate, though weak, officious hies.
> I spring preventive, and unbar the way,
> Then, turning, with a Smile of Pity say,
> Here, Friend!—this little, copper Alms receive;
> Instance of will, without the Pow'r to give.[13]

The conjunction of "Friend" with "little, copper Alms" is particularly distasteful, and the debased coinage of charity is immediately
apparent. Throughout the century countless poets retailed the
pleasures of charity. No doubt they all had a genuine humanitarian
feeling for the poor, but when they expressed these feelings in
verse, the stress fell on the act of charity, on the way this act placed
the "good man" in harmony with nature and God, rather than on
the plight of the poor man.[14] What Crabbe needed was a narrator
who could present the necessary detail while remaining discreetly
in the background. With his unobtrusive narrator Crabbe could
avoid "the graceful tear that streams for others' woes" in Mark
Akenside's *The Pleasures of Imagination*. John Armstrong went a
step further than Akenside when he equated charity with good
taste: "Of all Taste the noblest and the best" was to "behold in
Man's obnoxious State / Scenes of Content, and happy Turns of
Fate." Armstrong believed that the "Man of generous Mould"
exercises the most refined taste when he helps to bring content to
the poor, and as proof, he cites how these are "generous Deeds as
we with Tears admire."[15] Such poets implicitly assumed poverty
to be a part of the rightful order of things, with benevolence the
equivalent social virtue. But acquiescence in the poverty leads to

self-admiration and sentimentality in the benevolence. It becomes a kind of self-indulgence.[16] And this Crabbe wanted to avoid.

One can better understand Crabbe's vehement dislike of pastoral when it is realized that as a result of the emphasis placed on the feelings of the philanthropist, the poor were no longer described as distressed people, but pastoral shepherds idling in a green and merry land. Since poets wished to emphasize the beauty of the act of charity, they found it necessary to describe beautiful surroundings and not empty commons. The countryside in *The Pleasures of Imagination* contains "every charm." Its beauty is an emblem of the good life nature intends for the villagers. All too frequently the idea of picturesque poverty is conjured up in order to feel a glow at the thought of relieving it. And since poverty is always there, the glow is always possible.

Once one sees the connection between the pastoral and humanitarian poetry, Crabbe's attack on "sleepy bards" should be all the more understandable and his purpose in *The Village* easier to define. He is not developing the idea that the poor should be helped (the humanitarians had made this theme appear trite), but rather that one must recognize the poor and their conditions before attempting to help them. In many ways, Crabbe's *The Village* is anti-humanitarian, because in the 1780s "humanitarian" entailed a sentimental attitude to the poor. I am not saying that no genuine humanitarian poetry was written before Crabbe's time. Obviously sections of Pope's *Moral Essays* and Thomson's *The Seasons*, Johnson's *London* and Langhorne's *The Country Justice*, show a genuine concern for the poor. The point which needs stressing, however, is that the great mass of humanitarian verse, especially from 1740 to 1780, tended to organize the facts of the material world to create a warmth in the observer. In order to avoid the dangers of a trite humanitarian appeal to the conscience of the rich, Crabbe decided that a different organization of the facts was required, one that actually amassed some detail about the lives of the poor. It is to a discussion of the ways in which Crabbe presented this detail that I now wish to turn.

II

In attempting to distinguish the difference between Crabbe's treatment of the poor in *The Village* and that of earlier eighteenth-century poets, one is often driven to say that Crabbe's portraits are "realistic" or "naturalistic." Indeed, the demands by writers such as Johnson and Crabbe for a reformulation of the literary account of English country life can be seen exemplified in the "rise of the novel" as opposed to the old "romance." Yet terms such as "realism" and "naturalism" have become over-used in recent years; what is required is an explication of Crabbe's technique of portrayal. The most obvious point is Crabbe's choice of his native Aldborough as the setting of the poem. The importance of this lies not so much in the way the features of Aldborough differ from, say, Farnham in Surrey, as in the way the topographic details of a particular place give the poem a locus outside the customary poetic backgrounds. Beginning with the particular, and not with the universal or generic, Crabbe was creating his own world and its own values. In choosing to emphasize certain features of his own area, and thus giving them universal significance, Crabbe was one of the first of a long line of artists such as Thomas Hardy and Robert Frost who created their distinctive world from the particularized details of the surrounding countryside.

The choice of Aldborough as the setting supplied Crabbe with a host of details that could not easily be accommodated to the normal eighteenth-century picture of the world. Just as late eighteenth-century botanists were discovering vast numbers of new plants with new properties that were finally to overthrow their classification system and call into doubt the idea of special creation with each plant embodying its God-given logical essence,[17] so Crabbe's introduction of plants such as the blue bugloss and the slimy mallow forced him (or perhaps "allowed" is a better choice of terminology) to offer an alternative structuring of the world to that ordinarily accepted at the time. In contrast to most eighteenth-century poetry of natural description where the background is meant to suggest benevolence and harmony,[18] the setting of *The Village* creates a sense of inherent evil. Crabbe explains how he was born, not on an ordinary coast, but on a "frowning coast" where the countryside is filled with Manichean forces ready to thwart man's efforts:

> Lo! where the heath, with withering brake grown o'er,
> Lends the light turf that warms the neighbouring poor;
> From thence a length of burning sand appears,
> Where the thin harvest waves its wither'd ears;
> Rank weeds, that every art and care defy,
> Reign o'er the land, and rob the blighted rye:
> There thistles stretch their prickly arms afar,
> And to the ragged infant threaten war;
> There poppies, nodding, mock the hope of toil;
> There the blue bugloss paints the sterile soil;
> Hardy and high, above the slender sheaf,
> The slimy mallow waves her silky leaf;
> O'er the young shoot the charlock throws a shade,
> And clasping tares cling round the sickly blade;
> With mingled tints the rocky coasts abound,
> And a sad splendour vainly shines around.   (1. 63–78)

Mrs. Haddakin has said: "The function of the passage as a whole is to demonstrate that if you look closely enough into a picturesque landscape you are led, by way of agricultural problems, to consider the welfare of human beings."[19] But even more than this, Crabbe's description of "rank weeds" reigning over the land and defying all man's efforts to cultivate anything but the scantest garden for pleasure and use creates the terms by which man inhabits the world. Images such as "clasping tares" and the "slimy mallow" have been carefully chosen to convey the impression that, on the most primeval terms, man has to combat forces of destruction. The inhabitants of the village do not live in a "Happy Valley" where the design of nature is ordered to help man, but on a coast where the sea is swallowing the homes built upon the loose shingle.

The weeds may look splendid to the "sleepy bards" who do not see clearly, but they are a sad sight to the villager attempting to earn a living from the "thin harvest." Crabbe's own viewpoint is interesting, for unlike the labourers who can see only the sadness of the weeds and the sleepy bards who see only the splendour, Crabbe can see both sides. These weeds grow among the sustaining corn, and threaten it, but the principle of growth is there in both weed and corn. The thistles are noble in a way; the poppies are narcotics as well as pretty; the colours are striking; the leaves are "silky." Everything is involved with its opposite: beauty and wastefulness, use and want. "Sad splendour" sums it up.

Crabbe of course is himself open to the same sort of criticism that he made of the earlier "pastoral" poets; for just as they created an ethical universe in which man lives in harmony with nature, so Crabbe has created a universe in which an amoral force involves everything with its opposite to create "sad splendour." But every artist (indeed everyone) must have some organizing principle of selection; what matters is how well the principle accounts for the observed facts and how useful it is in helping to predict as yet unobserved phenomena. Part of what gives the early section of *The Village* so much power is the way the organizing principle that Crabbe posits in nature carries over into the people, or, to use a metaphor from botany, the way the people are rooted in their milieu.

The transition between the landscape and the people is made with devastating understatement. Like the weeds, the people have a sturdy and unruly vigour. But they are not civilized, and in their wild actions, they threaten to overcome the conventions and arts of society. The central notion of "sad splendour" evoked by the setting is seen to have a direct corollary in the people:

> So looks the nymph whom wretched arts adorn,
> Betray'd by man, then left for man to scorn;
> Whose cheek in vain assumes the mimic rose,
> While her sad eyes the troubled breast disclose;
> Whose outward splendour is but folly's dress,
> Exposing most, when most it gilds distress.   (I. 79–84)

Crabbe was never greatly influenced by theories of the natural goodness of man, so that having once established in *The Village* the idea that man as a part of nature is moved by a principle of growth which has little respect for ends, he does not hesitate to draw the conclusion that the people of the village are rude and lawless.

Critics such as René Huchon have made much of the way Crabbe, in Book II, shows his villagers to be brawling drunkards, as if this controverted the intention of Book I.[20] But Crabbe's wish to show the real picture of the poor by no means implies that he wanted to show good villagers living in harsh surroundings; rather he shows how the villagers reflect their environment:

> Here joyless roam a wild amphibious race,
> With sullen wo display'd in every face;
> Who far from civil arts and social fly,
> And scowl at strangers with suspicious eye.   (I. 85–88)

The village then is pre-eminently a place of hostility in which man's role is no different from that of other living things. Man's misery and his viciousness are explained as the counterparts of environment.

In choosing to describe villagers who live "far from civil arts and social," and showing them as a part of nature which has vigour and splendour, but which is amoral, Crabbe developed a view of man and nature which has little in common with the optimism of mid-century poets. Many eighteenth-century writers believed that the new science offered proof that one could see aspects of God through his harmonious and beautiful world. Thomson wrote of Isaac Newton:

> All intellectual eye, our solar round
> First gazing thro', he by the blended power
> Of *gravitation* and *projection* saw
> The whole in silent harmony revolve.[21]

An amateur scientist himself, Crabbe valued the principle of classification which Thomson praises so highly, but as Crabbe said in "Midnight," his was a "horizontal Eye" that saw "all things grey" (line 219). Whereas Thomson believed that Newton's "intellectual eye" gave man insight into the hierarchical laws by which God harmonizes the universe, Crabbe's "horizontal Eye" led to empirical observations that did not assume a moral universe. Thomson began with the assumption that Newton had been able to give a reason for everything, including, in his words, "the yellow waste of idle sands."[22] This traditional view in which man was seen as a unique creation with an immortal soul participating in an ethically organized universe is implicitly challenged by Crabbe's "scientific" method, where he begins by describing the particular, the barren soil of Aldborough, and from this particular attempts to draw conclusions. The difference is crucial and it should be no surprise to find that Crabbe draws the conclusion that man, like all other living things, has to battle in order to live. As an amateur scientist, Crabbe has offered a picture of man in terms of his observed outward actions with no mention of the usual moral and spiritual dimensions.[23]

Yet any description of man in terms of physical environment alone is of course incomplete, and so Crabbe shifts his stance to a second element to explain the villagers. The prosperous and important men of the village do not lend their aid to help the unfortunate poor. Instead, they seduce the poor away from honest attempts to wrest a living from the infertile soil to enlist them in the more lucrative trade of smuggling:

> Here too the lawless merchant of the main
> Draws from his plough th' intoxicated swain;
> Want only claim'd the labour of the day,
> But vice now steals his nightly rest away. (1. 89–92)

Crabbe shows that smuggling does not involve only one or two lawless people. The smuggled goods have to be transported across England, and in order to achieve this "lawless passport," numerous officials participate. Natural philosophers in the eighteenth century can often be divided into two categories: those who feel nature is evil and civilization good; and those who hold nature is good and civilization evil. Surprisingly enough, in Book 1 Crabbe shows himself to belong to neither school, since he advances the opinion that nature, society, and even the villagers themselves are all implicated in the sense of evil.

When Crabbe draws attention to the "lawless merchant" he is not mentioning a minor evil restricted to East Anglia, but a pressing problem badly in need of redress. R. W. Harris has described smuggling, in the second half of the eighteenth century, as "a major national industry" and estimated that it employed some forty thousand men.[24] When Crabbe wrote *The Village*, smuggling was at its height, constituting such a danger to the country that Pitt, when he came to office in December 1783, decided that the redress of smuggling must be among his first reforms. The "lawless merchant" is not a petty thief but a symbol or representative of a flourishing national crime which was contributing to the nation's economic problems.

In these examples of physical and social coercion, Crabbe can be seen in the process of formulating a tentative theory of the influence of environment on man, where man is not free to make himself what he wants to be, but is moulded into the person he is by the physical and social forces around him.[25] Nature and society force upon him a life of "Rapine and Wrong and Fear" (I. 111), about which he can do little.

III

The first part of *The Village*, to line 130, describes the poor of a small part of England, the Suffolk coast. The conclusion reached is that their poverty is basically the fault of the poor natural resources:

> But these are scenes where Nature's niggard hand
> Gave a spare portion to the famish'd land;
> Hers is the fault, if here mankind complain
> Of fruitless toil and labour spent in vain. (I. 131–34)

Quite legitimately, Crabbe's readers might have objected that his "real picture of the poor" described the plight of only a small number of unrepresentative villagers. As if to refute such an objection, Crabbe changes his perspective at line 135 to expand his subject by including inland scenes "more fair in view." In the more prosperous counties nature is no longer so hostile, but the labourers are still as poor. The reason is that they are now coerced by yet another unfriendly agent, employers:

> But yet in other scenes, more fair in view,
> Where Plenty smiles—alas! she smiles for few—
> And those who taste not, yet behold her store,
> Are as the slaves that dig the golden ore,
> The wealth around them makes them doubly poor.
>
> (1. 135–39)

If on the "frowning coast" poverty was the "fault" of nature, then inland, where the country is rich, the blame must be placed on the unequal division of property. Here Crabbe introduces the idea that poverty is the result of exploitation by the landed class. In his early poem, *Inebriety* (1775), Crabbe had compared women to slaves in order to emphasize their lack of intellectual freedom, but the comparison was only vaguely developed. In *The Village* the comparison is literal. As slaves dig the golden ore for their masters, so the English peasants till the fields of golden corn for the landlords. An invidious type of slavery, economic slavery, as unjust as the physical slavery of the West Indies, Crabbe suggests, can be found in England.

That the labourer was cut off from the ameliorating influences of society had been tentatively suggested at the opening of the poem when Crabbe denied that any connection existed between the work of the peasant and the work of the artist. At line 140, Crabbe develops this argument by implying that he is speaking directly to a defender of the pastoral. He asks this imaginary person—what possible profits do the poor gain from their part in the division of labour? The answer given by most defenders of the system, for instance the answer Soame Jenyns gave,[26] was that the poor lived a healthy life in the invigorating country air. Crabbe pretends to accept this answer when he again asks:

> Or will you deem them amply paid in health,
> Labour's fair child, that languishes with wealth?
>
> (1. 140–41)

But in refutation of such sentimentalism, he replies, showing the peasant's life to be one of unremitting labour:

> Go, then! and see them rising with the sun,
> Through a long course of daily toil to run;
> See them beneath the dog-star's raging heat,
> When the knees tremble and the temples beat;
> Behold them, leaning on their scythes, look o'er
> The labour past, and toils to come explore;
> See them alternate suns and showers engage,
> And hoard up aches and anguish for their age. (I. 142–49)

In conclusion, Crabbe demands that the landowners stop deluding themselves, and admit that long hours of toil are not only unpleasant, but possibly killing:

> Then own that labour may as fatal be
> To these thy slaves, as thine excess to thee.   (I. 152–53)

To all those people such as Soame Jenyns who attempt to find compensations for the poverty of the poor in their supposed peace of mind or health, Crabbe replies with indignation:

> Yet grant them health, 'tis not for us to tell,
> Though the head droops not, that the heart is well;
> Or will you praise that homely, healthy fare,
> Plenteous and plain, that happy peasants share?
> Oh! trifle not with wants you cannot feel,
> Nor mock the misery of a stinted meal—
> Homely, not wholesome; plain, not plenteous; such
> As you who praise would never deign to touch.
>
> (I. 164–71)

It is doubtful whether Crabbe saw this attempt on the part of the wealthy to paint the villager's life in rosy colours as malicious; when he speaks of "ye gentle souls, who dream of rural ease," he seems rather to have in mind poets as well-intentioned as Goldsmith, who, realizing that the modern villager was in difficult circumstances, still continued to think of an ideal village in terms of the pastoral. For Goldsmith, once the enclosures were stopped, Auburn would become again a village of "spontaneous joys, where Nature has its play" (255). As this remains an impractical alternative to his picture of empty commons, Goldsmith's criticism of the enclosures becomes enveloped in the mists of sentimentalized idealization. Crabbe, however, recognized the futility of comparing the empty commons with Auburn, since any contemporary farmer could tell you that the villagers had never enjoyed those halcyon days of "health and plenty" which Goldsmith thought he remembered.

For a moment, Crabbe's indignation with pastoralists who blithely talked about the rural poor, of whom they knew little, almost causes him to suggest a redistribution of wealth. In place of the purely descriptive lines:

> See them beneath the dog-star's raging heat,
> When the knees tremble and the temples beat (1. 144–45)

Crabbe had originally written the more revolutionary lines:

> Like him to make the plenteous harvest grow
> And yet not share the plenty they bestow.[27]

But Crabbe draws back from stating outright that the rich are to blame for the plight of the poor, and blames them only for failing to recognize the terrible conditions. In this way although a criticism is lodged against the social system, Crabbe nowhere suggests that his description of the situation is also the remedy. Yet, by placing the workers and employers in opposition, Crabbe's portrayal of village conditions hints at the class struggle which was to begin in earnest in the next decades.

That Crabbe does refuse to assume a radical voice to denounce the landlords perhaps accounts for the reluctance of many critics to credit Crabbe with any new perceptions. Arthur Sale phrases the criticism most openly when he asserts that Crabbe (and Langhorne as well) had nothing fresh to say since Dodsley had said it all decades before in his poem *Agriculture*: "The whole thing [had been] nutshelled still another twenty years earlier in a generously open order to 'reward / The poor man's toil, whence all your riches spring'."[28] But if one accepts Sale's challenge to examine poems such as Dodsley's *Agriculture*, one finds that they are far removed from both the themes and spirit of the first book of *The Village*. For instance, when Dodsley refers to the "poor" he means not the parish poor, the peasants or the labourers, but the farmers. Moreover, the farmer is only "poor" in comparison to the gentry. When Dodsley's views about actual labourers are investigated, one finds that he normally portrays them in the pastoral tradition of healthy, happy Arcadians. His favourite peasant remains the milkmaid Patty—"Her shape was moulded by the hand of Ease" (1. 161). Her lover is "Young Thyrsis." Far from stating the same themes as Crabbe, Dodsley rarely touches upon the conditions of the poor. When he occasionally mentions villagers without their pastoral disguise, he speaks of them with the contempt of the prosperous middle-class merchant.[29] But even if Sale were correct in his reading of Dodsley's portrayal of the agricultural worker, this would hardly destroy the uniqueness of Crabbe's poem. Crabbe is not interested in telling people how the village labourer should be treated. The great merit of Book 1 is that Crabbe gives no advice. The eighteenth-century reader had more than enough advice. Instead, Crabbe attempts to set down an impression of the people of the village. Inevitably the poem implies social solutions, but Crabbe is not so much interested in any single solution as he is in portraying villagers and village life so as to open people's eyes to the conditions that existed around them.

Yet as Crabbe realized only too well, many of his readers might easily remain unaffected by this account, since the attitude of the time could still be summed up in the Biblical statement: "Ye have the poor with you always." Acquiescence in poverty was especially easy, paradoxically enough, because both the social code and the law recognized that the poor had a claim on society. Ever since the passing of the Elizabethan Poor Law (Statute 43 Eliz. c.2), it had been accepted that the parish had a duty to care for its poor. Since it was well known that the poor were entitled to parish aid, many people took the attitude that the poor were already being helped sufficiently. For instance, Daniel Defoe in *Giving Alms no Charity* (1704) argued persuasively that more government aid to the poor would only increase their laziness. The perplexity of many people is exemplified in the Rev. Joseph Townsend's statement: "There never was greater distress among the poor: there never was more money collected for their relief. But what is most perplexing is, that poverty and wretchedness have increased in exact proportion to the efforts which have been made for the comfortable subsistence of the poor."[30] After Townsend, Robert Malthus in his *An Essay on the Principles of Population* (1798) was to become one of the main exponents of this theory that more charity to the poor would only create more problems. Recognizing that many people believed the poor already received enough, if not too much charity, Crabbe decided to show that the Poor Laws, as they were then administered, were by no means giving the poor the kind, and the amount, of relief that most people supposed. Again the poem expands, this time to add the Poor Laws to its growing progression of causes which were destroying the integrity of the poor.

To prove his point about the Poor Laws, Crabbe takes as his example an old peasant, a man who at one time had been "chief in all the rustic trade" (a figure we are to meet in a more developed form as Isaac Ashford in "The Parish Register"). When he ages and is unable to work any longer, his masters exploit him with callous brutality as a part of the "roundsman system."[31] In order that his readers would be in no doubt that the old man is a genuine case of distress, Crabbe added the following footnote to explain the system: "A pauper who, being nearly past his labour, is employed by different masters for a length of time, proportioned to their occupations."[32] The "roundsman system" was obnoxious for several reasons. First, the farmer often did not need the man at the time he was allotted, and thus the roundsman did nothing and was forced to bear the insults of the farmer. Secondly, the man often had to walk long distances to reach his place of work. Most important of all, the system degraded the poor by taking from them their integrity and status. They became labour pure and simple— distributed at the whim of the "kingly overseer."

In the figure of this old man Crabbe is attacking the myth that the parish adequately cared for its poor. No longer able to find work, the old man has turned to the parish, but in order to lower its costs, always a central concern, the overseer sends the old man on the rounds of the parish, giving him odd jobs for various employers. As he is not capable of a full day's work, the parish subsidizes his wages. The jobs allotted to the old man show how little consideration was given to his age:

> Oft may you see him, when he tends the sheep,
> His winter-charge, beneath the hillock weep;
> Oft hear him murmur to the winds that blow
> O'er his white locks and bury them in snow,
> When, roused by rage and muttering in the morn,
> He mends the broken hedge with icy thorn. (I. 200–205)

If the old man had refused this work, then the parish could have instituted even harsher action: "If such poor person shall refuse to work, or run away from such employment, the guardian shall complain to a justice, who shall on conviction commit the offender to the house of correction, there to be kept to hard labour not exceeding three calendar months, nor less than one."[33]

But all is not over, since the old man has still one more reward. After labouring all his life, contributing to the economic prosperity of which so many Englishmen were proud, he can retire to the parish poorhouse. What so appals Crabbe is the hypocrisy of the parish. The overseers and "Churchwarden stern" are proud that they have not left the old man to starve on the open hillside. But the poorhouse is the decrepit asylum of all society's undesirables—the lame, the blind, the sick, the mad. Although the intention of the Poor Laws—to find work and supply shelter for the poor—was admirable, Crabbe wished to show that these laws broke down badly in practice. Dorothy Marshall makes much the same point when she notes: "The distinguishing mark of the Poor Law administration, during these years, was the enormous gulf between theory and practice. . . . The latter was a miserable travesty of the former."[34]

The description of the old man in the parish poorhouse is one of Crabbe's most famous. Burke placed it in *The Annual Register* and it appeared in Knox's *Elegant Extracts*. Certainly Crabbe's description of the poorhouse appears to have come as a great shock to many of his contemporaries. This would indicate that *The Village*, although it did not disturb people's political or social assumptions, caused many individuals to look with new eyes at the phenomenon of poverty. Francis Jeffrey commented that he knew "more than one of our unpoetical acquaintances who declared they could never pass by a parish workhouse, without thinking of the description of it they had read at school in the Poetical Extracts."[35] The reason this description had such an effect on Crabbe's readers was that they had never taken the trouble to look into one of these poorhouses, or if they had, they tended to see it as one of the infinite stages in God's ethical universe. As it was, Crabbe's description of a poorhouse left many readers horrified:

> Such is that room which one rude beam divides,
> And naked rafters form the sloping sides;
> Where the vile bands that bind the thatch are seen,
> And lath and mud are all that lie between,
> Save one dull pane, that, coarsely patch'd, gives way
> To the rude tempest, yet excludes the day.
> Here, on a matted flock, with dust o'erspread,
> The drooping wretch reclines his languid head;
> For him no hand the cordial cup applies,
> Or wipes the tear that stagnates in his eyes;
> No friends with soft discourse his pain beguile,
> Or promise hope till sickness wears a smile. (1. 262–73)

The description is in terms we would now refer to as Dickensian, but long before Dickens hit on the idea of surrounding a character with objects which establish his inner state of mind, Crabbe had used this technique in *The Village*. The dilapidated condition of the House reflects the parish's degenerate social conscience. Moreover the images of decay and squalor used to describe the House serve as a corollary to the opening images of the sterile coast. The poorhouse represents all that is left for the poor villager after his defeat by the forces of evil.

What Crabbe objects to is not simply the terrible conditions of the poorhouse, but that all those unable to work, for whatever reason, were placed in the same category under the same roof. Although the passage describing the inmates of the poorhouse is long, I think it is worth quoting at length, both because of its intrinsic merit and because it so greatly influenced Crabbe's contemporaries:

> Theirs is yon house that holds the parish poor,
> Whose walls of mud scarce bear the broken door;
> There, where the putrid vapours, flagging, play,
> And the dull wheel hums doleful through the day—
> There children dwell, who know no parents' care;
> Parents, who know no children's love, dwell there!
> Heart-broken matrons on their joyless bed,
> Forsaken wives, and mothers never wed;
> Dejected widows with unheeded tears,
> And crippled age with more than childhood fears;
> The lame, the blind, and, far the happiest they!
> The moping idiot and the madman gay.
> Here too the sick their final doom receive,
> Here brought, amid the scenes of grief, to grieve,
> Where the loud groans from some sad chamber flow,
> Mix'd with the clamours of the crowd below. (I. 228–43)

In their failure to distinguish the poor as people, the overseers have fallen into the same error as the pastoralists. When the poetry of a period treats all the poor as happy shepherds, one can be sure that the administrators will show an equivalent amount of scorn.

Numerous people, including William Wordsworth and Sir Walter Scott, commented that this passage and especially the lines: "The lame, the blind, and, far the happiest they! / The moping idiot and the madman gay" affected them greatly.[36] That this description could have such an effect proves that Crabbe was correct in his belief that such facts were little known. Yet Crabbe was only pointing out what anyone might see in parish poorhouses, or what they might read in the Poor Laws. As the Statute 43 Eliz. c.2 made clear, "every poor, old, blind, lame, and impotent person, or other person not able to work" was entitled to relief. Crabbe's point is not to suggest that the Poor Laws fail to provide for the poor; as he says, "the laws indeed for ruin'd age provide." But he feels that because of the inept administration and "the cold charities of man to man" the "scrap is bought with many a sigh."

In the end, man, who has all along been at the mercy of forces of nature which act upon him with irreversible direction and force, is so manipulated by society that he loses even his desire for survival. The old man asks himself why he should live when nothing he can do will help and no one will aid him:

> Why do I live, when I desire to be
> At once from life and life's long labour free?
> Like leaves in spring, the young are blown away,
> Without the sorrows of a slow decay;
> I, like yon wither'd leaf, remain behind,
> Nipp'd by the frost, and shivering in the wind;
> There it abides till younger buds come on,
> As I, now all my fellow-swains are gone;
> Then, from the rising generation thrust,
> It falls, like me, unnoticed to the dust.   (I. 206-15)

When no answer is forthcoming, the old man finds life holds no further interest for him and so he gladly dies. The old man's life has been so determined for him that he has become little more than a natural object following inviolable laws. He is like the tree which flourishes, gives seed, and dies. His last comment is a recognition that his life has meant nothing to anyone:

> Then let my bones beneath the turf be laid,
> And men forget the wretch they would not aid!
>
> (I. 224-25)

Significantly enough, at the end of his description of the poor-house, Crabbe does not conclude, as Dodsley or Savage or Shenstone would have done, with a pat phrase that everyone must help his neighbour. He continues to remain in the background, quietly describing different features of the condition of the poor, leaving the reader to draw his own conclusions. In one sense the parish fulfils its legal responsibilities, since it supplies both a doctor and a priest. Yet the doctor who looks after the poor is a conceited quack:

> Anon, a figure enters, quaintly neat,
> All pride and business, bustle and conceit;
> With looks unalter'd by these scenes of wo,
> With speed that, entering, speaks his haste to go.
>
> (1. 276–79)

This "potent quack" (potent in the ironical sense that he is dangerous) is obviously to blame for at least part of the misery of the poor. Crabbe, however, emphasizes that the fault lies not only with the doctor; he is "paid by the parish" and protected by a "drowsy Bench." It will be recalled that the reason Crabbe had been employed at Aldborough as a doctor to look after the poor was because the other doctor, Raymond, had raised his prices. The parish chose Crabbe because he was poor, badly qualified, and therefore cheap.[37] Who is to blame? First, the doctor. Second, society. The "drowsy Bench" allows the quack to practise, and the parish employs him. But the individuals of the parish are themselves to blame for condoning the practice, for employing the quack in order to save a penny on the rates.

The parish priest who ministers to the poor proves to be no better than the doctor. He is the caricatured eighteenth-century vicar, riding to the hounds, playing whist, and drinking until he slips under the table. The priest is a "holy stranger" to the poor, and like the doctor, he refuses to visit them. Again one can see Crabbe's attempt to refute the sentimental approach to village life when he compares the priest of *The Village* with Goldsmith's good priest, "passing rich with forty pounds a year."

The difference between Crabbe's poem and the earlier poems which had taken up the subject of the poor can be seen in the following lines with the obvious allusion to Gray's *Elegy*:

> Now once again the gloomy scene explore,
> Less gloomy now; the bitter hour is o'er,
> The man of many sorrows sighs no more.—
> Up yonder hill, behold how sadly slow
> The bier moves winding from the vale below;
> There lie the happy dead, from trouble free,
> And the glad parish pays the frugal fee.
> No more, O Death! thy victim starts to hear
> Churchwarden stern, or kingly overseer;
> No more the farmer claims his humble bow,
> Thou art his lord, the best of tyrants thou! (1. 318–28)

In his *Elegy* Gray had generously allowed that all men were equal at death, and from this, had concluded that the rich and great had no right to feel superior to the humble. Yet this is sentimentality, no matter how pleasantly conveyed. Crabbe, on the contrary, declares that the poor are the slaves of the great, the tyrants. While Gray was content to formulate the proposition that all men are alike defeated by the tyrant death, Crabbe declares that death is by far the kindest tyrant of the poor. Moreover, Crabbe points out ironically how both rich and poor are equally happy: the poor man is happy to have escaped life; the rich man is happy to have escaped paying to support life.

When the ending to Book 1 of *The Village* is compared with the ending to Gray's *Elegy*, the conclusion is inescapable that *The Village* constitutes a reply. Both poems end with the bier being taken to the graveyard. Gray ended his poem with the villagers reading the epitaph on the gravestone; Crabbe's villagers explore "the mingled relics of the parish poor." At this point the tension in *The Village* relaxes for a few lines and one suspects that Book 1 may end in elegiac melancholy. But then Crabbe announces that the priest has refused the time to give the last benediction, and the poem concludes quietly but acidly:

> And, waiting long, the crowd retire distress'd,
> To think a poor man's bones should lie unbless'd.

The allusion to the beatitudes is surely intentional.[38]

IV

In any discussion of *The Village* a danger exists of treating Book I as a poem complete in itself, because in the second book Crabbe alters the direction to adopt what seems at first sight to be a platitudinous and somewhat sycophantic solution easily acceptable to everyone. René Huchon has argued that in the second part "the chaplain has spoilt the poet,"[39] because, in his opinion, Crabbe displays a "commonplace pessimism" which is out of keeping with the original design. This interpretation has been challenged, most recently by Oliver Sigworth, who has suggested that Crabbe's advice to the poor in Book II—not to envy the rich—was meant to balance the statement of Book I—that the rich should not envy the poor.[40] Yet the unhappiness of the wealthy is hardly of the same kind as the physical poverty of the villager, and to pretend that the villagers' basic economic problems are somehow compensated for by the problems of the wealthy is hardly satisfactory. Indeed, Crabbe himself says as much in Book I :

> Say ye, oppress'd by some fantastic woes,
> Some jarring nerve that baffles your repose;
>
> . . . .
>
> How would ye bear to draw your latest breath,
> Where all that's wretched paves the way for death?
>
> (I. 250–61)

Some of the apparent discrepancies between Books I and II disappear when attention is paid to Crabbe's tone of voice and the reasons why the tone alters. For instance, Book II begins as though it were going to continue the vein of Book I: "No longer truth, though shown in verse, disdain, / But own the Village Life a life of pain." The first surprise comes when, in the name of truth, Crabbe admits that he has himself oversimplified village life, and that probably the villagers enjoy some moments of "sweet repose." This phrase "sweet repose," with its connotations of pastoral, suggests that the pastoral is about to be readmitted. But the phrase soon proves to have ironic overtones when Crabbe describes the villagers on their day of rest. There is no "sweet Patty" playing at innocent diversions on the village green; Crabbe's villagers retire to an alehouse and erupt in a bloody brawl. Again, one can observe Crabbe's technique of first offering the conventional, sentimental response to the poor—their sweet repose—and then rebutting it by describing the opposite. Moreover, he does not seem to be exaggerating; for, as one economic historian has commented: "Throughout the eighteenth century there were but few recreations which appealed to any but the most material and least elevated side of human nature. In all ranks of society, high and low alike, drinking and gambling abounded. . . ."[41] The brawling, drunken villager is Crabbe's answer to the pastoralist who imagined that the poor "with rural games play'd down the setting sun" (I. 94).

While this argument that the villagers are as coarse in their play as in their work seems harmless enough when taken out of context, almost all Crabbe's critics have found the incident surprising, and have felt that it marks a turning point in the poem. Its importance becomes evident as soon as one observes that the incident is based on the assumption that everything is related, that nothing exists in isolation. And this concept of society leads Crabbe to ponder the hypothesis that if links exist between labour and leisure, may there not also be a link in the quality of life between rich and poor?

Of course there certainly may, and Crabbe goes on to describe how the labourers enjoy their day of rest, not because of, but in spite of, the efforts of the farmers and gentry. The "careful masters" would like to see Sunday outlawed so that the labourers could work every day of the week:

> Thus, as their hours glide on, with pleasure fraught,
> Their careful masters brood the painful thought;
> Much in their mind they murmur and lament,
> That one fair day should be so idly spent;
> And think that Heaven deals hard, to tithe their store
> And tax their time for preachers and the poor. (II. 19–24)

Physical poverty in one class is inevitably linked to moral and spiritual poverty in other classes.

In many ways Crabbe in Book II seems to set out deliberately to defeat the reader's expectations. The description of the poor in Book I leaves unanswered the question—who is to blame? When in Book II Crabbe begins to describe the vices of the poor, no doubt many readers hoped he would identify the culprits, perhaps the poor themselves. Indeed, in a copy of the second edition of *Poems* (1808) in my possession, someone in an early nineteenth-century hand has scratched out Crabbe's line:

> but Peasants now
> Resign their pipes and plod behind the plough (I. 23–24)

and has substituted his own version:

> but Peasants now
> Suck their tobacco pipes and hold the plough.

However, Crabbe's conception of society is based on the premise that the poor can exist only if the rich are poor. For instance, when Crabbe describes some of the village girls, not "so chaste as fair," he immediately proceeds to reveal that they are by no means unique in their lack of chastity:

> These to the town afford each fresher face,
> And the clown's trull receives the peer's embrace;
> From whom, should chance again convey her down,
> The peer's disease in turn attacks the clown. (II. 51–54)

The village girls lack chastity, which is not unexpected, but the "peers" bring with their licentiousness, disease. Just as the beautiful weeds are to be found everywhere amidst the corn, so is there a subtle mingling of the diseases of the rich amongst the fair village girls. When Crabbe describes the "injured peasant and deluded fair" standing before the stern judge, the moral most people would draw is that the judge was right in reprimanding the villagers. Henry Fielding, for instance, believed the poor required a stern hand. But before the scene ends, Crabbe shows how great and poor are in fact alike, when—

Some favourite female of her judge glides by,
Who views with scornful glance the strumpet's fate,
And thanks the stars that made her keeper great.

(II. 80–82)

Crabbe appears to wish to draw his readers on to the conclusion that the poor are vicious and lewd, and then to confront them with facts to show that the licentiousness of the poor was to be found also among the great.[42]

Certainly such an enlightened, if common sense, attitude was much needed in this period. When in 1787 William Wilberforce set up his Society for the Suppression of Vice and Immorality, he did so with the idea of reforming the conduct of the lower classes.[43] While the Society reprimanded people of low birth for swearing or drinking, the members rarely thought of giving the same reprimand to a person such as Richard Brinsley Sheridan or the Prince Regent, both of whom led notorious private lives. What Crabbe has done in Book II is to show that just as the poor cannot be singled out for special favour, so they cannot be given special rebuke.

The objection often brought against this part of the poem is that Crabbe's new premise—everyone is equally miserable and corrupt —seems to suggest that special attention to the poor is unnecessary. For anyone who values social equality for its own sake (and since the time of the French Revolution, this has meant an increasing number of people), Crabbe's second book must appear evasive. Yet suppose change is required. How is it possible in Crabbe's world? For changes to come about, they must be the result of either a radical consciousness among the lower classes or a reformist or paternalist attitude amongst the upper classes. But when Crabbe presents the poor as brawling drunkards and the rich as diseased libertines, change appears unlikely and the indignation is partly dispelled. Not only are the means to effect change missing, the motive is also absent. For almost two centuries now there has been a growing tendency to believe that a mere statement of the problems of society will put into motion the means for their correction. However, Crabbe's habits of mind are quite different. Although he describes with great accuracy man's social situation, he does so, not in order to offer new social objectives, but as a means to comment on man's moral and spiritual condition. Once the premises of *The Village* are fully worked out in all their implications, he is forced to the conclusion that all men, both rich and poor, live a life without meaning, blindly subject to the laws of the world, until they end "in the dust." The question then arises whether man is independent enough to formulate his own goals. In Wordsworth's terms, it is a question of man's ability to transform the prison house of the mind into a place of joy. Since Crabbe is much more interested in the question of man's place in the world than he is in questions of social equality (after all, equality is usually sought for the purpose of helping individuals), the central question—whether man is totally determined by physical causes or whether he can rise above them to live morally—takes over in Book II.

To understand why Crabbe becomes so concerned about man's condition, it will be helpful to look at the grounds on which previous humanitarian poets had urged reform. Social critics of the early eighteenth century had assumed that the vices of the town were the chief causes leading to man's corruption; like Cowper, they believed firmly that if men were given the opportunity to retire to a quiet life in the country, their good nature would come to the fore. Accordingly, it was believed that the essential factor in social reform was to eradicate man's follies by removing the false values of the city, especially the emphasis upon luxuries. Poets such as Dodsley, Shenstone, and Akenside generally accepted Virgil's formulation in his second Georgic that nature responded to man's pleasure and need, and concluded therefore that in the country man must be happy and virtuous. When Crabbe took up this essentially pastoral theory and showed it to be false, he in fact destroyed the basic premise of eighteenth-century social criticism —the optimistic view that man in the country was innocent and virtuous. Consequently, when in Book II Crabbe looked closely at the "simple life that Nature yields" he found a Hobbesian world of "Rapine and Wrong and Fear," and discovered that for his "poor, blind, bewilder'd, erring race," he had created a world in which the eighteenth-century ideal of benevolence could not exist. Crabbe would have been the first to admit that the lot of the poor was miserable and deserved to be ameliorated. But *The Village* (at least up to line 106 of Book II) allows no possible solution. Nature, and indeed the universe itself, offers no ideal which man need only acknowledge and approach to become virtuous.

Yet Crabbe does not close the poem at this point, but turns suddenly to offer yet another response to the problem in his famous, or rather infamous, threnody on Robert Manners. To see this eulogy as a purely selfish attempt on Crabbe's part to win the favour of his new patron, the Duke of Rutland, would be uncharitable, but not unreasonable, if it were not that the pattern of *The Village* with its abrupt shift in emphasis is repeated in many of Crabbe's later poems. As will be seen in the next chapter, "The Hall of Justice" contains a similar disjunction when it turns suddenly from the question of earthly justice to that of divine justice. Similarly, the sketches of individuals in *The Borough* and "The Parish Register" belie the public values enunciated by their narrators. In *The Village* the introduction of Robert Manners comes exactly at the point when Crabbe is face-to-face with the consequences of his empirical world. Significantly, Crabbe introduces Manners, not to show that he helped the poor, but because Manners's way of life demonstrates that "Life is not measured by the time we live" (II. 172). In this respect *The Village* resembles Wordsworth's *Resolution and Independence*. Both poems are concerned with the seeming futility of man's life and the way in which meaning can be found or given. Where Wordsworth speaks of the "cold, pain and labour" of a totally secular life, Crabbe speaks of "narrow views and paltry fears." And just as the old leech-gatherer gives Wordsworth new resolution so does Robert Manners provide Crabbe with hope. Manners is the noble "chief" who has accepted the fallen world, while still managing to experience joy. Crabbe tells the poor that if such great men exist "then let your murmurs cease, / Think, think of him, and take your lot in peace" (II. 113–14). Caution is necessary at this point, since at first sight it is unclear why the poor should cease complaining because of the discovery of one noble man. But assume the opposite to be the case; suppose it had proved impossible to find such a man. The conclusion would be that nothing anyone could do would have meaning.

It is against this background that Crabbe's introduction of Robert Manners with his Christ-like associations should be viewed. In a world of self-interest, Manners, the one noble man, brings everyone of the village—rich and poor alike—the evidence that man can rise above himself. Manners, it should be stressed, is necessary not simply because he was generous or happy, or even virtuous, but because he did not bow down to circumstances. He chose to die for the cause he believed in (Robert Manners died in a naval battle). Thus Manners's way of death offers proof that man is not merely another species of fauna, but can himself shape his own destiny. The introduction of Robert Manners also signals that Crabbe is now interpreting the Hobbesian world of the earlier part of the poem in terms of the Christian view of history where man is in a fallen state to be saved only by the intercession of a man-god. It will be recalled that many writers since the time of Pascal have been impelled toward a belief in God because a godless world seemed so unbearable. Although Christ is not actually introduced into *The Village*, Robert Manners is clearly an analogue. Crabbe's difficulty in managing the transition from one part of the poem to the other is evident in his imagery. While he does not forsake the nature imagery of the first part of the poem—Manners is likened to a "tall oak"—nature is no longer amoral, but ethical and protective. The "tall oak" is the "guard and glory" of the trees below.

Although this Christ-like figure, so suddenly and preposterously introduced, strikes almost all modern readers as vestigial, one can see how Crabbe's concern with "the real," which generated a description of man's condition extraordinarily similar to that of the Christian view of fallen man, left him with only the Christian solution as a means of escape from the labyrinth of Hobbes's world. Crabbe has posited a static world where man and society do not change, where in fact man's behaviour can be described in terms of unchanging natural phenomena. Under such conditions, the artist can describe man only as he was and always will be.

It would be as well to point out that Crabbe did not actually have to choose the Christ-like figure of Robert Manners as the solution to his "realist" dilemma. For, implicit in the writing of the poem is the assumption that Crabbe himself escaped and changed, and his work presumably will help to further the changes already in motion. Yet such a conclusion would have meant the creation of a narrator who participates in his own story, an innovation, for Crabbe, that was still in the future. Certainly, Crabbe does not press this point; indeed when he mentions Stephen Duck, an earlier eighteenth-century poet who rose from ploughboy to a favourite of Queen Caroline, he suggests that the trade of poet is perhaps even "poorer" than that of thresher (1. 27–30). At any rate, Crabbe accepts the static world of his eighteenth-century forbears, which, because it is now without value, is meaningless.

In his later work Crabbe often pursues this line of thought by describing in great detail the lack of meaning and emotional colour in everyday life. Many of his later characters flee this type of life with its banal mediocrity by resorting to neurotic aberration—a technique used by many twentieth-century authors. In poems such as "Peter Grimes," Crabbe, in a very Kafka-like way, is able to show how the typical details of everyday life, emptied of meaning, have a spectral character which evokes the sense of a disintegrating personality. Yet in other poems, such as "The Frank Courtship" and *Tales of the Hall*, Crabbe does permit a modicum of change in his characters, and thereby creates some of his finest comic poems. In dream poems such as "The Insanity of Ambitious Love," moreover, Crabbe goes on to explore the possibility of an earthly paradise as a counterpart to man's fallen estate, but his inability to conceive of the material and political exertion necessary to effect the change leads him to conclude with unsatisfactory repudiations. In *The Village* Crabbe refuses to accept the imaginative logic of his environmentally described world, and since he does not introduce a sense of personal or historical dynamic, he is left with the factitious Robert Manners in the abstract-idealist mode of thought to dispel the poem's oppression.

Although the figure of Manners does not resolve the poem's questions in the same empirical mode and voice in which they are asked, his introduction carries its own poetic logic. Ian Gregor has pointed out that the ending of Book II converts the poem into "a striking variation of a well recognized 'kind'—the elegiac pastoral."[44] It clearly resembles the ending of such poems as John Philips's *Cyder* where Philips encourages the young Harcourt to return to England to follow his father's example: "See! how the Cause / Of Widows, and of Orphans He asserts / With winning Rhetoric, and well-argu'd Law!"[45] I would suggest that the classical elegy in Book II affords a counterpart to the classical opening of Book I. It will be recalled that Crabbe opened the poem in the classical style; in Book II he closes singing of the "pure stream" which still flows on, "and shall for ever flow." In effect, the classical eulogy of the great man rounds out and completes the classical opening of the poem.

Yet since Crabbe employed the classical form at the beginning of *The Village* as an ironic device to contain anticlassical ideas, the classical ending, coming as it does after so much abjuration of the classical, also partakes of this ironic mode. Irony demands two points of view in conflict, and usually deliberate irony results when the author holds one of the views to be correct and the other false. What happens in *The Village* is that Crabbe introduces a conventional viewpoint—for instance, the "sweet repose" of the villager—pretends for a moment to argue its validity, and then turns round to show its falsity. From the beginning of Book II, versions of pastoral are suggested, and then rejected. At the end, the theme of the "great man" sweeps in and overwhelms the poem. Obviously the "great man" is a variant of pastoral just as was the "sweet repose" of the villager, but Crabbe bows to the inevitable, and permits himself a "pastoral" solution.

An illuminating biographical fact is Crabbe's personal experience of "the noble chief," the saving grace of the villagers: Edmund Burke actually rescued him from the threat of debtor's prison and perhaps even suicide.[46] Yet Crabbe, it must be said, was unfortunate in his choice of Charles, fourth Duke of Rutland, as his "great man" to carry on the example of his brother Robert Manners. The duke died four years later, aged only thirty-three. Nathaniel Wraxall's comments on the duke reveal him to have been a man who never "displayed any eminent talents," a pleasant but rather decadent member of the aristocracy.[47] Although today one tends to see the duke's character as additional evidence of the untenability of Crabbe's solution, agreement or disagreement with the philosophy of Crabbe's ending should not blind us to the obvious conclusion that in poetic terms, Crabbe is not offering the reader a felt response to an individual—Manners—but is depending on the ending's standard elegiac qualities to create in the reader an association with all the great men of the past—officers and poets alike—who have served their country.

Thus *The Village* combines Crabbe's perceptions of an empirically based world with his belief in man's ability to find values and goals. Fitting in with Crabbe's sense of things in his own life and concluding the classical manner of the poem, the elegiac ending informs the poem with those transcendent ideals for which Crabbe could find no place in the world of the village.

Chapter 2
By want on error forced

In 1785, five years after arriving in London, Crabbe appeared on the point of realizing all his ambitions. His poems—*The Library*, *The Village* and *The Newspaper*—had enjoyed success; Dr. Johnson had given him his blessing; and his appointment as chaplain to the Duke of Rutland had placed him in a respectable profession. His success had also enabled him, after an eleven-year engagement, to marry "Mira." Yet just when one might have expected Crabbe's literary career to flourish, he disappeared completely from the world of letters. With the exception of a sermon preached at the funeral of the Duke of Rutland, and a chapter in J. Nichols' *The History and Antiquities of the County of Leicester*, Crabbe published nothing from 1785 until 1807. Accordingly, the opening lines of *The Newspaper*, written in 1785—"A time like this, a busy, bustling time, / Suits ill with writers, very ill with rhyme"—deserve to be taken seriously, for Crabbe followed his own advice to eschew poetry.

Yet it would be incorrect to assume that Crabbe was mouldering in the country, writing nothing during his long silence, since his son mentions three novels that were consigned to the flames.[1] Crabbe seems to have been experimenting with problems of style and form, and by 1799 was sufficiently satisfied with some new poems to begin negotiations with Hatchard for an edition, but these he subsequently withdrew on the advice of his friend Mr. Turner. Crabbe's use and development of the novel's narrative technique will be seen in many of his later poems.

When Crabbe published *Poems* (1807) after twenty-two years of silence, not only had England changed a great deal, so had Crabbe. He was fifty-three years of age and a clergyman of the Church of England—unlikely qualifications for a poet noted for his probing into social and moral complexities. Knowing these facts, it is with some trepidation that a reader approaches the new poems, perhaps expecting to find a new conservatism to accompany the advanced years of the poet. After all, Wordsworth was hardly the exception when he lost his poetic nerve in his thirties.

To discover that most of the new poems of 1807—"Sir Eustace Grey," "The Parish Register," and "The Hall of Justice"—are fresh and original is thus both surprising and pleasing. "The Parish Register" amplifies Crabbe's best theme, the lives of common people, and develops further the interest in social types shown in *The Village*. "Sir Eustace Grey" attempts to reproduce something of the quality of the mind of a madman, a new and surprisingly different theme. But it is in "The Hall of Justice" where Crabbe shows unmistakably that during his years as a parish priest he had not forgotten the central problem of *The Village*—how to introduce a sense of purposive value in a world described entirely in causal terms. The tone of "The Hall of Justice," blunt and argumentative, suggests it is closer to the style of *The Village* than the objective probing attitude of "The Parish Register." Crabbe's statement in the preface that "nine years have since elapsed" since he wrote the poem,[2] confirms this impression.

"The Hall of Justice" is an interesting poem in many respects, not the least being that Crabbe here experiments with the octo-syllabic line and alternating rhyme. But my main reason for singling it out in this study is that it confronts the reader directly and openly with an issue that is central to Crabbe's thinking: how an individual can be said to choose freely, and therefore be responsible for his actions, when these actions have been determined by social circum-stance. While never explicitly stating the connection between poverty and crime in *The Village*, Crabbe had shown through his imagery that the wretches and criminals of the village were at least in part the product of their environment. In "The Hall of Justice"

Crabbe once again takes up this theme of the causal connection between environment and crime to show, in a particular case, how a woman with no education is finally forced into a life of crime in order to obtain bread.

This theme of "The Hall of Justice" was by no means new in 1807. Almost a century earlier, Daniel Defoe had insisted on a close connection between pauperism and crime. In his preface to *The History of Colonel Jack,* Defoe stated categorically of Jack: "Circumstances form'd him by Necessity to be a Thief."[3] Again, in *The Fortunate Mistress,* Roxana's maid, Amy, expresses much the same sentiment: "Poverty is the strongest incentive; a Temptation against which no Virtue is powerful enough to stand out. . . . As to Honesty, I think Honesty is out of the Question when Starvation is the Case."[4] While this interest in the connection between poverty and crime was alive at the beginning of the century in the writings of people such as Defoe and Mandeville, by the middle of the century it had lost most of its original force. Although the idea remained current throughout the eighteenth century, poets were mainly interested in the feelings of the philanthropist rather than those of the criminal. When Savage said: "Hence Robbers rise, to Theft, to Murder prone, / First driv'n by Want, from Habit desp'rate grown,"[5] and Johnson in *London* commented how the "midnight murd'rer" is "cruel with guilt, and daring with despair" (238–39), neither wished to explore the social implications of society's complicity in the criminal's guilt.

When most eighteenth-century poems paid only lip service to the idea that necessity offers an excuse for crime, it is no surprise that Crabbe's exposition, in which he raises the question in a court of law, should have created a great impact on his readers. Jeffrey found the poem "very nervous—very shocking—and very powerfully represented."[6] Such a reaction was only to be expected when one considers that "The Hall of Justice," by raising questions of natural law during the period of the Napoleonic Wars, called into question the entire basis of English judicial law.

Although the theme of the "Hall of Justice" is presented in a radical manner, it should come as no surprise to those familiar with

The Village to find that the conclusion of the poem seems deliberately ambiguous and even conservative. Crabbe's intention appears to have been to raise the issue of the influence of social conditions on crime without forcing his readers to the conclusion that society is responsible for the acts of criminals. Like many of Crabbe's poems, "The Hall of Justice" works obliquely, leaving much unsaid, and indeed, leaving much that appears to be purposely ambivalent. The poem tells the story of a vagrant woman who has been caught stealing. Before the judge sentences her, she asks that the story of her life may be heard in the hope that her circumstances will be taken into account. Reluctantly the judge agrees to listen, but by the time the woman has finished her story of hardship and misery he has been moved to compassion. The opening lines in which the vagrant begs that her story be heard are bold and dramatic; their style and tone suggest not a cowed criminal begging for mercy, but an aristocrat demanding justice. "Impetuous and lofty" is Jeffrey's description. To the constable, who thinks he can treat vagabonds with disrespect, the vagrant speaks contemptuously:

> Take, take away thy barbarous hand,
> And let me to thy master speak;
> Remit awhile the harsh command,
> And hear me, or my heart will break. (I. 1-4)

The language is strong, and the words "barbarous" and "harsh" carry a degree of irony, being spoken in a courtroom—supposedly a hall of justice. That the judge should be termed the constable's "master" is a fine touch, indicating the woman's perceptions of the relationships within the court.

The passage gathers even more effect when one recalls that Crabbe has the woman speak on her own behalf, not simply to add drama to the scene, but because under the law at this time, a person accused of a felony was not permitted to employ a lawyer to make his defence in the courts.[7] Of this law forbidding counsel to speak for those accused of felonies, Sydney Smith said: "We are called upon to continue a practice without example in any other country, and are required by lawyers to consider that custom as humane, which every one who is not a lawyer pronounces to be most cruel and unjust—and which has not been brought forward to general notice, only because its bad effects are confined to the last and lowest of mankind."[8] Lacking education and all knowledge of the law, the vagrant woman is forced to conduct her own case against a judge who is in all probability little disposed to be charitable to a gypsy wanderer. By giving the vagrant woman the ability to make a strong and impassioned speech in her own defence, Crabbe manages to show what can, in exceptional circumstances, be said to extenuate a crime. That the judge is surprised by the woman's speech is clear from his replies, and thus Crabbe is able to indicate how trials, as usually conducted, neglect to take into account an important aspect of the case—the defendant's situation.

At the beginning of the poem Crabbe presents the judge as stern and unbending. Nor is he exaggerating in the least. Although many judges were undoubtedly compassionate in their private lives, in their public capacity they were notoriously strict with the "unworthy poor." When the judge finds that the woman wishes to plead her case, he asks incredulously what she can possibly say on her own behalf. Because of her "deeds of sorrow, shame, and sin," the judge concludes that she is past help. His interpretation of the law is literal: since the woman has been found guilty, and has no character to plead, all that remains is to pronounce sentence. Yet Crabbe has the judge emphasize the word "deeds," leaving the way open to a possible discussion of motive.

When the woman begins her speech—a speech on which her life may depend, since stealing goods worth more than five shillings was punishable by death—Crabbe introduces a decidedly radical proposition. Explaining first that she stole the food to feed herself and her baby, the woman acknowledges that she broke society's law, but claims to have followed "a stronger law." In effect, this claim challenges the validity of England's system of jurisprudence by appealing to natural law or the law of self-preservation:

> My crime!—This sick'ning child to feed,
> I seized the food your witness saw;
> I knew your laws forbade the deed,
> But yielded to a stronger law.
>
> Know'st thou, to Nature's great command
> All human laws are frail and weak? (1. 9–14)

Surprisingly, Crabbe withdraws this argument before it has time to be fully developed. Seeing the judge frown, the woman realizes that she is losing his sympathy, and abruptly stops discussing natural law: "Nay! frown not—stay his eager hand, / And hear me, or my heart will break" (1. 15–16). The vagrant then gains the judge's sympathy by another course, by describing the difficulties she and her baby have encountered.

The momentary introduction of the argument commits neither Crabbe nor the vagrant to its validity. That the judge refuses to listen to arguments involving natural law is only to be expected, since the doctrine was literally outlawed. Concerned that the French Revolution would spread to England, the government had endeavoured by every means within its power to stop the circulation of ideas about natural law and natural rights. The publication of Thomas Paine's *Rights of Man*, by far the most influential book amongst those of the lower classes who were attempting to articulate their desire for a better life, had been banned in 1792, the year following its publication. Even Locke's well-known statements on natural law, which at the time of the Glorious Revolution had seemed self-evident and even innocuous, a century later appeared full of revolutionary venom.[9] What the reader is meant to make of the vagrant woman's brief appeal to the theory of natural rights is by no means easy to define. A naive reader might conclude from the judge's objection to the subject, that Crabbe himself did not want such an "offensive" topic introduced, and that he mentions it only because it was appealed to by reformers. But this view is untenable, for the poet gave the argument to the vagrant in the first place. Had he not wanted the issue of natural rights raised, he could have ignored the argument completely. In a poem such as "The Hall of

Justice," where the central concern is the relation of the individual's needs to social justice, the momentary introduction of the argument from natural rights allows the idea its full force without any overt endorsement. An analogous situation occurs when a clever lawyer suddenly introduces inadmissible evidence to sway a jury. Although the jury may be directed to disregard the point, obviously the effect cannot be completely erased. In Crabbe's poem, the judge is moved to sympathy by the tale of the woman's suffering, not by her plea of abstract natural rights. Crabbe of course knew from his own experience that the way to gain sympathy was to arouse compassion. In his first letter of appeal to Burke, he had openly said, "Let me, if possible, interest your compassion."[10]

Although Crabbe does not press the abstract issue of natural rights, his next argument supporting the woman's case shows him willing to argue extenuating circumstances. The woman begins, with a great deal of rhetoric, to describe the plight of her child, and once the judge's interest has been regained she proceeds to argue that she has been the victim of her circumstances and lack of education:

> Taught to believe the world a place
>   Where every stranger was a foe,
> Train'd in the arts that mark our race,
>   To what new people could I go?
> Could I a better life embrace,
>   Or live as virtue dictates? No!   (I. 47–52)

In the same way as Defoe observed in *The History of Colonel Jack* how Jack had "Never been taught any Thing, but to be a Thief,"[11] so also does Crabbe stress the woman's lack of education. She is "a child of sin, conceived in shame, / Brought forth in wo, to misery born" (I. 35–36). As a means of self-preservation, the vagrant turns to crime—"by want on error forced"—taking from society only what she needs to stay alive. Significantly, in the first edition Crabbe had written "on Want and Error forced" and only later changed it to the much stronger version "by want on error forced," for this latter version brings out clearly that the woman's poverty forces her to commit "error."

What is important to note here is the way Crabbe is building into his poem two conflicting views on the nature of man that were *simultaneously* held by many thinkers throughout the eighteenth century. While accepting the idea of the formative influence of education, most people cherished a second belief in man's ability to find and make his own happiness. One of the best examples of this confusion can be seen in John Locke's *Thoughts Concerning Education* (1693). On the first page, Locke says: "Men's Happiness or Misery is for the most part of their own making," and on the next, he says: "I think I may say, that of all the Men we meet with, Nine parts of Ten are what they are, Good or Evil, useful or not, by their Education."[12] In Lockeian terms, the vagrant's life of evil is the manifest result of her faulty education: "Like them, I base and guilty grew" (1. 42). But at the beginning of "The Hall of Justice," the judge has Locke's alternative theory uppermost in his mind, and since he believes that the woman is responsible for her own irregular conduct, he intends to sentence her accordingly. When the woman begins to convince the judge of her inability to lead a good life, then the two beliefs—that man can fashion his own happiness, and that education makes a man what he is—come into conflict. In day-to-day life, most people appear to have chosen whichever of the two theories was the most applicable to their present need, and to have conveniently forgotten the other. By the end of the century, however, the contradiction between the two models of personality was rapidly becoming apparent. In *A New View of Society* (1813), Robert Owen pointed out the dangers to society—especially with regard to concepts of punishment—arising from the conflict of these two views on the formation of human character, and asked his readers urgently to reconsider the subject.[13] More recently, both Nietzsche and Sartre have echoed this warning. The conflict has by no means been resolved.

In order to convey the full force of the dilemma, Crabbe gives each of his speakers one of the conflicting theories. To make the situation extreme, he portrays one speaker as a judge, the other as a gypsy. Groups of gypsies travelling together constituted a separate community, ruled by their own laws. When Crabbe describes how the vagrant involuntarily joined one of these bands, he ensures her separation from the normal habits of English society. As a member of a gypsy band she belongs to a different world: for all intents and purposes she might be in Bohemia or Asia.

Certainly the woman's story of her gypsy life earns her the compassion of the magistrate, especially when she emphasizes how the entire band was at the mercy of the band leader. Thus, when the gypsy leader demands her favours, she has no other recourse but to obey. That she is entrapped in an alien society where arbitrary laws prevail would undoubtedly gain the vagrant support from among Crabbe's readers. Englishmen at this time were only too ready to lend their help and pity to those unfortunate enough not to be born under England's humane laws.

Ironically, neither the judge nor most people of this time (clearly Crabbe means the judge to stand for the opinions of society) would have stopped to consider whether the woman's situation among the gypsies was not similar to her position in the court of law. In both cases she is in an alien society, forced to obey laws she had no hand in making. For her, the judge is as much a despotic ruler as was the gypsy leader. Among the gypsies the woman was forced to live by her wits, and in English society, where laws were made to protect property, her situation is no different.

So strongly has Crabbe insisted on the influence of the vagrant's past life, that even though her wild story has little to do with the theft of which she has been accused, the woman gains the judge's sympathy. He says:

> I hear thy words, I feel thy pain;
> Forbear awhile to speak thy woes;
> Receive our aid, and then again
> The story of thy life disclose.
> For, though seduced and led astray,
> Thou'st travell'd far and wander'd long;
> Thy God hath seen thee all the way,
> And all the turns that led thee wrong.   (I. 101–108)

At the beginning of Part II, he again shows that the woman's sorrows have touched him deeply when he claims that "the sinner's safety is his pain." But curiously enough, the vagrant wins the judge's compassion, by appealing to him as a Christian and not as a judge. When he, in turn, asks to hear her "sins," he sounds very much like a confessor:

> Come, now again thy woes impart,
> Tell all thy sorrows, all thy sin;
> We cannot heal the throbbing heart
> Till we discern the wounds within.   (II. 1–4)

The vagrant, primarily interested in saving the small child, pleads that the judge forget her sins and intervene on behalf of the child, but the judge is not nearly so interested in the child as in the woman's feelings of guilt. The important fact is that throughout her difficulties she has been able to distinguish right from wrong, and has lacked only the will and power to flee the gypsies:

> True, I was not to virtue train'd;
> Yet well I knew my deeds were ill;
> By each offence my heart was pain'd—
> I wept, but I offended still;
> My better thoughts my life disdain'd,
> But yet the viler led my will.   (II. 69–74)

Thus Crabbe has by no means described the vagrant in terms of the true "child of nature." While the woman was forced into a life of crime by circumstances, she has not become amoral.

Since the judge appears now to be compassionate, the reader naturally expects him to show mercy, but the judge's conception of mercy comes as something of a shock, for he assumes completely the role of priest and urges the woman to seek God's pardon:

> Recall the word, renounce the thought,
> Command thy heart and bend thy knee.
> There is to all a pardon brought,
> A ransom rich, assured and free;
> 'Tis full when found, 'tis found if sought,
> Oh! seek it, till 'tis seal'd to thee.   (II. 127–32)

Crabbe has shifted the theme from a social to a theological level so that now the judge is concerned not with a legal pardon, but with the possibilities of spiritual salvation. Somehow the social and economic problem has been dissolved in the spiritual, leaving the ending enigmatic. The judge never says whether he will help the child or pardon the mother; instead he turns his attention to assuring the vagrant that she need not despair of finding grace.

It might be assumed that Crabbe has intended the legal pardon to be found included in the spiritual one. But as he does not explicitly say so, the shift away from economic and legal concerns remains bothersome, since it leaves the problems raised at the beginning of the poem unresolved. Does the woman succeed in convincing the judge that the difficult circumstances of her early life made virtue impossible? Nowhere does Crabbe resolve the problem of whether crimes of necessity should be punished. The difference between God's justice and man's is not a minor one. At this time in England many people (perhaps even most) were capable of admitting that the social order was riddled with injustice, while rationalizing that God's justice would rectify this state of affairs in the next world. Paley, Wilberforce, and Burke all held this view in one form or another.

Obviously the poem permits several interpretations, but Crabbe's problem remains clear: while he wants to see mercy shown to the vagrant, he does not wish this single case to be turned into a precedent for general theory. Many writers had already expressed their horror at any relaxation of the principle of individual responsibility. At the time of the rebellion of 1745, the anonymous writer of *A Serious Address* had shown his dislike of theories placing responsibility for criminal acts on society rather than on the individual criminal: "But sure every Body sees the Weakness and Folly of this Excuse; it is as good in the Mouth of a Thief and a Robber, when he tells you he must either *Steal* or *Starve*; or of a Murtherer, that he must either *kill* or be *hang'd*."[14] Such writers felt social standards were challenged by ideas of corporate responsibility. Crabbe was obviously fascinated with problems in which his sense of individual responsibility conflicted with his observation of the ways in which individuals were socially determined. But he was fascinated, not only with the problem itself, but with ways of embodying the contradiction in his poetry so that he could present the paradox in which both truths coexist. By emphasizing that the woman's pardon falls upon her own shoulders (in religious terms), he avoids the admission that anyone other than the woman is at fault, while still offering her the possibility of a pardon for her actions. Strictly speaking, this introduction of God's remission is irrelevant since it does not guarantee society's forgiveness, but rhetorically the reader's expectations are partially met, because the way to a pardon "assured and free" is shown to the woman. The poem is so arranged that it appears as though the rules of society will conform "to the will of God."[15]

The presupposition that God would rectify the inequalities of this world in the next was widely accepted and in itself was innocuous enough. Yet often writers were tempted to use this belief to justify social inequality, or to go one step further and disallow reform by arguing that changes in this world would upset God's plans in the next. In James Grahame's "The Sabbath" (1804), for instance, Grahame argues that in the present difficult times, guiltless people were kept prisoners as felons (Grahame had been a lawyer before he became a clergyman). But he concludes that "'tis not ignominious to be wronged"[16] since Judgment Day will see them with the angels. In "The Hall of Justice" Crabbe utilizes this tradition without ever sanctioning it, thus creating an ironic counterpoint.

Crabbe is particularly skilful in anticipating the contemporary issues and situations which would allow him to present his view of moral and social paradox. At the time of publication of "The Hall of Justice" a new interest was being taken in the gypsies and their lack of Christian faith.[17] In 1831 the Reverend James Crabb (no relation to George Crabbe) published *The Gypsies' Advocate* in which he stated that his object was to furnish a work that "might be the means of exciting among his countrymen an energetic benevolence toward this despised people."[18] He argues that although the gypsies were often vicious, they could not help themselves because they lacked the benefit of Christianity: "Among this poor and destitute people, instances of great guilt, depravity and misery are too common; nor can it be otherwise expected, while they are destitute of the knowledge of salvation in a crucified and ascended Saviour."[19] Similarly, when Crabbe's magistrate discovers that the vagrant does not fit his stereotype of the usual sort of vagabond, but was unable to help herself because of her pagan life amongst the gypsies, he feels he ought to reclaim her. Even James Crabb, although clearly moved to pity the gypsies' condition, is interested more in converting them to Christianity than in helping to better their conditions. A story is told of George III which typifies this attitude. Apparently the king saw a gypsy woman dying with her children around her. Going to her, the king attempted to help the woman and tell her of the grace of God. According to James Crabb, the king "saw her expire cheered by the view of that redemption he had set before her."[20] But of the children left motherless there is no mention; their earthly fate was not, apparently, of interest. Clearly Crabbe is portraying much the same missionary zeal in the magistrate's concern for the woman's soul.

Although most modern readers probably feel uneasy with Crabbe's dissolving rather than resolving the issues raised, nevertheless "The Hall of Justice" is remarkable in the way it poses an extremely forceful and radical question—are the poor wholly responsible for their crimes?—while cloaking the equally radical answer in respectable religious terminology. The ambivalent ending allows Crabbe to acclaim social accountability for the criminal without ever seeming to challenge the belief in individual responsibility and freedom of choice. In his later poems, as will be seen shortly, he finds ever more skilful and successful ways of embodying this paradox.

Chapter 3
This is the life itself

I

Although in "The Hall of Justice" Crabbe begins to develop the personalities of the vagrant and the judge, the poem's main concern is with a conflict of ideas. As has been seen, the question is whether an individual can be responsible for his actions when the social group to which he belongs is influenced strongly by powerful social and natural forces. As portrayed in "The Hall of Justice," the question offers no real resolution: when looked at from the personal perspective, the individual has freedom to choose; but from the social viewpoint the individual is moulded by his environment. Like most eighteenth-century satirists such as Hogarth and Fielding, Crabbe wanted to have both explanations; where he differs is that he was also interested in posing the contradiction and creating a resolution.

The poems that follow "The Hall of Justice" show Crabbe's interest slowly turning from characters who are portrayed so as to reveal ideas to characters who are portrayed as people interesting in themselves. This move is a natural refinement of Crabbe's intention in *The Village* to present the "real" facts of social life. There he had described the people in general; in "The Parish Register" (1807), *The Borough* (1810), and *Tales* (1812), he begins to look ever more closely so as to examine the individuals who compose the group. As will be seen, this move also permits Crabbe to deal with social problems as they are created, developed, and maintained by individuals' failures in relationships with one another.

But it should also be recalled that Crabbe's move to portraiture was not made in a single leap, for in both "The Parish Register" and "The Borough" he employs a narrator who offers sketches of people and places in order to build up a composite sketch of community life. Moreover, these narrators not only describe individuals and places, they also offer *general* views on the quality of life. Consequently, these abstractions are assailed as soon as the particularized exploration of people and places begins.

The Borough seems more successful than "The Parish Register" as a poem, largely because of the more highly developed narrative technique, yet Crabbe's attempt both to assert fundamental moral truths and to create free characters who respond naturally to their social situations can clearly be seen in "The Parish Register," and I shall briefly describe what happens there before passing to a more detailed consideration of *The Borough*. At the beginning of "The Parish Register" Crabbe expresses a number of abstract generalizations, which he suggests will be implicit in the following survey of the people's "tempers, manners, morals, customs, arts." With regard to his first point, which follows directly from *The Village*, there cannot be much argument: "Auburn and Eden can no more be found." However, this "fact" no longer plunges Crabbe into the bleak world of "Rapine and Wrong and Fear"; instead, it leads him to take over a theme from "The Hall of Justice," to assert that the individual must assume responsibility and employ his will to fashion a life for himself based on free choice. Although this emphasis on the will obviously contains something of an existential component, Crabbe does not envision man inhabiting a value-free universe, but one of "good and evil mix'd." Man is said to have the skill and power to part the good from the evil if "he feels the will."

Implicit in this view of a world susceptible to rational analysis is the assumption that the good or wise man who chooses well can expect reward. If this were not the case, the rationality of the universe would be called into doubt. In normal Christian terms the reward is often postponed until the after-life since another world is required to explain the inequalities of this world. But at the beginning of "The Parish Register" Crabbe's gaze is focused upon man in this world (although in rather abstract terms) and thus, like Milton in the last books of *Paradise Lost*, he stresses the possibilities that depend upon man's will.

Crabbe shows his readers around the homes of the industrious peasants who live a good life in "fair scenes of peace." All those who are honest and diligent occupy cottages, with adjoining land which the lord of the manor has given for their private cultivation (1. 129). While the cottages are not palaces, they are pleasant and clean; the walls are decorated with prints, and each cottage has a supply of books. By eighteenth-century standards, these cottagers lead a life that might well be called "pastoral." But this idyllic life is only for the industrious peasant; for the "idle peasant," Crabbe reserves the "infected row" where everything is dirty and ugly. The idle peasants consist of "the sot, the cheat, the shrew," and many are thieves and smugglers. These descriptions of the idle and industrious peasants—so akin to Hogarth's progress of "Industry and Idleness"—obviously embody the popular eighteenth-century assumption that, if a man were poor yet assiduous, he could always earn a decent living. One of the better-known exponents of this philosophy was William Paley, who eulogized the pleasures of the working man on low wages, and maintained: "All the provision which a poor man's child requires is contained in two words, 'industry and innocence'."[1]

Paley's position certainly contains some truth: under many circumstances the industrious man was more likely to succeed than the lazy one. Like all such statements of the obvious, however, it has little to say about actual conditions—in this case, the difficulties experienced by the poor even at the best of times. In his prologue, Crabbe adopts a more sensible position when he asserts that the "State of the Peasantry" is only "*meliorated* by Frugality and Industry" (my italics). Yet the beginning of "The Parish Register" uncharacteristically abjures altogether the social explanations for poverty offered in *The Village*, and takes over Paley's position, when it shows that *only* the vicious and improvident are poor, a conclusion that does not necessarily follow, since it is possible for a man with all the will in the world, and with industry and frugality to boot, to remain poor. Only when poverty itself becomes a sin or a sign of sin is it true that all the poor are sinners.

Many people have quite rightly criticized this depiction of the poverty-stricken at the beginning of "The Parish Register," and recently W. K. Thomas has claimed that this passage shows Crabbe was not really "nature's sternest painter," as Byron had commented, since Crabbe refused to show that both the industrious and the idle peasants lived in near-poverty conditions.[2] Yet the picture of the poor at the opening of "The Parish Register" is so obviously naive and so obviously out of keeping with the complexity of the picture presented in *The Village*, that it should arouse suspicions as to whether it is Crabbe's complete view. The answer of course is that it is not, for it fails to take into account the many individualized character sketches (which constitute the bulk of the poem) depicting the complicated processes by which individuals participate in social situations. The over-all effect of Crabbe's poetry often modifies internal didactic statements. Only an insensitive reading could fail to appreciate the extent to which "The Parish Register" qualifies its opening statements.

For instance, the narrator explores a whole host of complex personalities ranging from young girls such as Phoebe Dawson, who find themselves poor because they are kind, passionate, and imprudent, to men like Isaac Ashford, the model peasant, who, at the end of a virtuous life, finds himself faced with the horror of the workhouse. That "The Parish Register" describes these complex situations is of course its strength. It would have been a poor poem, indeed, had Crabbe included many exemplary characters such as the model labourers Reuben and Rachel and the model farmers Robert and Susan. These people are so prudent that they become unbelievable. Their pleasure or "content" is of the sort described by being "ready with the rent" (1. 417–18). Crabbe does not want to deny the value in the lives of honest, hard-working people who always live within their means (both emotionally and economically). In fact, he wants to encourage others to follow their example. But when he turns from the world as it ought to be (Reuben and Rachel) to the world as it is (the tenement) the moral prescriptions seem inapplicable. Crabbe's problem, then, is to find some sort of a balance between the telling and showing.

In "The Parish Register" Crabbe is not always successful in keeping this balance. Some of the difficulties apparently stem from the poem's having outgrown Crabbe's original conception. Although he begins and ends saying that he is describing the parish poor, in fact most of the character sketches are about the middle and upper classes. In spite of weaknesses and the obvious need for revision of the type Crabbe's friend Turner gave to early drafts in 1799, the poem's general shape is evident. "The Parish Register" begins with statements about the world's rationality, where men are responsible for their actions, and reap their due rewards, but as happens to Job, this sense of the world is shaken by new perceptions of what actually happens to people who are left free in the midst of a welter of choices. The complexity of life is constantly overflowing the categories in which the poem attempts to confine it. This is certainly the case with the narrator's reaction to the sudden death of Farmer Frankford's young wife. He cries out:

> Oh sacred sorrow! by whom souls are tried,
> Sent not to punish mortals, but to guide;
> If thou art mine (and who shall proudly dare
> To tell his Maker, he has had his share?)
> Still let me feel for what thy pangs are sent,
> And be my guide and not my punishment! (III. 629–34)

The effect of the experience has been to overwhelm his earlier confidence, and to leave him praying for some sort of rationale.

Nor is this an isolated case. From the beginning of the character sketches, a process is set in motion which serves to undercut the narrator's supposed reason for telling the stories. Crabbe *says* that his first portraits will describe births, presumably the most cheerful section of the register; but in the first story, Crabbe *shows* the miller's daughter being courted by a fortune hunter, seduced, forsaken, thrown into a tiny cottage, and finally going mad. Surely this very first sketch refutes the simplistic idea that the good prosper and the bad suffer. Who is good in this case? and who is bad? The miller is a tyrant, but he manages to keep his money and a hard-hearted mistress as well. If anything, the sketch demonstrates that people with open hearts and generous sentiments suffer because of their innocence. The development of the poem is a continual modification of the original link between poverty and vice, with the individual sketches showing a marked progression of pessimism about man's ability to fashion his own happiness. It is all very well to assert that the individual, by means of his will, can employ religion, reason, and work—the nineteenth-century trinity—to find significance, but this is valid only if there is assumed to be a unity to the moral world. In many of Crabbe's sketches this assumption of unity is challenged by the "naked and unveiled character" of his physical descriptions (preface to *Tales*) which exist, as it were, independently of any ordering principles. The progression from abstract to particular is not just a matter of Crabbe learning to express his wisdom in less conventional terms; rather the poem is for the reader an experience in which an initial abstract idea is modified under the continual testing of individual exploration.

The reader's perception must expand through this testing and his conclusions be drawn without help from the narrator who remains in the background objectively reporting. As the narrator's personality does not colour the poem significantly, and his opening views on the rationality of the world become—without his knowledge—seriously undermined, the poem's focus is somewhat fuzzy. The lack of a narrator participating in and thus being changed by the events he describes considerably weakens the poem. Although in *The Village* this objectivity succeeds, the greater complexity of "The Parish Register" requires a more flexible narrative technique.

II

With the publication of *The Borough* (1810), three years after "The Parish Register," Crabbe moved yet another step towards the creation of a narrative style in which he could encompass his perceptions of the contradictions inherent in presenting social questions on both the macro scale, involving people as seen in groups, and on the micro scale, where the individual, in his relations to others, is the focus. Whereas "The Parish Register" describes the people of the parish by means of births, marriages, and deaths, *The Borough*, as its title suggests, takes as its subject matter a particular town, with its institutions of schools, almshouses, hospitals, inns, and with its professional people such as aldermen, doctors, lawyers, priests. The magnitude of the endeavour is immense, and *The Borough*, running to 7,742 lines, is only a few hundred lines shorter than *The Prelude*. With Crabbe's reputation as a poet of the poor, the title no doubt raised expectations in the minds of many readers of 1810 that the poem would be about "rotten boroughs" and placemen, but both in his preface and his poem, Crabbe establishes that his intention is not to satirize political corruption but to describe as accurately as possible a particular borough and the flavour of life found among its inhabitants.

Yet Crabbe was learning that accurate description, rather than being easy, required multiple viewpoints. A major step forward from "The Parish Register" to *The Borough*, and one that solves many of Crabbe's problems in combining conflicting attitudes, is his creation of what he called a "man of straw" narrator, whose relation to Crabbe is by no means clear.[3] In the preface, Crabbe explains that he has called to his aid "the assistance of an ideal friend" to narrate the poem, yet when this ideal friend is "a residing burgess in a large seaport," and one recalls that the reputation in literature of the businessman or "cit" was not high,[4] one can be pardoned for entertaining some suspicions about the degree to which this narrator speaks for Crabbe. At several points throughout the poem, mocking comments are made about "merchant-maxims" (VIII. 134), and Crabbe generally pokes fun at the businessman whose first concern is with the prudent arrangement of life and fortune. That this "man of straw" narrator tells the borough's story has the effect of making any inferences or conclusions dependent on his perception. This, of course, gives Crabbe a degree of detachment.

Although in *Tales of the Hall*, Crabbe develops fully a number of narrators among whom he divides his own views, in *The Borough* his "man of straw" is only partially developed as a personality. As a result, there are times when the narrator speaks directly for Crabbe, and times when he does not; times when he is satirized and times when he is not. In many ways *The Borough* is a transitional poem. While Crabbe often uses his burgess to speak openly and directly as a social critic in the style of *The Village* (as will be seen in the following discussion of the letters on medicine and workhouses), *The Borough* never gives the sense of having been written to support a particular belief about borough life. Indeed, the views expressed by the narrator are so diverse, and there is so much social statement that is not borne out by his description, that the reader is forced to see the poem as a series of loosely joined sketches in which any single "truth" is contingent for its validity on the inferences available from the rest of the poem. The poem continually demands that the reader reassess his expectations.

In *The Borough* Crabbe can be seen to be moving towards poems such as *Tales* and *Tales of the Hall* in which social views are contingent on personality, and yet he has not completely left behind the forms of social statement expressed in *The Village* and "The Parish Register." He appears to be in somewhat the same position that Herbert Davis describes when he says of Jonathan Swift: "Just as with all his other later disguises, Swift simply makes use of a mask as it suits him; it is never permanently moulded over his face, and it always allows him to use his own voice."[5] Similarly, in Crabbe's case, although at times he speaks openly through his narrator, for most of the poem the narrator's perspective is not the final ordering principle of the poem. This being the case, Crabbe has committed himself only to the ordering principle that no such definitive principle is final.

Indeed, at the beginning of *The Borough*, Crabbe even manages to raise the fundamental question of whether verse can present adequate visual images:

> . . . can we so describe,
> That you shall fairly streets and buildings trace,
> And all that gives distinction to a place?   (I. 2–4)

Since the poem patently goes on to attempt such a description, it is rather surprising to find the answer—"This cannot be." Crabbe's solution to this apparent dilemma has been embodied in the form of the poem: he presents the narrator's account as a series of letters to a friend living in the country, a friend who has requested the description, and who can be counted on to use his "fancy" or imagination to help interpret the meaning of the descriptions. At the very beginning of the poem, by means of the rhetorical structure of letters to a friend, Crabbe reminds the reader of the relation between the percipient and the perceived object, and of the active role the reader must play in making manifest what is described.

While this element of the poem's form may at first sight seem irrelevant to Crabbe's social commentary, in fact it controls the sort of social commentary being offered. Instead of attempting to present definitive truths in terms of abstract propositions, Crabbe presents situations that permit the reader to evaluate social problems from a number of different points of view, thereby revealing how generalizations about social issues depend upon both the selection of available data and the person doing the selecting. A relatively unimportant but clear example of this occurs at the beginning of Letter II when the narrator asks: "What is a Church?" He finds that the question can receive many answers, all of them correct, depending on the attitudes of the people asked. The vicar replies that the church is a flock, "whom bishops govern and whom priests advise; / Wherein are various states and due degrees" (II. 6–7). The sexton has quite a different view: "'Tis a tall building, with a tower and bells" (II. 12). And in the abstract, the church is:

> The faithful, pure, and meek;
> From Christian folds the one selected race,
> Of all professions, and in every place.   (II. 2–4)

Since each of the answers is correct, and the poem admits or accepts them all, the reader is challenged to see many different impressions and to overcome the temptation to look from an "either-or" perspective. This is very different from the opening of *The Village* where Crabbe had been intent on capturing the one "real" view.

Throughout *The Borough*, Crabbe often impresses upon his readers the difficulties in arriving at objective conclusions, in distinguishing appearance from reality. For instance, the memorial to Jacob Holmes claims that Jacob was worthy and virtuous, that his wife loved him, and that he was "liberal, kind, religious, wise." But the narrator asks, "What is the truth?"

> Old Jacob married thrice;
> He dealt in coals, and av'rice was his vice;
> He ruled the Borough when his year came on,
> And some forget, and some are glad he's gone;
> For never yet with shilling could he part,
> But when it left his hand, it struck his heart. (II. 152–57)

As shall be seen, one of the main themes of *The Borough* is the discovery of how complex and difficult is the search for "the truth" concerning borough life.

Moreover, it was becoming clear to Crabbe that verse itself was inimical to historical narrative. In his sketch of the vicar, for instance, Crabbe notes that he has no intention of sequentially explaining everything about the man—this "let historians show" (III. 6). Although Crabbe is often thought of as writing short stories in verse that might equally well have been written in prose, one has only to attempt the experiment of transcribing some of his character sketches from verse into prose to see how much is lost. With its sharp juxtapositions of briefly-mentioned character traits, the verse can be fruitfully suggestive and ambivalent while the same technique in prose appears flat and unfinished. It is important to remember that *The Borough* cannot be regarded merely as rhymed history from a single perspective; Crabbe is continuously altering his point of view within the poetic structure.

For instance, when the narrator describes the effect of the ocean on the habits of mind of the inhabitants, he cannot, in his comments on this description, achieve the largeness of conception necessary to order the poem's vision. When he first describes the sea, it is tranquil, but soon a storm arises, a storm in which a ship is wrecked and many men drown. Significantly enough, the people of the borough can do nothing to help the drowning sailors. The women beg their husbands and sweethearts not to put out the lifeboats, but their pleas are unnecessary, since the force of the storm immobilizes human intervention. Curiously enough, the sense of helplessness is reinforced, and the narrator's own position becomes contained within the purview of the poem, when one discovers the narrator, after his moving description of the shipwreck (including the corpse on the beach and the cries of the dying sailors) falling into platitudes:

> But hear we now those sounds? Do lights appear?
> I see them not! the storm alone I hear:
> And lo! the sailors homeward take their way;
> Man must endure—let us submit and pray.
>
> Such are our winter-views; but night comes on—
> Now business sleeps, and daily cares are gone;
> Now parties form, and some their friends assist
> To waste the idle hours at sober whist;
> The tavern's pleasure or the concert's charm
> Unnumber'd moments of their sting disarm. (1. 267–76)

The lack of connection and the sense of incongruity here between the strength of the storm, the weakness of the narrator's response, and the concluding waste of "idle hours" clearly evokes the disjunction in the world at large.

In *The Borough*, the sea, in its pervasive influence on the lives of the people, quite obviously has emblematic as well as topographic significance, and thus creates an atmosphere in which the later social commentary is firmly located. This influence is pointed out in many places, but in none more subtly than Letter 1 where the narrator attempts vainly to escape its influence by going inland. When he at last comes to a garden surrounding a cot, he concludes that he has finally left the influence of the ocean behind, but he is mistaken:

> This gives us hope all views of town to shun—
> No! here are tokens of the sailor-son:
> That old blue jacket, and that shirt of check,
> And silken kerchief for the seaman's neck. (1. 139–42)

So important is this role of the sea it seems almost unnecessary to stress its influence; and so it would be, had not many of Crabbe's critics overlooked the point altogether. For instance, Oliver Sigworth has claimed that Crabbe meant the sketch of the ocean and the shipwreck to be seen almost wholly as topographic description: "We can imagine how Wordsworth or Thomson would have concluded the passage. The description would probably have led them somehow to a series of reflections upon man and the universe. Not so Crabbe."[6] Considering the emphasis which in late years has been placed on the analysis of images it seems rather ridiculous to have to point out the obvious truth that Crabbe could suggest ideas through descriptions and images without didactically explaining his intention. Crabbe might well have answered Sigworth's comment in the words of Rhodophil in *Marriage à la Mode*: "I am not so ill a painter that I need to write a name beneath the picture."

Crabbe's use of the ocean creates in the reader a whole host of reflections on man and the universe, and prepares him for later portraits of individuals, such as the prisoner who dreams of being overwhelmed by a huge wave as he walks by the seemingly peaceful shore. Not that Crabbe's ocean is anything but an ocean. He never—as a writer such as Conrad might—allows the particularity of the ocean to disappear into symbol. But in descriptions such as that of Jachin, the parish clerk, Crabbe's topographic setting powerfully locates the texture within which borough life goes on:

> In each lone place, dejected and dismay'd,
> Shrinking from view, his wasting form he laid;
> Or to the restless sea and roaring wind
> Gave the strong yearnings of a ruin'd mind.
> On the broad beach, the silent summer-day,
> Stretch'd on some wreck, he wore his life away;
> Or where the river mingles with the sea,
> Or on the mud-bank by the elder-tree,
> Or by the bounding marsh-dyke, there was he.
>
> (XIX. 270–78)

The river mingling with the sea is usually an image of eternal life, but Crabbe's inclusion of the mudbank and the elder tree twists the conventional religious image so that now it suggests Jachin's complete dissolution of body and soul.

Crabbe believed that most novelists and poets failed to do justice to the degree of violence, sudden change and senseless, unjustified horror which he saw as a part of life. As he says of his fellow writers:

> Life, if they'd search, would show them many a change,
> The ruin sudden and the misery strange!
> With more of grievous, base, and dreadful things,
> Than novelists relate or poet sings.   (XX. 21–24)

Once it becomes evident that one of the main aims of *The Borough* is to elucidate disparate ways of looking at community relations, and that the ever-changing ocean stands as part of the objective correlative for the never-ending process of evaluation and re-evaluation, then it should come as no surprise to find that, in those cases where the narrator attempts to draw inferences from what he sees, his conclusions tell the reader as much about the narrator as about the scene he is describing. When this occurs, neither the narrator nor the other characters appear to represent Crabbe's own viewpoint; at times, even, the suggestion is that Crabbe does not have a single viewpoint, but eclectically develops as many different facets as possible.

A good example of this procedure occurs in Letter V, where the subject is corrupt elections. Most of Crabbe's critics in the early nineteenth century disliked this letter. Even Jeffrey, who usually found something to praise in Crabbe's poetry, commented, "The letter on the *Election*, we look on as a complete failure,—or at least as containing scarcely any thing of what it ought to have contained." [7] What it ought to have contained, according to these critics, was scathing criticism of political patronage. Although the letter begins promisingly enough—"Yes, our Election's past, and we've been free, / Somewhat as madmen without keepers be" (v. 1–2)—criticism of corrupt elections soon declines into a tale of woe about the inconveniences such elections occasion the good people of the town. Moreover, the narrator's tone of voice is that of the "genteel" *Spectator* essays, rather than that of the vitriolic political controversies concerning the reform of corrupt boroughs raging in the years before the first Reform Bill. Yet what the early critics overlooked is that the narrator is not so much interested in the corruption and bribery of elections as he is in the loss occasioned to his own dignity as a result of his supporting a candidate in his own borough election. When this happens, the narrator becomes a character in his own story, as open to criticism as any of the other characters. Crabbe's attitude towards the narrator in this letter is by no means always clear, and this creates some fuzziness of focus, but Crabbe's delight in characterization and his sense of a multiplicity of viewpoints definitely leads him to undercut or satirize the narrator's own statements. For instance, once the villagers learn that the narrator supports a particular party, he receives numerous social calls from voters who make demands on his time. But as the narrator explains at length how he disapproves of "party-friendship" which forces him to entertain people who "make your house their home," and how he hates being forced to be polite to the "wretch" who prates "your wife and daughter from the room," his tone becomes one of self-pity. This is especially true when he notes how the opponent's side rakes up family scandal to sway the voters.

In other words, the narrator is not so much criticizing corrupt elections as complaining about the way the election forces him to become involved, suffering all the indignities while allowing him none of the glory. Crabbe might well have taken this opportunity to voice some forceful criticism, for the narrator condemns the way in which freedom is equated in the minds of the people with the freedom to bribe, coerce, and level all distinctions. But the incipient criticism is largely dispelled when Crabbe shows the narrator refusing to discuss principles by keeping to personal complaint—his dislike of the "shame and toil" the "riot and abuse." Quite clearly, Crabbe is more interested in characterizing a personal view of the situation than he is in developing an argument.

Crabbe must have felt this himself, for in his preface he stated: "An Election indeed forms a part of one Letter, but the evil there described is one not greatly nor generally deplored, and there are probably many places of this kind where it is not felt."[8] When the letter is read attentively and without preconceptions, it is discovered that it includes much material which is irrelevant to the subject of corrupt elections, but which is quite informative about the personality of the narrator. At line 127 the narrator interrupts his criticism of elections to give a long description of the town's mayor.[9] Although the narrator treats this man seriously as the borough's "worthy mayor," the reader soon realizes that the mayor is not so "worthy" as the narrator believes. For instance, the narrator sees the mayor as a person having at heart the best interests of the borough:

> Our worthy mayor, on the victorious part,
> Cries out for peace, and cries with all his heart;
> He, civil creature! ever does his best,
> To banish wrath from every voter's breast;
> "For where," says he, with reason strong and plain,
> "Where is the profit? what will anger gain?"   (v. 127–32)

The reader, however, is able to perceive that the mayor's being "on the victorious part" accounts in large measure for his good nature and restraint. The pun on the word profit in the mayor's question, "Where is the profit?" alerts us to the possibility that the mayor might wish to see party animosity continue if it led to profits. The narrator reports noncommittally the mayor's rise from poor fisherman to man of riches, and quietly explains how the most important event of his life was the day he discovered that money could earn interest. The mayor's reaction at learning money will breed is: "I begin to live." In order to emphasize this ironic treatment of the mayor and ensure that none of his readers would mistake the mayor for a praiseworthy figure, Crabbe inserted a footnote in which he pointedly refers to the questionable legality of the mayor's corporation doles.

Thus, by the end of the letter, Crabbe has developed his narrator sufficiently well that we can see the list of election complaints as the result of the narrator's personal desires and ambitions. The closing lines assert his hope that his own poetry will attain glory (in the service of humanity, no doubt!) and that the good vicar, the borough's "male lily," should have "less to do." The last line— "And our good vicar would have less to do"—surely strikes one as intentional bathos on Crabbe's part. The narrator's "concern" for the election strife is no more than one would expect of any good burgess interested in maintaining "that old ease." Jeffrey's comment about the letter's "timidity" is really beside the point, for he misses the way in which Crabbe, by means of his characterization of the narrator and the mayor, locates his "social" criticism in the humanity of the individual characters. As a result, Crabbe's criticism here is not the didactic kind which sets out what is wrong; rather he displays the way in which the corruption of the elections is inherent even in those who hate the corruption, since they appear to be unable to rise above their petty, selfish concerns to a statement of first principles. For the portrayal of such an interaction between the social and the human, it is apparent that Crabbe could not really use his own voice as narrator, since the point was to show even the critic criticized, and thus to present issues in a multi-faceted human context.

Letter XXIII, "Prisons," offers an excellent example of the way in which Crabbe manages to manipulate the narrator so as to offer a number of insights into questions concerned with mercy and justice. The letter opens with the bland statement: "'Tis well that man to all the varying states / Of good and ill his mind accommodates" (XXIII. 1–2). In normal conversation one might expect this piece of moralizing to be followed by a comment on how all men are susceptible to hardships and misfortunes. A few such misfortunes might even be mentioned, such as those associated with extremes of heat and cold, disease, accidents, etc. Surprisingly enough, the example cited is that men often go to prison. The very assurance with which this statement is posited strikes one as odd, since a term in prison is not normally in the same category of natural misfortunes as that of, say, childhood diseases.[10]

As soon as the narrator begins to describe the prison, however, the reader understands his reason for accepting prison life as a possible part of every man's experience. In the borough's prison all different types of offenders are grouped together. When serious and trivial offences may equally result in a prison sentence, there is some reason for regarding a term in prison as not unlikely. Even to use the word "offence" is misleading, for many of the prisoners have committed no offence other than that of being unfortunate enough to fall into debt. The narrator goes out of his way to point out the differences among the various types of prisoners: "Thus might we class the debtors here confined, / The more deceived, the more deceitful kind" (XXIII. 36–37). Such statements force the reader to see how foolish and wrong it is to treat a man who has spent a lifetime in hard work on the same footing as a man who has set out to deceive his creditors. And thus Crabbe's social observations are left implicit, ready for the reader's discovery.

Nor is this interest in finding examples of injustice in Crabbe's prison merely a twentieth-century penchant. The narrator himself may appear insensitive to the injustice of the prison, but as he proceeds with his account, he comes to perceive the absurdity of imprisoning certain classes of debtors. Of the small shopkeeper who fails in business because he does not have sufficient goods to sell, the narrator says: "Debtors are these on whom 'tis hard to press, / 'Tis base, impolitic, and merciless" (XXIII. 82–83). He realizes that in many instances the causes of bankruptcy do not lie altogether with the merchant, but can be traced to external causes such as a general depression in trade. At this time a small business-man could still be made or broken by the patronage of one or two well-known neighbouring families. That Crabbe wishes his readers to feel pity for the prisoners is clear, for he has one of them express the following sentiment:

> Go to thy world, and to the young declare
> What we, our spirits and employments, are;
>
> . . . .
> And bid them haste to join the gen'rous tribe.
>
> (XXIII. 193–98)

Crabbe himself often went to the King's Bench to administer relief.[11]

The letter itself, consisting of a series of vignettes, has a cumulative effect so that the interest and pity given to minor criminals is extended even to those who have committed a serious crime. Notably enough, the woman under sentence of death, because "she fired a full-stored barn," is not condemned. Rather, her life is shown to be a chain of violent actions leading to the desperate act of firing a barn (regarded as something akin to child-murder), which in turn provokes the authorities to even greater violence when they commit her to prison and condemn her to death:

> She was a pauper bound, who early gave
> Her mind to vice, and doubly was a slave;
> Upbraided, beaten, held by rough control,
> Revenge sustain'd, inspired, and fill'd her soul.
>
> (XXIII. 217–20)

That the narrator sees and explains the way social causes have contributed to the woman's act does not mean that he or the reader condones the act, but such an explanation permits insights which make outright moral condemnation less likely.

In fact many of the examples seem to have been selected for the express purpose of forcing the reader to recognize how little many of the prisoners merit a prison sentence. In this category is the man who pledged his bond for a friend:

> And there sits one, improvident but kind,
> Bound for a friend, whom honour could not bind;
> Sighing, he speaks to any who appear,
> "A treach'rous friend—'twas that which sent me here:
> I was too kind—I thought I could depend
> On his bare word—he was a treach'rous friend."
>
> (XXIII. 96–101)

Automatically one feels sympathetic towards such "kind" people forced to spend perhaps a lifetime in "a damp prison, where the very sight / Of the warm sun is favour and not right" (XXIII. 22–23).

Nor were such cases uncommon. A few years later Crabbe had occasion to see the poet Thomas Moore placed in a similar situation when he had to flee the country for two years after his deputy in Bermuda had made him liable for a debt. At that time Crabbe commented, "Mr. Anacreon Moore is obliged to go abroad on Acct. of the decision which calls on him for £6000, a Debt contracted without a Fault on his part and almost without a Possibility of Avoiding it."[12]

In all these sketches one cannot help noting that Crabbe's use of the narrator constantly edges forward considerations of justice. Furthermore, Crabbe ensures that this question of justice is brought into the framework of the poem by actually raising the question in connection with the last and most dangerous of the criminals, the highwayman. Although the narrator generally attempts to dissociate himself from the questions of mercy and justice, at one point he recognizes that his comments are inadvertently raising the questions, and he asks the rhetorical question:

> "But will not mercy?"—No! she cannot plead
> For such an outrage;—'twas a cruel deed:
> He stopp'd a timid traveller;—to his breast,
> With oaths and curses, was the danger press'd:—
> No! he must suffer; pity we may find
> For one man's pangs, but must not wrong mankind.
>
> (XXIII. 245–50)

The method of introducing the question, of allowing it to flicker across the narrator's mind, only to have it stopped in mid-sentence, suggests that Crabbe wanted the possibility of reduced prison sentences only to be hinted at. A similar instance of this technique has been seen already in "The Hall of Justice." But whether or not the narrator wishes to discuss the question of mercy and justice, and from the way he stifles it he clearly does not, Crabbe certainly wished the reader to be aware of its presence. One might even say that the manner in which the narrator forcibly ends any further consideration of the question makes the reader even more aware and suspicious of the implications of the question than if he had been offered a longer and more prosaic treatment.

The device Crabbe uses to gain his reader's interest in and sympathy for the highwayman is to show the highwayman dreaming of his happy youth:

> The house, the chamber, where he once array'd
> His youthful person; where he knelt and pray'd.
> Then too the comforts he enjoy'd at home,
> The days of joy; the joys themselves are come—
> The hours of innocence—the timid look
> Of his loved maid, when first her hand he took
> And told his hope . . . . (XXIII. 277–83)

The highwayman's "early prospects" were happy and good; had circumstances proved different, he would probably have developed into a good citizen. But the dream suddenly changes to show the highwayman en route to the gallows: "Some heartless shout, some pity, all condemn" (XXIII. 269). No doubt this condemnation is what the highwayman could have expected in actuality as well as in dream, but the reader, having seen what the highwayman once was, and perceiving his despair at the thought of the gallows, cannot now so easily join the ranks of those who condemn. The sketch forces the reader to see both past and present simultaneously, so that in forming an opinion of the highwayman, the reader cannot, as the judge has done, take into account only the single felonious action on the highway. As Crabbe himself points out in the preface, his intention was to "excite in some minds that mingled pity and abhorrence which . . . ties and binds us to all mankind by sensations common to us all, and in some degree connects us, without degradation, even to the most miserable and guilty of our fellow-men."[13] But in the sketch, Crabbe is able to do all this without ever once seeming to *tell* the reader his intention.

However, even some of the most perceptive of Crabbe's readers have failed to make the imaginative leap necessary to reconcile the *two* pictures of the highwayman. Jeffrey, who singled out the details of the felon's dream as an example of "the exquisite accuracy and beauty of the landscape painting," found "an unspeakable charm from the lowly simplicity and humble content of the characters."[14]

Yet when Jeffrey quoted this section of the poem, he stopped at line 329, omitting the last four lines of the poem where Crabbe shows the "unspeakable charm" to be all in the past. Jeffrey ended his quotation at the point where the young man and his beloved were dallying by the ocean; he did not include the lines describing the dreamer awakening to find himself a convicted felon. The two aspects of the man's life must be taken together; to follow Jeffrey, and focus on the aspect of the highwayman's life which is particularly appealing, is to misread the poem. Always intent on seeing life whole, Crabbe was not content to portray the prisoner only as a highwayman; he wanted his readers to see that in any one man there were actually a great many different men. Yet Jeffrey's mistake is a natural one, since the description of the early life of the highwayman is given at great length. The seemingly disproportionate amount of space given to the highwayman's happy youth compels the reader to base his opinion of the man mostly on these early years.

The treatment of the last section of the letter is extremely artful. As has been seen, Crabbe permitted the narrator to state specifically that mercy could not be shown to the criminal. Yet the narrator's assertion is qualified by the long description of the highwayman's pleasant youth, which captures the reader's interest, and as Jeffrey noted, makes him feel "how deep and peculiar an interest may be excited by humble subjects."[15] After having aroused this interest in the highwayman as a young boy amidst his pastoral landscape, Crabbe changes suddenly to the present, when in the last four lines of the letter he shows the prisoner awakening from his dream. The effect of the sudden transition is to give the reader some idea of the prisoner's despair, and to transfer the interest and affection which he had felt for the youth to the condemned felon. And thus even in the extreme case of the highwayman, Crabbe has managed to question the processes by which moral decisions are taken.

The narrator's own conclusion is that—"Pity we may find / For one man's pangs, but must not wrong mankind" (XXIII. 249–50). Yet this is not very different from the reaction of the crowd: "Some pity, all condemn," and is hardly a resolution of the conflict. The effect of the letter is to create the maximum amount of sympathy for the prisoners on an individual basis without ever jeopardizing the general principle that crime must be punished. The antithesis between the two themes—crime must be punished, and individuals should be spared—is never resolved. Yet the conflict permits the reader to perceive how differently the decision to punish appears to the judge and the accused. What does the letter suggest should be done? It does not suggest any one answer. But through his manipulation of narrative, Crabbe offers an arresting insight into social problems for the reader who perceives that "What is done" changes when seen first through the judge's eyes and then through the eyes of the accused.

One of the great delights of both "The Parish Register" and *The Borough* is their profusion of detail, conveying not only a sense of the richness of life, but of the importance and significance of each particular, each individual. Crabbe enables us to see people and things afresh, unencumbered by the usual social, moral, and religious paraphernalia. For instance, in Letter xvi, "Benbow," the narrator first prepares the reader to dislike Benbow and all his ideas by portraying him as a drunken profligate, but as soon as Benbow takes centre stage in his own right, he captures attention, and we discover that he has some quite remarkable observations to make. The reader is told that Benbow is an unworthy member of the alms-house, that Sir Denys committed an error of judgment in admitting him. Yet when Benbow tells the story of old Squire Asgill and his son, his response to life carries conviction, and the reader disregards the narrator's comments. Undoubtedly Benbow has faults, and Crabbe wished his readers to appreciate these faults, but to a degree Benbow usurps the narrator's role as Crabbe's mouthpiece so that the reader's attitude towards Benbow constantly varies, leaving Crabbe's own position uncertain.

For the purposes of this chapter, my main interest in Benbow lies in his account of old Squire Asgill and the change which took place in the Asgill estate when the young squire assumed control. Benbow's reasons for praising the old squire and disparaging his son are almost always connected with the old squire's love of hospitality. Benbow lays particular emphasis on the way the old squire refused to make a great distinction between himself and his servants:

> No pride had he, and there was difference small
> Between the master's and the servants' hall;
> And here or there the guests were welcome all.
>
> (XVI. 73–75)

The old squire, with his conviviality and hospitality, seems a much better human being than the new-style farmers whose sole interest is reaping the maximum amount of profit from their land. For instance, old Asgill does not attempt to restrict the game to his own table: "Of Heaven's free gifts he took no special care; / He never quarrel'd for a simple hare" (XVI. 76–77).

Like Squire Western in *Tom Jones*, old Squire Asgill is interested primarily in his own pleasures, and these are of the simple and crude country variety. A drinking tenant pleases him more than one who wishes to enclose the land for greater profit. Consequently his gruff good nature benefits his poor neighbours. As far as Benbow is concerned, the old squire—a Tory and a churchman—is the perfect example of England's landed gentry. That he keeps a mistress instead of a wife is a sign, not of corruption, but of high spirits in the best tradition of the novels of Fielding and Smollett.

This is not to say that the reader cannot appreciate that old Squire Asgill is an extremely limited person, a man who is probably as narrow as Squire Western and with a sense of humour as crude as that of Fanny Burney's Captain Mirvan.[16] But for all that, surely Crabbe meant the reader to agree with Benbow in preferring the father to the son:

> The father dead, the son has found a wife,
> And lives a formal, proud, unsocial life;—
> The lands are now enclosed; the tenants all,
> Save at a rent-day, never see the hall;
> No lass is suffer'd o'er the walks to come,
> And, if there's love, they have it all at home.
>
> (XVI. 120–25)

The old squire's generosity to guests and servants alike has been replaced by his son's penurious system of economy so that, as Benbow remarks, if the ghost of the old squire could return, it would no longer find the house filled with song and the smell of food cooking:

> There would it see a pale old hag preside,
> A thing made up of stinginess and pride;
> Who carves the meat, as if the flesh could feel,
> Careless whose flesh must miss the plenteous meal.
>
> (XVI. 136–39)

A large part of the reason why we side with Benbow is that he has all the good lines. Benbow's ability to manipulate language to create graphic scenes worthy of Hogarth predisposes us to dislike the straightened lives of the new squirearchy. His comments on love and his descriptions of the carving of the meat embody the *joie de vivre* of pre-industrial England, and give a felt reason for disliking the economies of the new style "cash nexus."

As Crabbe indicated in "The Parish Register," however, the changing styles of life brought the small farmer a higher living standard, allowing him to buy Wilton carpets and to grace his walls with prints of Werther.[17] This no doubt partially accounts for Crabbe's refusal to commit himself entirely to Benbow's belief that the old order was better in every way. On the other hand, in Benbow he has created the right sort of character to present his criticisms of the new order, for Benbow's perspective is that of "below stairs." He is interested, not so much in the efficiency of the farm, as he is in his own well-being and the happiness of those around him. Much of the hardship caused by enclosures could not be measured in pounds, shillings, and pence, but was to be found in the changed "style of life." Benbow, as a member of the lower classes, could value the hospitality of the old squire, and could appreciate his generosity in little things. For instance, Benbow notes how, under the old squire, the borough maidens were allowed into the fields to pick flowers, whereas the new squire denies them this right. The right to pick flowers is a small matter, but when the labourer lived close to subsistence level such privileges often meant the difference between living in frugal comfort or slavish poverty.

This matter of children being allowed into the fields and parks for their own enjoyment, to pick flowers and berries, was a point touched on in the debate over enclosures. It occasioned a dispute in *The New Monthly Magazine* among three men signing themselves Publicola, Veritas, and Humanity. The debate arose when Publicola complained that the squires were setting mantraps and spring guns against poachers, thus closing the fields and parks to the innocent diversions of the country people. Humanity felt the issue to be serious enough to warrant the following answer:

> I cannot at all agree with VERITAS when he terms PUBLICOLA'S complaints relative to cottagers' children not being permitted to gather berries "too frivolous to reply to." Deprive the rich and luxurious man of his pines and grapes, and he will feel how frivolous is the complaint of the child of poverty when deprived of his haws and sloes.[18]

Benbow was by no means alone in his insistence that the labourers had lost a great deal with the disappearance of the old rural economy. Many people recognized that if all the labourer's rights were taken away, he soon became a slave (like the barn-firer). As Benbow is primarily interested in his own pleasures, he is quick to appreciate the dangers inherent in a capitalistic attitude to land and wealth, but it is his ability to formulate his criticisms in terms of the plain facts of everyday life that makes his argument so convincing. Yet there is always the danger in such discussions of becoming solemn and misrepresenting Crabbe's tone. Like Marvell, Crabbe often seems to undercut even his most serious points, as if to remind the reader that life as it is really lived denies all manner of fences. Even as he advances the point about the borough damsels picking flowers in the open fields, he undercuts it with irony by noting that they took their walks for flowers at night. No doubt old Squire Asgill also picked flowers.

III

In any attempt at a descriptive survey of a place or time, a writer requires both freshness of insight and accuracy of language if he is to avoid falling into platitudes. Much description is simply enumeration of the obvious punctuated with exclamations on its beauty or ugliness. In both *The Village* and "The Hall of Justice" Crabbe had been able to give his descriptions resonance by playing off various traditions—the pastoral against the empirical, the social against the individual. In *The Borough* he faced the problem of describing a community for the sake of its own intrinsic interest, and therefore could not avail himself of his earlier technique. But as D. H. Burden has noted, Crabbe builds into *The Borough* a number of implicit comparisons and allows them to interact, and this in part resolves the difficulty.[19] For instance, at the beginning or the poem, when the narrator is preparing to describe the borough's river, he asks his friend in the country to call to mind his quiet, winding stream, so reminiscent of the pastoral. The narrator asks this, not because the borough's river is similar, but because it is entirely opposite. Instead of the casual, leisurely angler of the inland stream, the borough has a poor oyster dredger:

> Nor angler we on our wide stream descry,
> But one poor dredger where his oysters lie:
> He, cold and wet, and driving with the tide,
> Beats his weak arms against his tarry side,
> Then drains the remnant of diluted gin,
> To aid the warmth that languishes within;
> Renewing oft his poor attempts to beat
> His tingling fingers into gathering heat.   (I. 53–60)

No comment is made on the incongruity of the comparison, but the effect is to leave the reader slightly uneasy about the implied differences. This is especially the case when the narrator describes how at evening, the wealthy, with all their "comforts spread around," hear "the painful dredger's welcome sound" (I. 65–66). The verse is here forcing together contraries—comfort and pain, wealth and poverty—in a most unusual manner.

Similarly, in Letter X, when the narrator and his friend discuss the sorts of entertainment to be found in the borough, the rich friend in the country imagines that they must be gay, sociable, and interesting. The narrator, however, points out their boring qualities, how on a good evening at a typical club, time is merely consumed in eating, drinking, and playing cards. He concludes that much of the conviviality is superficial and spurious. While this denigration of the town's social life is a common eighteenth-century theme, the surprising feature is that the account does not end with the usual panegyric on country solitude, but with some muted praise of the pleasures to be found in a Friendly Society, a Benefit Club of the sort much under discussion at the time and greatly feared by many as an institution of insurrection.[20] Compared with the clubs of the wealthy, the poor man's club is a great success. Again the reader has been forced to drop his normal perspective as he is jarred into seeing things from a new and unusual angle.

Perhaps the best and most extensive use of this change of perspective comes in the accounts of the borough's welfare institutions. An early nineteenth-century reader would have found Crabbe's borough amazingly well supplied with such institutions. It has a system of parish out-relief, a private almshouse, lifeboats, a modern gaol, and a hospital. If Chadwick's commissioners had investigated the borough, no doubt they would have written a glowing report.[21] Crabbe, however, opens another dimension when he asks the interested observer to inspect the borough's pleasant almshouse:

> Leave now our streets, and in yon plain behold
> Those pleasant seats for the reduced and old;
> A merchant's gift, whose wife and children died,
> When he to saving all his powers applied.   (XIII. 1–4)

But is this first impression of a benevolent and well-endowed almshouse borne out by the facts? Several things suggest that it is not. The first point to arouse suspicion is that the almshouse is not the gift of a magnanimous squire, but of an eccentric, lonely, old man. Crabbe acknowledges that the benefactor was genuinely interested in helping people, but points out that he built the almshouse while starving himself (in the manner of the eccentric Thomas Day, the author of *Sandford and Merton*, who also had a taste "to give and spare").

Of course there was nothing wrong with someone like Day wishing to live penuriously, while devoting all his money to charity. Richard Lovell Edgeworth remarked that Day "was the most virtuous human being" he had ever known.[22] And Crabbe certainly speaks warmly of the merchant who lives Day's sort of life in order to build an almshouse. But Crabbe's picture of the benefactor is by no means the customary picture of the well-balanced country gentleman setting aside a portion of his income for the poor. In order for this almshouse to be built, one man had to deprive himself of everything.

Leaving aside for the moment the benefactor's eccentricities, one can admit that he created an admirable almshouse based on sound and generous principles:

> Within the row are men who strove in vain,
> Through years of trouble, wealth and ease to gain;
> Less must they have than an appointed sum,
> And freemen been, or hither must not come;
> They should be decent and command respect
> (Though needing fortune,) whom these doors protect,
> And should for thirty dismal years have tried
> For peace unfelt and competence denied.   (XIII. 62–69)

Even Malthus would probably not have objected to such deserving people receiving a pension in recompense for a lifetime of effort. But Crabbe disappoints those of his readers who were looking for confirmation of their belief that all was well with society when he shows how the practice of the almshouse differs from its precepts.

The success or failure of almshouses depended almost wholly on their governors. The usual reason for their failure, and certainly the reason cited by Crabbe, was a lack of proper control at the administrative level. In Crabbe's house the original founder had tried to prevent corruption by ruling that six guardian-directors were to administer its affairs at all times.[23] In theory this idea seems excellent, but Crabbe shows that: "Numbers are call'd to govern, but in fact / Only the powerful and assuming act" (XIII. 231–32). Although six are supposed to succeed the founder, *in fact*, the one with power—Sir Denys—takes charge. Sir Denys is not vicious or cruel; like many autocrats, he is merely inept. In a letter to Mary Leadbeater, Crabbe remarked that Sir Denys was of all his characters "the nearest to real life."²⁴ Sir Denys' social position has given him power for so long that he now refuses to listen to evidence, and brutishly forces on the rest of the community his own ill-thought-out opinions. Well-intentioned though he may have been, Sir Denys' inability to form judgments on the evidence produced must have made him appear an arbitrary monarch to those over whom he ruled:

> View then this picture of a noble mind:
> Let him be wise, magnanimous, and kind;
> What was the wisdom? Was it not the frown
> That keeps all question, all inquiry down?
> His words were powerful and decisive all;
> But his slow reasons came for no man's call.
> "'Tis thus," he cried, no doubt with kind intent,
> To give results and spare all argument.   (XIII. 132–39)

In order to show that Sir Denys is exactly the sort of man to gain the public's approbation, Crabbe develops a rhetorical structure in which the "voice of the public" is allowed to speak. The public is wildly enthusiastic about the various amenities that Sir Denys has given the town:

> He raised the room that towers above the street,
> A public room where grateful parties meet;
> He first the life-boat plann'd; to him the place
> Is deep in debt—'twas he reviv'd the race;
> To every public act this hearty friend
> Would give with freedom or with frankness lend;
> His money built the jail, nor prisoner yet
> Sits at his ease, but he must feel the debt.   (XIII. 148–55)

Although Crabbe agrees with the public voice that in many ways Sir Denys is an admirable person, the irony inherent in the repeated comment that the borough is "deep in debt" to Sir Denys suggests that it may owe him more than gratitude; it may owe him hard cash. That the "public voice" speaks these lines and not Crabbe or his narrator also indicates Crabbe's lack of complete approval of Sir Denys. The point is not that Crabbe disdains the public actions of Sir Denys; in fact he says: "I grant the whole, nor from one deed retract" (XIII. 159). But the public's emphasis upon these actions has obscured the real character of Sir Denys, and has perhaps misled many in their evaluation of his contribution to the community. Again Crabbe is asking the reader to make a sophisticated evaluation of a borough community; to do this one must step behind the external appearances of the borough to observe the real motives governing the actions of the borough rulers.

Our final opinion of Sir Denys depends to a large extent on the opinion we form of his directorship of the almshouse. Only in the following three letters, when Crabbe shows Sir Denys filling the vacancies in the almshouse, do we see some of the results of his term as director:

> Three seats were vacant while Sir Denys reign'd,
> And three such favourites their admission gain'd;
> These let us view, still more to understand
> The moral feelings of Sir Denys Brand.   (XIII. 336–39)

The people whom Sir Denys chooses are certainly an odd group: Blaney, "a wealthy Heir, dissipated, and reduced to Poverty"; Clelia, a frivolous woman of pleasure; and Benbow, a literary descendant of Shakespeare's Bardolph. In permitting such people a place in the almshouse, Sir Denys has destroyed its original plan. The founder had meant it to be a place of refuge for those persons bankrupt in spite of their best efforts; Sir Denys has turned the house into a home for those fallen through their own dissipation. As Crabbe acknowledges, Sir Denys is not a bad man, but his good intentions work against the best interests of the community.

In his portrait of Sir Denys, Crabbe manages to overturn some of the conventional judgments of his time. In a Fanny Burney novel, Sir Denys would have been portrayed as vain but essentially good. In *The Borough* he becomes an insidious force weakening society. On the other hand, Laughton, who succeeds Sir Denys in the position of guardian of the almshouse, is the sort of character generally portrayed in contemporary literature as dangerous:

> At length, with power endued and wealthy grown,
> Frailties and passions, long suppress'd, were shown;
> Then, to provoke him was a dangerous thing;
> His pride would punish, and his temper sting;
> His powerful hatred sought th' avenging hour;
> And his proud vengeance struck with all his power.
>
> (XIII. 286–91)

In a Richardson novel, Laughton would have been portrayed as was the arrogant and ruthless Sir Hargrave Pollexfen—a man with no redeeming features.[25] Yet Crabbe shows Laughton fulfilling all his duties in connection with the almshouse: "He never to this quiet mansion sends / Subject unfit, in compliment to friends" (XIII. 326–27). Because of Laughton's ambition and cruelty, one would expect Crabbe to condemn him as a cause of social injustice. On the contrary, for his work in the almshouse, Laughton becomes an object of praise.

Crabbe's technique is to present one side of a question, and then to alter the focus of the poem so that another side comes into view. In the case of the almshouse, he begins by praising its principles but then reveals that its function controverts these principles. Theoretically there are six guardians, in practice, one. And people such as Clelia, Blaney, and Benbow pervert the original intention of the almshouse. Superficially the almshouse may resemble a model poorhouse; in fact it is ruled by two successive tyrants— Sir Denys and Laughton. Neither is compassionate, and the best one can say for Laughton is that he is rigorously just. Systematically, while seeming to do the opposite, Crabbe demolishes our good opinion of the borough's almshouse—society's ideal of the charitable institution.

If we can imagine the Poor Law Commissioners being pleased with the almshouse, then they would probably have waxed ecstatic over their tour of the hospital. In the records it would be entered as the gift of a generous individual, the natural conclusion being that once again man's Christian love for his brother had triumphed over self-interest. Chadwick would have noted that here was an instance where man felt responsible for those less fortunate than himself. Certainly the opening lines of the letter suggest that the narrator wishes to see the hospital as the product of such charity:

> An ardent spirit dwells with christian love,
> The eagle's vigour in the pitying dove;
>
> . . . .
> Her utmost aid to every ill applies,
> And plans relief for coming miseries.
> Hence yonder building rose . . . .   (XVII. 1–13)

But is the word "hence" appropriate?

At first the narrator seems to indicate it is, but when the question is asked, "How rose the building?" the answer reveals that it rose at least as much from self-interest as from compassion for the unfortunate. True enough, the idea of the hospital was conceived by a genuinely pious man. But this man required financial aid, and so turned for help to a second man, a person filled with remorse for his ungenerous treatment of a brother. He contributes to the hospital as an act of penance. The third man to contribute is one who:

>   never grieves
> For love that wounds or friendship that deceives;
> His patient soul endures what Heav'n ordains,
> But neither feels nor fears ideal pains.   (XVII. 202–205)

And the fourth man to help is a type of utilitarian who gives funds to the hospital in order to balance the debit side of his ledger with God.

Crabbe of course never criticizes these men for helping to build the hospital. As poet, he

> . . . almost dreads their failings to detect;
> But truth commands:—in man's erroneous kind,
> Virtues and frailties mingle in the mind;
> Happy, when fears to public spirit move,
> And even vices to the work of love!   (XVII. 273–77)

The point is that Crabbe wished to show that much of what passed with the public for pure charity was actually inspired by other motives. The structure of the letter suggests a continual movement away from perfection. At the beginning of the letter, the narrator gives the view of the optimistic Christian who believes that Christian charity was transforming the injustices of British society. But the progression of the poem reveals that the highly praised Christian charity plays only a small role in the building of the hospital.

As a parish priest, Crabbe cared for the sick, and thus he came to learn a great deal about the working of hospitals. When he visited Edinburgh in 1822, Crabbe was more interested in the Royal Infirmary and Bedlam than in the "historic sights"—much to the surprise of Lockhart who served as his guide: "Mr. Crabbe repeated his visits several times to the Royal Infirmary of Edinburgh, and expressed great admiration of the manner in which the patients were treated. He also examined pretty minutely the interior of the Bedlam. I went with him both to the Castle and Queen Mary's apartment in Holyrood House; but he did not appear to care much about either."[26] Crabbe's knowledge of the social welfare institutions of his day was obviously fairly extensive, and one might have expected him to load his poems with minutiae. However, he rarely develops his sketches of these institutions in any detail, since he prefers to emphasize their relation to people—the financiers, the administrators, and the poor. Only in their social relations can the working of these institutions be discerned, and their effects on the community evaluated.

Since the institutions of the borough differ so greatly when seen from different viewpoints, it should come as no surprise to discover that the same holds true for the poor themselves. For instance, at the beginning of Letter XVII the narrator describes the poor and the parish out-relief in fairly glowing terms. Yet before the end of the letter is reached, this cosy belief is dispelled when the narrator turns to describe "the narrow row," where the poor live in terrible conditions. Interestingly enough, this division of the letter into two parts—the first describing in general terms the good care given to the poor, and the second describing actual poor people in miserable conditions—mirrors the same type of division which has already been noted in *The Village* and Part I of "The Parish Register."

In "The Parish Register" Crabbe had beckoned the reader to follow him into the poor sections of town where most people refused to go: "Come! search within, nor sight nor smell regard; / The true physician walks the foulest ward" (I. 212-13). In the second half of Letter XVIII of *The Borough* he also emphasizes that what he is about to describe is the little-known side of life among the poor: "Here our reformers come not; none object / To paths polluted, or upbraid neglect" (XVIII. 274-75). In order that the parish might distribute poor relief effectively, the overseers were supposed to visit the poor. Crabbe points out that since few officials bothered with the visits, little was known about those who were seriously and chronically poor.[27]

Whereas at the beginning of the letter the narrator had implied that the poor were happy and well cared for, the later sections indicate that they live a life which is apart from and relatively unknown to the rich. The fisherwoman is a good example. As a young girl, she had been clean, decent, and modest. But when she married a sailor, and had to live amidst the uproar of the row, she soon assumed habits fit for the row:

> But, when a wife, she lost her former care,
> Nor thought on charms, nor time for dress could spare;
> Careless she found her friends who dwelt beside;
> No rival beauty kept alive her pride:
> Still in her bosom virtue keeps her place;
> But decency is gone, the virtues' guard and grace.
>
> (XVIII. 322-27)

Without any condemnation at all, Crabbe indicates how the changed circumstances of the woman alter her style of life, the conclusion being that circumstances affect manners and thereby influence standards of morality. Crabbe's own visits to the homes of the poor had shown him a section of the poor that was virtually unknown to the average educated Englishman, and was to remain so for at least several more decades. As Crabbe's son comments: "At Stathern, and at all his successive country residences, my father continued to practise his original profession [of apothecary] among such poor people as chose to solicit his aid. . . . He grudged no personal fatigue to attend the sick bed of the peasant, in the double capacity of physician and priest."[28]

The description of the tenement shows both that the borough contains extensive poverty and that the narrator is in no position to change the situation. Although he attempts to reason with the owner, the dialogue reveals the entrepreneur's power and cunning as well as the narrator's essential helplessness:

> Nor will he sell, repair, or take it down;
> 'Tis his—what cares he for the talk of town?
> "No! he will let it to the poor—a home
> Where he delights to see the creatures come."
> "They may be thieves;"—"Well, so are richer men;"—
> "Or idlers, cheats, or prostitutes;"—"What then?"—
> "Outcasts pursued by justice, vile and base;"—
> "They need the more his pity and the place."
> Convert to system his vain mind has built,
> He gives asylum to deceit and guilt.   (XVIII. 334–43)

Indeed, the passage seems to give the best of the argument to the owner, his terse comments carrying as much persuasion as the narrator's longer argument.

The effect of the extended description of the filth of "the dusty row" is further to overpower the narrator's previously optimistic remarks. In addition, the sketch incorporates several sardonic allusions to the Goldsmith-like comments of the earlier part of the letter. In his description of the tenement the narrator says:

> Above the fire, the mantel-shelf contains
> Of china-ware some poor unmatch'd remains;
> There many a tea-cup's gaudy fragment stands,
> All placed by vanity's unwearied hands.   (XVIII. 392–95)

This passage contains an obvious allusion to Goldsmith's: "While broken tea-cups, wisely kept for shew, / Ranged o'er the chimney, glistened in a row" (*Deserted Village*, lines 235–36). Where Goldsmith had used the teacups as a sign of the owner's frugality and industry, Crabbe allowed the cracked teacups to represent the broken lives of the poor.

The reason Crabbe can state at one moment that the poor are well cared for, and at the next, that they live in terrible conditions, is that he alters the focus of the poem. When the narrator praises the life of the poor, he is speaking in general terms of a class of people, "the worthy poor." But when he describes the miserable lot of the poor, he turns to individuals whom even many of the most advanced and progressive thinkers of the day deemed to be outside the consideration of society.[29] What this method of presentation does is first to confirm the reader's natural inclination to believe that the community is fulfilling its obligations to the less fortunate, and then to subvert this approach by suddenly subsuming under the phrase "all our poor," the many poor who have been conveniently forgotten so that England can be thought of in terms of the metaphor of the family. Crabbe's dual focus has the effect of forcing the reader to see that at least one member of the family has been neglected, while never calling into doubt the value of the metaphor. Interestingly enough, it was often people, such as Crabbe, of liberal sympathies and a conservative temperament, who were most helpful in pointing out the true relations of the poor to the community. The reactionaries and radicals both had a stake in portraying the lower classes so as to further their own political aims. Robert Southey, who is often similar to Crabbe in his attitudes, observed: "Understand me! I admit that improvements of the utmost value have been made, in the most important concerns: but I deny that the melioration has been general; and insist, on the contrary, that a considerable portion of the people are in a state, which, as relates to their physical condition, is greatly worsened, and, as touching their intellectual nature, is assuredly not improved."[30] This same split observed by Southey is reflected in the narrator's vision of his borough: when thinking of the town's prosperity, he paints the provisions for the poor in glowing terms; but when he comes to describe individual cases, the prosperity begins to appear somewhat superficial.

The total effect of *The Borough* depends on the juxtaposition of life as the narrator would like to have it—the conventional view that the British constitution was the best possible—and Crabbe's realization of the horror and misery which lay below the surface of respectable society. Crabbe's great merit as a social poet lies in his ability to allow his readers to see the bad aspects of society without denying their good counterparts. To ignore Crabbe's representation of the tenement on the grounds that it is "unsuitable to poetry" is to fall prey to the nineteenth-century weakness for cant. The letter, which begins as a panegyric on the state of the poor, ends with the lines:

> High hung at either end, and next the wall,
> Two ancient mirrors show the forms of all,
> In all their force;—these aid them in their dress,
> But, with the good, the evils too express,
> Doubling each look of care, each token of distress.
>
> (XVIII. 404–408)

And Crabbe's poetry has the effect of these strange mirrors— mirrors in which he portrays the good, but doubles "each look of care."

IV

A problem confronting all writers who suggest that the objective world is dependent to some extent on individual perception is that social evils lose some of their hard edges or "reality," with the result that the sense of urgent need for the correction of the evil is dispelled. In recent times this has been the basis of a telling criticism of the twentieth-century novel by both Georg Lukács, the Marxist critic,[31] and the novelist-philosopher, Iris Murdoch.[32] All of Crabbe's later poems show him grappling with this problem, but one can see it particularly well in Letters VI and VII of *The Borough* in which he discusses the professions of law and medicine. Moreover, these two letters complement one another. In Letter VI, on the law, Crabbe achieves a fine comic effect when he investigates the individual causes of corruption in the law. Yet this comic tone is upset when he shows that legal malpractices are serious and current; for the expectation of reform undercuts the humour. In Letter VII, on the other hand, he calls out strongly for reform of medicine, but allows the declamation to be softened when he shows how individuals are themselves responsible for creating the social ills. One letter leans towards social action; the other towards individual change.

In his letter on the law, Crabbe begins light-heartedly, reminding his readers that the subject touches his own interests, for if he is careless, some litigious lawyer might make him account for the satire in his poetry:

> —Law shall I sing, or what to Law belongs?
> Alas! there may be danger in such songs;
> A foolish rhyme, 'tis said, a trifling thing,
> The law found treason, for it touch'd the king. (VI. 31–34)

Of course there is actually little "danger" for Crabbe in this satire, but by pretending the opposite, he creates a tone of mock-seriousness which allows him to keep his social criticism at the level of light satire. Incidentally, it should be noted that in choosing to satirize lawyers for using the law to further their own ends, Crabbe was giving himself a difficult subject, since lawyers had been a standard source of fun and criticism for centuries. The important point, however, is not whether the criticism is new but whether the artist can make it new. After all, in the 1850s Charles Dickens was still able to make the law the subject of one of his greatest novels. Moreover, like most self-conscious satirists, Crabbe recognized that the subjects of satire had remained remarkably unchanged over the centuries.[33] After offering his own criticisms of the devious methods of lawyers, he pretends to overhear someone commenting on his hackneyed subject:

> "Nay, this," you cry, "is common-place, the tale
> Of petty tradesmen o'er their evening-ale.
> There are who, living by the legal pen,
> Are held in honour—'honourable men'." (VI. 81–84)

Even here, in his admission of how widespread was criticism of the law, Crabbe prepares the way for his own criticism when he employs Mark Antony's ironic comment on the assassins—"So are they all, all honourable men"—to question the rejoinder that many in the legal profession are honourable.

However, as soon as Crabbe introduces his first examples of fraudulent law, the tone changes significantly, for he is discussing a contemporary social evil which he knows and dislikes. In his comments on the way parishes go to law over any and every case in which their responsibility is in doubt, he was striking at what we now can see to have been one of the great issues of the time:

> There is a doubtful pauper, and we think
> 'Tis not with us to give him meat and drink;
> There is a child, and 'tis not mighty clear
> Whether the mother lived with us a year;
> A road's indicted, and our seniors doubt
> If in our proper boundary or without:
> But what says our attorney? He our friend
> Tells us 'tis just and manly to contend. (VI. 93–100)

In this short space Crabbe mentions three of the most troublesome duties of the parish. The first is the "doubtful pauper," about which there is little need to comment, since the records of the time are full of the thousands of cases in which parishes wrestled with the problem of responsibility. Although in theory the Poor Laws gave a subsistence to everyone in need, in actual fact, the Law of Settlement made it extremely difficult for those who wished to move from one parish to another to gain the settlement necessary to entitle them to poor relief. About the people who had at one time paid rates, and who later became "decayed housekeepers," there was little doubt; such people deserved weekly help or even an annual pension. But for most people, the day labourers, lodgers, and migrant workers, there was no settled policy. In parishes where the overseer was particularly harsh, the case would be taken to law to find a loophole which would enable the parish to deny responsibility.[34] The Webbs note that "half the time of the Court" was spent "in splitting hairs as to pauper settlements." When the parish was threatened with the charge of a new pauper it "rushed to lodge an appeal . . . frequently persuaded by the village attorney."[35]

The second serious case Crabbe mentions, that of the mother with child, was a particularly delicate one. Parishes attempted to keep out any new woman at all likely to give birth in the parish to a child she could not support, since under the law, the child deserved a settlement in the parish of his birth. Many tales are told of women in the last stages of pregnancy being carted from one parish to another. The parish officials of Bath were alleged to peruse their female visitors with a keen eye to ensure that no poor children were likely to be born within the boundaries of the city.[36]

Crabbe's third example, the construction of roads, was also a subject of much litigation. The expanding commerce of the eighteenth century demanded better transportation facilities, with the result that a vast program of road reconstruction was undertaken over the period from 1750 to 1810.[37] The capital for many of the roads was raised on the turnpike principle, and in certain instances the turnpike could more than pay for itself. But in most cases, the construction of roads remained an onerous and expensive task laid on the parish by the central government. Wherever possible, parishes attempted to pass the responsibility for road building to their neighbours.

Quite clearly, then, Crabbe's examples of legal abuses are serious enough to create indignation in the reader; indeed, when the vast number of cases in which the parishes went to law over paupers and settlements is recalled, Crabbe's verse makes one wonder why more criticism was not aroused.[38] Given Crabbe's admirable and timely choice of abuses in the law, it was quite possible for him to have turned the letter into a propagandist poem designed to convince the reader of the necessity of immediate action. Indeed, in his early years as a poet, Crabbe imagined that it was this type of social protest poetry that he would be writing. In "An Epistle to a Friend" (1780) he had shown himself to be so outraged with the social abuses he had encountered in London that he had angrily declared his plan to go "To Court on wings of agile anger . . . / And paint to freedom's sons each guileful deed" (21–22). In the years following, Crabbe learned to avoid the over-generality and "poetic diction" of these lines, and in so doing, learned that the function of poetry was not necessarily to urge action on issues, but to illuminate the issues from all sides. Certainly in the letter on law, Crabbe recognizes that although the abuses are serious, it would be unfair (and untruthful) to lay all the blame on the lawyers.

Repeatedly, Crabbe observes that the lawyers thrive only because man himself is selfish. When Crabbe introduces a good lawyer, Archer, we discover that he has seen so much of man's duplicity that he has become a cynic. Archer has been involved in so many devious cases,

> And seen so much of both sides, and so long,
> He thinks the bias of man's mind goes wrong.
> Thus, though he's friendly, he is still severe,
> Surly though kind, suspiciously sincere:
> So much he's seen of baseness in the mind,
> That, while a friend to man, he scorns mankind;
> He knows the human heart, and sees with dread,
> By slight temptation, how the strong are led;
> He knows how interest can asunder rend
> The bond of parent, master, guardian, friend,
> To form a new and a degrading tie
> 'Twixt needy vice and tempting villany.   (VI. 178–89)

The portrait of Lawyer Archer is a measure of Crabbe's grasp of the social situation. While Crabbe dislikes the Lawyer Swallows who ingeniously cheat people out of their money, and is ready to criticize them, he also implies that people generally receive the type of lawyer they deserve. The description of Lawyer Archer—"while a friend to man, he scorns mankind"—is reminiscent of Swift's attitude, and is evidence of the typical Swiftian ambivalence found in Crabbe's poetry.

When Lawyer Swallow dupes the Dissenters out of their church fund, the reader cannot wholly sympathize with the victims, since Crabbe has shown that they were prepared to dupe themselves by believing that Swallow had actually become their convert. These people can see that Swallow is a fraud: "He drank—'twas needful his poor nerves to brace; / He swore—'twas habit; he was grieved— 'twas grace" (VI. 350–51), but so anxious are they to claim Swallow as a convert, and have him lay out their fund at interest, that they deceive themselves about his honesty. The reader is invited to criticize not only Lawyer Swallow, but his clients as well. Even in the court case involving responsibility for the pauper, Crabbe begins by showing the villagers themselves ready to follow the line of least resistance. Their attorney has no trouble in persuading them to take the case to court. It is interesting to note that Crabbe himself seems to have been a little inclined to Lawyer Archer's point of view. Joanna Baillie noted: "I have sometimes remarked that, when a good or generous action has been much praised, he would say in a low voice, as to himself, something that insinuated a more mingled and worldly cause for it."39

In Letter VI Crabbe is giving two explanations for evil. The first is a social one, that the legal profession is corrupt and should be corrected. The second is a psychological one in which individuals are shown to create the social evil by means of their own narrowness and greed. The letter offers a blend of the explanations, the reader being left with a mixed reaction—whether to dislike the lawyers for their corruption or whether to see their activities as evidence of the natural corruption of all mankind.

In Crabbe's next letter on the professions, he is also inclined to describe humorously the avarice and fear of individuals, but in this case he leans in the other direction, and the humour is minimized when he speaks out openly against corrupt doctors. As a result, this letter seems much more emphatic and direct, close to the sort of satire on medicine that Crabbe had been writing thirty years earlier in *The Library*. But this letter also lacks subtlety since the language tends to be abstract, and the argument, didactic.

Crabbe levels a number of criticisms against the medical profession, but his main concern is to bring home to the public the serious consequences of allowing quack doctors to hand out unknown drugs (a topic of interest even today). One might think that in an age when doctors could not cure diseases anyway, and when many people relied upon folklore remedies, Crabbe is being too harsh. As G. E. Mingay has so rightly remarked: "Medical treatment was one of the few human needs in which the wealthy classes had little or no advantage. Even the best medical advice and the most costly treatment were not necessarily more effective than simple care or old wives' remedies."[40] Yet Crabbe is not attacking the village apothecary rich in his knowledge of helpful herbs and salves,[41] but the unlicensed drug-makers and dispensers who lived off the sale of pretended wonder drugs. The reason he felt that these people were dangerous in a way that the charlatan doctor of the early eighteenth century never could have been, was that they sold their drugs on a large scale as scientifically prepared medicine. Crabbe explains how these people invest large sums of money in newspaper advertising and then acquire famous and distinguished people to act as patrons to the drug. What particularly bothered Crabbe was the manner in which many of these people, entering business on a large scale, had become fabulously wealthy and influential. There may be some envy in the lines:

> How strange to add, in this nefarious trade,
> That men of parts are dupes by dunces made:
> That creatures nature meant should clean our streets
> Have purchased lands and mansions, parks and seats.
>
> (VII. 91–94)

But they also express Crabbe's concern with the scale upon which the quacks operated.

Crabbe mentions few of the different panaceas that were marketed, but he does notice and criticize the use of alcohol as a cordial and certain "pills" which would supposedly prevent venereal disease. Concerning the pills, he feels that all the puffs amount to no more "in plainer English" than "if you mean to sin, / Fly to the drops, and instantly begin" (VII. 203–204). His anger is aroused most of all by the "sleeping cordial," presumably opium, which was given indiscriminately in various forms to men, women, and children.[42] Opium was widely used in the treatment of diseases at this time, a reason why so many people unwittingly became addicts. Mingay notes that laudanum was one of the few "reliable and effective" drugs which doctors possessed.[43] Since Crabbe had himself begun taking opium some years previously,[44] possibly his own experience had shown him the great danger consequent upon taking this drug.

Although Crabbe once again undercuts his social criticism by showing that quacks thrive because of the foolishness and the misplaced trust of the populace, this time he does not allow the fact of human fallibility to prevent him from mounting a strong attack on quack medicine. Quite clearly Crabbe is here speaking in his own voice, urging that officials should take steps to halt the corrupt medical practices. And yet Crabbe was also beginning to recognize that a poem such as *The Borough* was hardly the place for calls to direct action. In order to prevent the poem from dwindling into a didactic tract, Crabbe has the narrator mull over the problem and "think out" the best solution. The narrator's first thought is that men of station and distinction should be asked to refrain from lending their names in support of the drugs, but he then realizes that his poem would little change the situation in this respect, for drugs appeal to those who "weakly reasoning, strongly feel" (VII. 283). He then discusses the possibility of regulating the malpractices by creating new laws, but changes his mind, when he recognizes that "in this land of freedom, law is slack / With any being to commence attack" (VII. 286–87). Consequently, when he turns finally to the men of science with the suggestion that they should be enlisted in the effort to expose the fraudulent basis of the panaceas, the suggestion appears the narrator's own, and as such belongs to the poem. What this indicates is that Crabbe wanted to press for social action but was looking for narrative machinery to incorporate such social criticism within the poem's structure. He is not altogether successful because the "solution"—involving the men of science—is clearly meant to apply to the outside world, but its phrasing leaves it as a contemplative suggestion by one who recognizes only too well the difficulty in overcoming the ordinary individual's need for quackery.

Neither of the letters on the law and medicine is entirely successful, although, like the curate's egg, they are good in parts. Crabbe's dilemma, whether to present social ills from the outside as "facts" or from the inside so as to discover the psychological reasons for their existence, seems to have no easy solution. Indeed, the argument as to which perspective is correct or how to combine both continues in our own day.

v

One of the most interesting devices that Crabbe employs to bring direct social criticism into *The Borough* without appearing to harangue the reader occurs in Letter XVIII, where the narrator argues with his friend in the country about the workhouse. Obliquely, the reader senses he is overhearing a conversation rather than being addressed directly. The passage is quite dramatic, because it is one of the few places in the poem where Crabbe describes at length something outside the borough. The scene opens as if the narrator is already in the midst of a conversation, answering a hypothetical question—"Our poor how feed we?" (XVIII. 5). He gives a brief answer, describing the usual type of parish out-relief, but then suddenly turns to launch an attack on the workhouses to be found in his friend's part of the country— "Your plan I love not" (XVIII. 109)—and proceeds to set out his objections to the workhouse.

The setting is so dramatic, in fact, that it might be thought that Crabbe is using the device to drag into the poem yet another description of a poorhouse in order to remind his readers of his famous description of the parish poorhouse in *The Village*. But a moment's thought will reveal that the type of poorhouse in *The Borough* is very different from that formerly described in *The Village*. In the earlier poem Crabbe had included the description of the poorhouse in order to protest against squalid and unhealthy conditions:

> Theirs is yon house that holds the parish poor,
> Whose walls of mud scarce bear the broken door;
> There, where the putrid vapours, flagging, play,
> And the dull wheel hums doleful through the day.
>
> > (*The Village* I. 228–31)

In *The Borough*, however, Crabbe's protest is aimed against the magnificent size of the poorhouse and the practice of herding the poor into one building, where they are forced to live estranged from their old friends and family. Whereas previously he had objected to the walls of mud, in *The Borough* he complains of palatial conditions. In some lines prefixed to the letter, Crabbe addresses the following admonition to the rich:

> Show not to the poor thy pride,
> > Let their home a cottage be;
> Nor the feeble body hide
> > In a palace fit for thee;
> > Let him not about him see
> Lofty ceilings, ample halls,
> > Or a gate his boundary be,
> Where nor friend or kinsman calls.

Certainly this warning against fitting out large houses for the poor seems a little odd, coming as it does after Crabbe's earlier criticism of the parish for allowing the poorhouse to be so mean.

The modern reader may well be a little startled by this apparent change of attitude, and since palatial workhouses were uncommon in Britain, he may also wonder what Crabbe is doing. However, Crabbe included in the preface a short account of the letter which offers a partial explanation of the scheme he is criticizing:

> I am aware of the great difficulty of acquiring just
> notions on the maintenance and management of this
> class of our fellow-subjects [the poor], and I forbear to
> express any opinion of the various modes which have
> been discussed or adopted: of one method only I venture
> to give my sentiments, that of collecting the poor of a
> hundred into one building. This admission of a vast
> number of persons, of all ages and both sexes, of very
> different inclinations, habits, and capacities, into a
> society, must, at a first view, I conceive, be looked upon
> as a cause of both vice and misery; nor does any thing
> which I have heard or read invalidate the opinion;
> happily, it is not a prevailing one, as these houses are,
> I believe, still confined to that part of the kingdom
> where they originated.[45]

In a note to the 1834 edition of *Poetical Works* Crabbe's son adds that these "odious Houses of Industry" were to be found "only in Suffolk, near the first founder's residence."[46] From these observations one may infer that Crabbe was describing a type of workhouse characteristic of East Anglia, a supposition which is confirmed by modern scholarship. The Webbs note: "It was the General Mixed Workhouse of the Suffolk Incorporations—not, as is commonly assumed, of the ancient poorhouse of the parish—of which Crabbe [in *The Borough*] gave such a terrible description."[47] This explains the seeming discrepancy between the description of the poorhouse in *The Village* and that in *The Borough*. In the earlier poem, Crabbe had described the old-style parish poorhouse, prevalent throughout England and Wales, while in *The Borough* he described the relatively new East Anglian experiment.[48]

Crabbe's rationale for attacking the workhouse is particularly effective as part of *The Borough*—a poem devoted to developing different viewpoints—because the criticism points out that, although the motives of the originators of the scheme were good, the workhouse failed because it did not take into account the desires, needs, and perspective of those it was designed to help. The workhouse also offers a fine contrast to another large building, the almshouse. It will be recalled that the almshouse deteriorated, not because the scheme was ill-conceived or failed to take into account the needs of the people, but because of poor administration. With the workhouse, we witness how even "charity, the virtue's crown and grace," is undermined when organizers allow their theories to take precedence over facts.

Throughout this section there is a sense of the narrator continually contrasting different treatments of the poor, answering contemporary questions, and posing many of his own. The verse is thick with question marks. As has been mentioned, the narrator begins with a matter-of-fact description of the sort of "out-relief" practised over most of England throughout the eighteenth century. And to this he contrasts the vast size of the house of industry of the Suffolk type. But there is no outright condemnation of the workhouse. In fact, Crabbe spends considerable time weighing the good and bad features of these "pauper-palaces." He acknowledges that the poor in such houses were well provided for, and that they were given ample opportunity to offer suggestions and express grievances. Perhaps recalling his previous objections in *The Village* to the squalid conditions in the old-style parish poorhouse, he agrees that hygienic standards in the new workhouse were high:

> Be it agreed—the poor who hither come
> Partake of plenty, seldom found at home;
> That airy rooms and decent beds are meant
> To give the poor by day, by night, content.
>
> (XVIII. 119–22)

His objection is to the way in which the poor of the workhouse were cut off from their old ways of life, and thus from any sense of individuality. But Crabbe also recognizes that this objection might seem somewhat trivial and sentimental, for after all, at a time when the poor rates were soaring, some sacrifices had to be made. Yet, as Crabbe points out, in hundreds where such workhouses existed, they were usually the only means of poor relief,[49] with the result that, no matter what a person's needs or abilities might be, he was treated in the same general manner. A person might require relief for many reasons: he might be old, disabled, infirm, orphaned, or simply out of work for a short time. The directors made no distinction. They placed all people requiring relief into one category, "the poor," and bundled them off to the house. In time, even the most fervent exponents of these workhouses were forced to admit that criticism such as Crabbe's was well founded, since the failure to take into account the different abilities of the inhabitants soon created an uneconomic enterprise and forced its end.

At many points the poem seems to offer direct answers to contemporary arguments, a feature that can be easily overlooked if nothing is known about the background. For instance, critics of the workhouse were not long in observing that one of the main reasons the workhouses failed to operate effectively was their amateur administration. In many cases this criticism was true, since the directors were local squires and farmers who could not be bothered to attend meetings, or concern themselves with the details of day-to-day affairs. However, spokesmen for the scheme replied to the critics that supervision by interested persons was unnecessary:

> The public is in no danger of losing at any time any of the advantages which a former zeal had promised, or a past vigilance has procured. For should that zeal hereafter abate, or that vigilance relax, the institution, *by means of its General Rules, remains like a machine,* which, having its springs of motion within itself, will with but an ordinary attention, and only common application, go on to perform without interruption its accustomed functions, and to produce without variation its usual benefits [my italics].[50]

It was this machine-like aspect of the workhouse which Crabbe, as one of the scheme's opponents, disliked so much:

> Who govern here, by general rules must move,
> Where ruthless custom rends the bond of love.
> Nations, we know, have nature's law transgress'd,
> And snatch'd the infant from the parent's breast;
> But still for public good the boy was train'd,
> The mother suffer'd, but the matron gain'd:
> Here nature's outrage serves no cause to aid;
> The ill is felt, but not the Spartan made.   (XVIII. 187–94)

Included in this comment is the assumption of yet another argument in favour of the houses—the argument from utility, which asserted that although harsh, the houses were necessary to train the children of the poor to industry. Crabbe agrees about the harsh conditions, but denies the public benefits—the system was not creating "Spartan" citizens, only demoralized ones. What he is referring to, of course, is the avowed use of the houses to keep the poor in order. Influential persons such as Arthur Young believed that the poor were demanding too many rights; in order to counteract this new spirit of independence, they advocated the repressive house of correction, which was remarkably like the workhouse. Young commented that more parishes should build workhouses of the Suffolk variety because "the lower orders of the kingdom are now pressing on the next; and the toe of the peasant truly galls the kibe of the courtier."[51]

When the house of industry was so closely tied in people's minds to the house of correction, it was to be expected that the general character of the building, especially with its large size and general rules, would come to resemble a prison. And this Crabbe points out:

> That giant-building, that high-bounding wall,
> Those bare-worn walks, that lofty thund'ring hall!
> That large loud clock, which tolls each dreaded hour;
> Those gates and locks, and all those signs of power:
> It is a prison, with a milder name,
> Which few inhabit without dread or shame.
>
> (XVIII. 113–18)

From the point of view of the poor who had to live in these houses, no doubt they did seem like prisons, with the "lordly overseers" as the keeprs, but if Crabbe had been content to portray this perspective alone he would have been doing an injustice to the houses, and indeed, to the good intentions of those who began them. The houses of industry were started, not to do the work of prisons, but to provide an economically viable, humanitarian alternative to indiscriminate welfare. The planners of the time felt that the cost of caring for the poor could be reduced if parishes were encouraged to pool their resources in order to construct a large workhouse capable of housing all the poor from the various parishes concerned. The idea was that the large size of the institution would permit the poor to work at profitable small-scale manufactures, so that instead of giving them indiscriminate and often arbitrary doles, the parishes would use the money to set up a business in which the poor could be profitably employed. Grouped together into viable economic units the poor would no longer be a drain on the economy. An early experiment in Bristol seemed to suggest that the scheme was feasible, so in 1756, as a result of Admiral Vernon's energy and persistence, a local Act was passed "which set up, for these two hundreds of Carlford and Colneis [in Suffolk], a new local governing body, empowered to erect a workhouse, and practically to take over, from the officers of the twenty-eight parishes concerned, the whole administration of the Poor Law."[52] Apparently by 1785 the administration of the Poor Law over the greater part of Suffolk and Norfolk "had been withdrawn from the parish officers and vested in fourteen new bodies of Incorporated Guardians of the Poor."[53]

In theory, these new workhouses—clean, well planned and spacious—seemed to offer a far better alternative to the parish dole. Crabbe takes care to point out the good intentions inherent in the houses, and even suggests that in many cases the guardians are kind:

> Grant indeed that the guardians of the place attend,
> And ready ear to each petition lend.   (XVIII. 125–26)

But he notes also that there is nothing the guardians can do to alleviate the situation when the fault lies with the very conception of the house itself. The poor "live repining, for 'tis there they live" (XVIII. 136). As George Rose had argued a few years earlier, the very form of the houses gave them an inhuman feeling: "The avowed policy of workhouses, in many instances, is a mixture of maintenance, and punishment by imprisonment."⁵⁴ It is worth noting that Crabbe's objection is not the sentimentalist's aversion to organized charity. Many people disapproved of any sort of organized relief on the grounds that it prevented the Christian from practising individual charity. Crabbe's point is not that charity should be dispensed *by* individuals, but *to* individuals.

At the back of his mind, Crabbe seems to have been thinking of the case of Isaac Ashford described three years earlier in "The Parish Register." Near the end of the section on workhouses he describes a person very like Isaac, in order to show the injustice of sending such a person to the workhouse:

> Here the good pauper, losing all the praise
> By worthy deeds acquired in better days,
> Breathes a few months; then, to his chamber led,
> Expires, while strangers prattle round his bed.
>
> (XVIII. 211–14)

Here, ideas implied in "The Parish Register" are further developed. It will be recalled that Isaac, although a "noble peasant" living an honest and hard-working life, had in his last days been confronted with the workhouse. Crabbe had "solved" the problem by having Isaac die before actually entering the workhouse. Whereas in "The Parish Register" Crabbe only implied that a new scheme was needed to help people like Isaac, in *The Borough* he goes a step further to develop strongly the case that people such as Isaac should be provided for in their own homes. He argues that the poor should be given a reasonable pension which will allow them to live out their final years in comfort.⁵⁵

A curious feature of Crabbe's portrayal of the workhouse is that he nowhere mentions the inmates being forced to work at some employment. Since the workhouses were established largely to "set the poor on work," this omission seems strange. But to expect Crabbe to deal with every aspect of the matter is to expect the wrong thing. Poets are rarely interested in writing what Leslie Stephen has termed "a Blue Book done into rhyme,"[56] in which everything about a particular social situation is developed in detail. Yet there is a more substantial reason for this lack of description of the poor "set on work," and one that bears out Crabbe's criticism of the houses. The Webbs indicate that by 1810 (the date of publication of *The Borough*) many of the houses of industry had already failed in the experiment to carry out manufactures. When the parishes realized that manufactures were no longer profitable, the workhouses ceased to be used as places of employment, and if they were not torn down altogether, they were used as centres to which the unfit could be sent. The Webbs note:

> As the expense per head in the House of Industry was high, each parish saw its way to save money by giving small doles of outdoor relief, rather than augment its numbers in the House. Finally, the quondam "House of Industry" became for the parishes only a sort of co-operative hospital for the sick, an orphan asylum for the deserted children, and a place to which the Overseers could send any able-bodied poor to whom they did not choose to allow the weekly dole.[57]

Crabbe's description of a workhouse of 1810 records a period of transition when the workhouse was still operative but when the attempt to have the poor work at profitable manufactures had already been given up. At this period, such houses must have been incredibly bad, because they brought a large number of people together and gave them nothing to do. Or, as Crabbe notes:

> What, if no grievous fears their lives annoy,
> Is it not worse no prospects to enjoy?   (XVIII. 170–71)

The organizers of the time were quite right in attempting to alleviate the needs and fears of the poor as a group within society, but

as Crabbe points out, the solution of group problems may ultimately be destructive to the individuals who constitute the group.
It is of great interest to see Crabbe, at a time when the institutional-
ization of large numbers of people was becoming popular as a
treatment of social problems,[58] objecting to such schemes on the
simple but profound basis that they treated individuals as means,
not ends.

VI

Although interesting, Crabbe's treatment of general social issues
such as the law, medicine, and workhouses does not constitute the
centre of *The Borough*. Had the poem consisted entirely of attacks
such as that on doctors, then it would definitely be uninteresting
as a poem, whatever merit it might have as a social document. *The
Borough* is a long poem, however, and readily incorporates a number of such sections without harm; indeed, the tone of outright
indignation helps to change the pace—something which is much
needed in a long poem, as both Wordsworth and Byron discovered.

Yet direct social criticism is the style of Crabbe's earlier writings,
and his emerging techniques of ambivalent perspective and voice,
to be effective, demanded as their counterpart the creation of fully
developed characters who could present their own points of view.
In *The Borough*, the characters do not often speak at length, but as
they assume importance in their own right the narrator begins to
record detail so as to suggest the inner life of the character, and
ceases to edit from a detached point of view. We have already
encountered a partial example in Benbow, but I wish now to turn
to the best-known character of *The Borough*, Peter Grimes. Peter is
especially interesting for this study because of the subtle ways in
which personal and social life are connected. By demonstrating
how the "social" grows out of the "human," Crabbe was also able
to solve a problem that had been with him from the time of *The
Village*—how to describe processes at work within society. The
solution, of course, is to show how individual actions help to forge

the future from the present. Indeed, this is the approach that dominates his later work.

At first sight "Peter Grimes" may appear to contain little, if any, social criticism, since the central concern is with the story of Peter. Yet in this superb portrait, where the development of character and situation approaches that of a short story, Peter's own personality and actions are themselves a criticism of society. The fisherman Peter Grimes clearly inhabits the same hostile coast as was seen in *The Village*, and as a character he evinces the powerful instincts and amoral forces that made the landscape there so threatening to man's precarious civilization. Little is given as explanation of Peter's personality; in some ways he seems like Iago a figure of unredeemed and unexplained evil. Or perhaps it is better to say that he represents the aspect of man's personality that seeks self-gratification by means of power over everything around. Peter's father, a kind and loving man, has the will but not the strength to stand up to his son. When Peter rebels, his father tells him to follow the Bible—"it is the word of life"—but Peter retorts with a blow that lays his father low, and the reply—"This is the life itself." As has so often been observed in the twentieth century, realism, or life itself, is characterized by "might is right."

In many ways Peter resembles the villain in the gothic tale, someone without a social conscience, who feels no responsibility for friends or relations. Yet in Crabbe's hands, this interest in the potentiality for evil of unleashed human desire is made to appear human, not necessarily an aberration as is usually the case with the gothic novelists. Like the villain in a gothic novel, Peter is cruel:

> With greedy eye he look'd on all he saw;
> He knew not justice, and he laugh'd at law;
> On all he mark'd he stretch'd his ready hand.
>
> (XXII. 40–42)

Unlike the villain, who is in opposition to the law, Peter finds that the law sanctions his cruelty; when Peter decides that he needs someone to help with his fishing, a person whom he can totally control, he does not have to turn kidnapper and place his victim under lock and key. He simply applies to a workhouse for an apprentice:

> Peter had heard there were in London then—
> Still have they being!—workhouse-clearing men,
> Who, undisturb'd by feelings just or kind,
> Would parish-boys to needy tradesmen bind;
> They in their want a trifling sum would take,
> And toiling slaves of piteous orphans make. (XXII. 59–64)

Had Peter been a conventional fictional character, the novelist would have condemned him as an outrage against mankind; Crabbe's presentation shows that Peter's attitudes and assumptions are little different from those of the social institutions of his countrymen. The workhouse-clearing men are as "undisturbed" by kind feelings as is Peter.

It is noteworthy that Crabbe's characterization of Peter (the way he makes him human) is not by means of details of his past, nor by descriptions of his thoughts—the usual resources of writers. Instead, he shows Peter acting out the ordinary assumptions of people who are clearly normal. Paradoxically, this makes Peter human but abnormal. For instance, the reader's first reaction to Peter's desire for a slave is that Peter is simply giving evidence of his cruel instinct to master others. Certainly one expects a moral comment on Peter, but as Howard Mills has noted: "Crabbe never 'sums up' Grimes: he avoids analysing motives and impulses, suggesting that his cruelty is inexplicable in those terms and so even more horrifying."59 What Crabbe does is to extend his technique of *The Village* (where he had shown the effect of nature and society on the poor *as a group*) to show that Peter, almost by a process of osmosis, has the same values as his surroundings and institutions—Peter's desire for a "slave" being the master's desire for an apprentice.

Throughout the letter, Crabbe continually mentions how the "good people" and the overseers of the parish were prepared to give Peter every opportunity to exercise his cruelty. Peter does not have to pay the workhouses for the apprentice or pay the apprentice wages; the workhouse directors pay Peter to take the boy off their hands:

> Such Peter sought, and, when a lad was found,
> The sum was dealt him, and the slave was bound.
>
> (XXII. 65–66)

It is the play on the word "bound" that permits Crabbe to introduce "slave." Any of Crabbe's readers who wished to condemn Peter for his cruelty would find themselves in difficulty, because Crabbe makes clear that, if blame is to be apportioned, the workhouse directors deserve as much as Peter. Even the "liberal" willing to find fault both with Peter and the workhouse directors might discover that he had been taken in by Crabbe's subtlety. When Crabbe turns to describe Peter's treatment of the apprentice, he implicates the entire borough community in Peter's crime:

> Some few in town observed in Peter's trap
> A boy, with jacket blue and woollen cap;
> But none inquired how Peter used the rope,
> Or what the bruise, that made the stripling stoop;
> None could the ridges on his back behold,
> None sought him shiv'ring in the winter's cold;
> None put the question—"Peter, dost thou give
> The boy his food?—What, man! the lad must live:
> Consider, Peter, let the child have bread,
> He'll serve thee better if he's stroked and fed."
>
> (XXII. 67–76)

Anyone believing that he had the right to condemn Peter would find from this description that, unless he had already raised his voice against the apprentice system, he fell into the same category as the people of the borough who turned a blind eye. A further subtlety is that, since the people of the borough are incapable of raising even pragmatic objections (such as—the boy will work better if he is fed), idealistic objections are out of the question.

There is a sense in which Crabbe's account of Peter capitalizes on the many sensational stories of the time about apprentices.

Indeed, Crabbe's son notes: "The original of Peter Grimes was an old fisherman of Aldborough, while Mr. Crabbe was practising there as a surgeon."[60] And even if most of Crabbe's readers would never hear of this obscure fisherman in Aldborough, the press carried many other bizarre examples to catch their notice. For instance, the *Annual Register* for June 1801 told the story of a master who had ill-treated his apprentice, Susannah Archer. Apparently this master had taken seventeen apprentices even though he was "so poor as not to be able to subsist himself." Lord Kenyon, who tried the case, asked the man, "Why beat these poor wretches when their bodily strength was not able to do as much work as you expected?" and mentioned that, "it appeared from the evidence of the neighbours that great wails [*sic*] appeared upon their backs, and their shrieks calling out for mercy were heard in the neighbourhood." In true Grimesian fashion, the man replied that he had "struck them with moderation." Lord Kenyon pointed out, however, that the situation was by no means all the master's fault: "The overseers ought to visit these places, and see they are properly taken care of, not once a year, but frequently. They stand *in loco parentis*. They are in the situation of parents with respect to these children, and should take the same care that parents would."[61] It was not that people were unaware of the great cruelty of the apprentice system. Like Peter's neighbours, they "reason'd thus":

> and some, on hearing cries,
> Said calmly, "Grimes is at his exercise."   (XXII. 77–78)

Here "cries" by means of "Grimes" has been converted into "exercise."

Sensational though the facts of Peter's story may be, in Crabbe's hands the poem gains its power from the understatement of events, which are made to seem almost everyday occurrences. And surely this is the point. Grimes does not think he is doing anything out of the ordinary: nor do his fellow citizens. And in fact he is not. He is taking advantage of an accepted system. His individual savagery reflects the savagery of the society. Where he differs is that he takes advantage of the system to do what it permits, instead of availing himself of the system and modifying his behaviour through moral considerations. The savagery is immediately obvious to the reader, but not for a long time to the townspeople. The reason is partly that Crabbe keeps Peter before our eyes continuously, but also that the townspeople are so used to the savagery of the system that they do not perceive the boys as we do. The savagery has been concealed for them by social convention so that they do not see bruised children, only uncared-for apprentices.

Even though the poem is itself a thorough denunciation of the apprentice system, it will prove helpful to give the bare facts of the system so as to clarify how Crabbe is drawing upon it. First, apprenticeship was common throughout the period. M. Dorothy George has noted: "Apprenticeship, in one of its many forms, was still in the eighteenth century the most general way of giving a child a start in life."[62] In theory, the system was praiseworthy, since children were taught a trade; in practice it broke down badly. Until 1691 the Law of Settlement stated explicitly that children gained a settlement in the parish in which they were found. However, the Act of 1691 created a new means by which parishes could free themselves from the onerous care of vagabond, bastard, and pauper children. It recognized that a person having served an apprenticeship of at least forty days gained a settlement in the parish of his apprenticeship. Dr. Burn described how, as a result of this new ruling, the overseers of populous parishes (especially those of London) made it their special object "to bind out poor children apprentices, no matter to whom, or to what trade, but to take especial care that the master lived in another parish."[63] Not all cases of apprenticeship were of this type; many businessmen and artisans took apprentices with a genuine desire to teach them a trade. But by the end of the eighteenth century, when the poor rates were causing increasing concern, overseers had for some time been using the apprentice system as a means of disposing of large numbers of unwanted children.

The system was, of course, open to a vast amount of abuse. Because the parish officers were commonly uninterested in the welfare of the child, the poor apprentice had few, if any, safeguards.

M. Dorothy George notes: "Any person, master or journeyman, man or woman, housekeeper or lodger, who would undertake to provide food, lodging and instruction, sometimes also clothes, medicines and washing, could take an apprentice, all the earnings of the apprentice, whether for the master or a third person, being the property of the master."[64]

What is perhaps more surprising than the savagery of the system is the way in which normally humanitarian people allowed the system to continue. The great defects of apprenticeship were widely known, and from the beginning of the eighteenth century one can find a series of angry outcries against particular instances of the maltreatment of apprentices.[65] How was it then that the system remained unchanged? Ordinary people, even ordinary people of the eighteenth century, are not naturally cruel to children. The problem was to find a better system of "setting the poor on work," and since no one could suggest a simpler method of employing all the unwanted children, the system of apprenticing remained. The majority of people found themselves accepting the bad treatment of apprentices and even their mysterious disappearances.[66] Like the people of *The Borough*, they came to equate cries with exercise, and in time probably did not even see what was before them.

What Crabbe does is to accept the system at face value, and then to show Peter acting on its very principles. For instance, when Peter's apprentice dies after three years as a result of harsh treatment, Crabbe again takes the opportunity of noticing how easily Peter can accomplish his design:

> Another boy with equal ease was found,
> The money granted, and the victim bound;
> And what his fate?—One night, it chanced he fell
> From the boat's mast and perish'd in her well.
>
> (XXII. 102–105)

After this second death, the magistrates question Peter closely, "but sturdy Peter faced the matter out"; not until a third boy mysteriously dies are the borough people forced to recognize the situation. They then turn against Peter, and the magistrates prevent him from taking additional apprentices. Even then, Peter's neighbours do not recognize their own complicity in the crimes, but throw all the blame on Peter. As is well known, his exile slowly drives Peter mad, and he returns to the marsh, the "slimy channel," where the "sidelong crabs had scrawl'd their crooked race" (XXII. 193). Here he dies seeing hallucinations of the dead apprentices.

At the end, Peter seems, to the strangers who seek him out to ask whether he repents, quite dazed by what has happened to him. In his final madness, he both confesses and defends himself in such confusion that it is impossible to fathom his reactions. He feels guilt, but seems unsure of what. Through it all runs the image of his father whom he obviously fears and who seems to represent arbitrary authority in Peter's mind. As happened in *The Village*, "the life itself" becomes so dominant and so pervasive that "the word of life" appears imposed entirely from without, and without reason. To a person such as Peter, this is the law's appearance: with regard to apprentices, the law encouraged their wholesale disposal, but punished anyone who acted according to the letter of the law.

Crabbe's vision is sometimes said to be pessimistic, yet he portrays the gulf between life itself and the word of life without moving entirely out of the world of conscience. At the end of "Peter Grimes," one does not put down the poem feeling that man lacks the capacity for goodness. The people of the town may be blind, they may be slow to act, but they do have compassion. This is seen at the time Peter is dying:

> Our gentle females, ever prompt to feel,
> Perceived compassion on their anger steal;
> His crimes they could not from their memories blot;
> But they were grieved, and trembled at his lot.

(XXII. 257–60)

These were the same women who, once they realized that Peter was treating his third apprentice badly, attempted to help the boy. But the emotion here is virtually without intelligence, and is aroused by all victims of distress. Crabbe seems to be suggesting that, while this raw emotion of sympathy is what ennobles human life, unless it is given some intelligence or direction, man will never understand the connections between distress and the conditions that create distress. The women pity Peter at his death, which is admirable, and yet this indiscriminate emotion is extremely limited and limiting. The women never understand the part the borough has played in causing the apprentices' deaths.

In "Peter Grimes," Crabbe presents the problem of the apprentice system with great clarity, leaving no doubt about the changes he feels are necessary for reform.[67] But Crabbe never states that these changes should, or would, be made. In fact the poem reveals Crabbe's belief that such changes will always be difficult to effect. Partly this pessimism about the possibility of change may be a reaction to the over-optimism of liberal reformers. People like Thomas Paine and William Godwin believed that social problems had only to be clearly formulated to be solved. Paine once said: "On all such subjects [of reform] men have but to think, and they will neither act wrong nor be misled."[68] Clearly such idealism has little in common with human experience. From his own observation, Crabbe knew well that habits played a large part in man's actions, and that little could be expected from wishful thinking about a sudden benevolent change in man's nature. Just as Crabbe reveals how complex and subtle are the causes behind Peter's actions, so he indicates that the evils of the apprentice system must be traced ultimately to the individual's mode of perceiving himself and his relations to others.

If one thinks of social criticism only in terms of those situations where an artist sets out to attack an abuse and recommend its correction, then "Peter Grimes" fails to qualify. But the definition of social poetry need not be so limited. In "Peter Grimes" Crabbe manages to delineate a social situation involving an abuse—the apprentice system—and at the same time suggest the reasons why the abuse has persisted so long. But the explanation is developed in terms of a human situation, which necessitates the blame being attributed to people, not to systems. Crabbe does not divide man into psychological, social, moral, and religious aspects but creates an aesthetic unity in which they are presented as ways of seeing man. In so doing, Crabbe comes close to achieving the impossible, writing social criticism which does not place all the onus for the trouble on "society," but which reveals that the economic forces of society are themselves rooted in man's perception of himself. The social reformer generally deals with the social causes, the artist with the human. Only rarely are they combined successfully; "Peter Grimes" is an outstanding example of such a success.

Chapter 4
Upon yourselves depend

Crabbe's interest in individual characterization, so marked in *The Borough*, is considerably expanded in his later poetry. And as the discussion in the preceding chapter revealed, Crabbe generally develops his sense of character in terms of social circumstance. It is misleading, therefore, to contend that when Crabbe describes individuals, the interest must be "psychological . . . rather than sociological."[1] Crabbe was writing in the early nineteenth century long before the twentieth-century divorce between the social and psychological aspects of man's character.[2] Yet in developing his characters in terms of their social context, Crabbe was faced with a difficulty, for one of his central concerns was the portrayal of individuals who attempt to repudiate social conventions. The combination was by no means always easy to achieve, as is evidenced by the number of stories in Crabbe's next book of poems *Tales in Verse* (1812) that are not wholly successful in treating the subject of ambition. "The Gentleman Farmer," "Arabella," "Jesse and Colin," "The Struggles of Conscience," and "The 'Squire and the Priest" are the most most obvious examples. Indeed, *Tales* is something of a paradox. Although it has generally been regarded as one of the highwater marks of Crabbe's art, when the volume is considered closely, its reputation is seen to rest on a handful of poems. Moreover, these often succeed precisely because Crabbe avoids the larger social implications in the lives of the individuals he creates. For instance, in both "The Frank Courtship" and

"Procrastination," Crabbe develops domestic situations with precision and finesse, but in comparison with the sort of problems raised in earlier poems and soon to be developed more fully in *Tales of the Hall*, they remind one of the work of an artist accustomed to massing large tracts of experience who has taken time out to compose sketches illuminating particular moments. Brilliantly done, they lack the resonance that we have come to associate with Crabbe.

It goes without saying, however, that the best of *Tales* are splendid examples, in miniature, of Crabbe's story-telling art. "The Frank Courtship," "Procrastination," "The Convert," and "The Patron" are among my favourite Crabbe. In several of these Crabbe is most skilful in portraying individuals wholly caught up in a domestic web. In "Procrastination," for instance, Rupert and Dinah are presented as young lovers too poor to marry. Rupert sets out to seek his fortune in the new world while Dinah stays at home to nurse a wealthy aunt. Crabbe shows successfully how life amidst the aunt's riches transforms Dinah from a lover of Rupert to a lover of comfort, with the verse itself creating the effect of riches on Dinah's sensibility:

> Around the room an Indian paper blazed,
> With lively tint and figures boldly raised;
> Silky and soft upon the floor below,
> Th' elastic carpet rose with crimson glow;
> All things around implied both cost and care;
> . . . .
> Above her head, all gorgeous to behold,
> A time-piece stood on feet of burnish'd gold;
> A stag's-head crest adorn'd the pictured case,
> Through the pure crystal shone th' enamell'd face;
> And, while on brilliants moved the hands of steel,
> It click'd from pray'r to pray'r, from meal to meal.
>
> (IV. 160–79)

The carpets, lush and elastic, are seen as traps for Dinah who becomes spellbound by the regular monotone of the beautiful clock, ticking away her well-fed life, leaving her dependent on the ordered habits that the care of wealth makes necessary and attractive. Rupert's attempted reunion with Dinah rings true, for Crabbe captures the almost physical repulsion that Dinah has for Rupert as a result of her newly-found fastidiousness. Her rejection of Rupert has little to do with reasons of self-interest, but goes deeper to preconscious habits. The story's pointed ending, with the reference to the "Levite," dramatizes tellingly the effects of wealth on emotion.

Similarly, in "The Frank Courtship," Crabbe portrays a particular moment in a family situation, and, it may be added, with a tone remarkably similar to that of Jane Austen. Crabbe has a striking ability to use the subtle indirection of physical detail to characterize people. The rigid father of this tale is sketched humorously and definitively in the opening two lines:

> Grave Jonas Kindred, Sybil Kindred's sire,
> Was six feet high and look'd six inches higher.   (VI. 1–2)

To create the conflict between father and daughter, Crabbe has Sybil go to live with an aunt who moves in far more liberal circles than the father suspects. The result is that some years later when the father wishes his daughter to marry a grave young man of their sect, Sybil objects. The meeting between Sybil and the young man, with mother and father hovering anxiously in the background, is brilliantly achieved: the father is in a position where power and threats are useless; the daughter finds herself admiring the suitor, but disliking his affectations of sobriety; and the man himself, while liking Sybil, is wary of her vanity. The conflict is played out (in both senses of the verb) with no one allowed to be wholly right, so that each has the opportunity for self-improvement—under duress of course—creating a fine comic effect.

Striking and original as "The Frank Courtship" and "Procrastination" may be, an uneasy feeling persists that what Crabbe has gained in sharpness of definition and polish of language he has lost in scope. The characters come alive as individuals, but they exist only within the limited parameters set by the poems. This is particularly evident when such poems are compared with "The Convert" (Tale XIX) where the pressure of outflowing personality continually forces the poem's form to accommodate new experience. John Dighton is a poor orphan who makes his way in the world by relying solely on his wits. But falling ill, he becomes terrified of an after-life. A friend comes to his rescue by leading him to religion and "lively hope," so that soon John is a faithful member of chapel, living a humble and hard-working life as a bookseller. What happens next bears out John Wesley's comment that his religion, which made men sober and hard-working, also made them rich, with the consequence that the work of religious conversion had to begin again. John grows wealthy because his scrupulous attention to business leads the brethren to buy from him. But his affluence affects his personality; he loses his humility as he begins the search for ways of increasing his business. He engages in dubious lotteries and the sale of every kind of book that people will buy. Crabbe traces his end to a sad death in which John finds that his concern with business has left him personally empty and solitary.

To my mind, Crabbe rather mars this fine tale at the end by suggesting that John's problems would have been solved had he been instructed by a proper churchman who could show that there was no need to scorn worldly goods as the Dissenters, in their puritan way, demanded. But when Crabbe in his own voice contends that no conflict exists between John's worldly aspirations and his personal morality, he states but does not show. Since at the very basis of the story lies the assumption that man's problems are created by the interaction of the personal and social, it will not do to set an abstract moral doctrine to oppose the working out of conflicting desires and duties. Yet this is a problem which arises time and again in *Tales* when Crabbe attempts to portray an individual who is definitively present in a social context but aspiring to live beyond social definition as a person of independent value. "The Convert" is a near success in this endeavour, and as I hope to show shortly "The Patron" (Tale v) creates a fine dramatic structure to deal with the question.

For the most part, *Tales* reveals that Crabbe was having difficulty in treating characters and situations that raised fundamental problems of social and religious allegiance. And I think this accounts for our feeling about *Tales*, that, for all its strengths, Crabbe has often narrowed the structure of feeling in which the characters exist. In poems such as "The Gentleman Farmer" or "The Struggles of Conscience" where the individual directly challenges the social order of which he is a part, there is a decided danger of the story becoming polarized with the social detail presented as mere stage machinery for the individual's intellectual aspirations. In other cases where an individual ambitiously attempts to escape restrictions imposed by his social situation, Crabbe's narrative point of view seems often to exclude the individual's own sense of distress. For instance, in "Procrastination" (Tale IV) the actual painful attempt to achieve financial independence is shunted off-stage and not dramatically presented. In "The Parting Hour" (Tale II) the distress is portrayed, but the pain has become something to be contemplated, not an emotion experienced in social stress. In both cases, the young man chooses to try and win his "fortune" by turning to the sea or going overseas to take his chances in the lottery of new-world adventures, so that there is little sense of an actual struggle with a given social situation. The individual's lack of success is ascribed to bad luck, and he is left to cope as best he can. In several of the other tales, such as "Arabella" and "The 'Squire and the Priest," Crabbe begins or ends by stating that the individual making demands is a victim of pride or weakness of character, and this editorializing diminishes the force of the individual's feelings. Yet Crabbe's continuing return to these questions of individual rebellion reveals that the clash between the individual and society was a deeply felt concern, the crux for Crabbe in any significant development of an individual's character. After all, Crabbe could simply have refused to treat such questions altogether, but his nature was otherwise, and throughout his life he sought the artistic means to express his attitudes towards ambition.

The subject of the individual's relation to his society is, of course, to be found in the literature of any period, but that it occurs frequently in Crabbe's poetry is no accident. Writers of the late eighteenth and early nineteenth centuries were particularly concerned with the ways and means of keeping society stable while allowing the individual to pursue his ambitions. The subject of pride, eternally popular in western literature, received a new and particularly social colouring between the period of the French Revolution and the First Reform Bill, when at times a popular uprising was feared in England. At this period many pens were employed to support or disprove Edmund Burke's description of ambition—"one of the natural, inbred, incurable distempers of a powerful democracy."[3] Yet the bulk of the literature of the period implicitly repudiates Burke's conservatism by accepting instead the individual's own voice as the starting point. One thinks of Wordsworth's *Prelude* and, a little later, Charlotte Brontë's *Jane Eyre*, both of which make claims for the individual's exclusive viewpoint which cannot be disputed because the inner life is so intensely realized and experienced. For Crabbe, the problem was to present the individual's inner life without destroying an external response to the insistent "I am and I feel." Although the artistic solution to this problem of the individual and society is not fully realized until *Tales of the Hall*, Crabbe's portraits of ambition are revealing in their own right. And not unexpectedly, some of the most illuminating and instructive examples of his attempt to find artistic resolutions occur in poems that he chose not to publish. A comparison of two such poems—"The Insanity of Ambitious Love" and "David Morris"—with a successful poem from *Tales* such as "The Patron" (Tale v) offers an opportunity to understand Crabbe's creation of individuals whose lives extend the language of endeavour rather than exist within it.[4] As Crabbe himself said in writing "Sir Eustace Grey"—"Be it granted to one who dares not to pass the boundary fixed for common minds, at least to step near to the tremendous verge."[5]

In some ways the most revealing of the three poems, although the least successful in creating an artistic whole, is "The Insanity of Ambitious Love," in which the vigorous depiction of toil, drudgery and madness leads Crabbe into new areas of concern. Any comment on the poem must take into account that it was left unrevised, and that Crabbe might have had to change it out of all recognition to put it in a final, acceptable state for publication. [6] Yet the challenge to Crabbe is clear enough, for at the centre of the poem is the experience of a man bred in a factory who sees his life in terms of "either-or"—either unrelenting labour as a factory worker or a life of luxurious ease as a member of the leisure class.

In the form that the poem has come down to us, the man's story is set in a frame, although it was almost certainly conceived originally as a separate entity. In the first section of forty-five lines, the rector Jacques mentions a madman he knows, and a few days later suggests that he take the narrator (presumably Richard—the younger brother of *Tales of the Hall*—although this is not certain, and indeed, of no great concern) to visit the madman. On their return, the squire asks about the visit, and the narrator agrees to tell the madman's story. Although the narrator explains that he will retell the story, the man himself actually tells it, and as will be seen, this has a significant effect on one's response to the poem. The story of the "madman" takes up the rest of the poem, with sixty lines added at the end, when Jacques breaks in to try and convince the man of his madness. The forty-five line introduction is in Crabbe's usual couplet; the tale itself is in the form of eight-line stanzas, with the rhyme scheme ababbcbc.

The madman's story, obviously the most important part of the poem, commences when he welcomes the visitors to his home, which he believes to be a mansion decked with expensive purple velvet, Persian carpets and gold-inlay decorations. But the crux of the matter is that in his youth he lived in totally different circumstances:

> Within a Father's vast Machine,
> Where Springs & Spindles ratling rang,
> And whizzing Wheels, a noisy row,
> And loud the busy Damsels sang,
> While, roaring, rushed the Flood below.   (73–77)

The "ratling," "whizzing," and "roaring" of the factory offer little in the way of opportunity, and he soon leaves to seek his fortune in more auspicious scenes. Here the poem moves into the realm of the supernatural, for the young man makes a visit to the gypsies, and it soon becomes apparent that the story's interest lies, not so much in the man's psychology, as in the prophetic element of his experience.

As soon as the supernatural begins to dominate the poem—the man describes a mysterious cave where he met a beautiful Gypsy-Queen who prophesied his future—the similarity between Crabbe's poem and "La Belle Dame Sans Merci" of Keats (1819) becomes apparent. Both poems illustrate the sad consequences of placing too much trust in the promise of a life of love and beauty. Like Keats, Crabbe obviously felt the power of attraction in this promise of unending happiness; his picture of the world deprived of "la belle dame" is as forbidding and hopeless as Keats' "cold hillside." But Crabbe's poem, unlike Keats's, is based on closely observed social detail. The Gypsy-Queen's first alternative to the young man—a Dantesque hell of unrelenting toil and unhappiness[7]—agrees well with many nineteenth-century descriptions of the life of the labourer. The section is long, but worth quoting in full to give the sense of anger and dismay:

> I look'd, and I beheld a Plain,
>   Bare! trodden! worn on every Side,
> And there were Men, who wrought with Pain,
>   And to the meaner Tasks applied.
>   They comb'd, they wove, they span, they dyed,
> While pale Clerks, pensive at their Seats,
>   Earn'd the poor Pittences & sigh'd.
> This, this, the pay that Labour meets!
>
> There Labour brought the pond'rous Ore!
>   There took from the eternal Heap,
> Now strove to melt the stubborn store,
>   Now forc'd the fire its Rage to keep.
>   Lo yonder Docks, cut wide & deep,
> Where toil'd the Slave! whom Death must free,
> Where half-starv'd Wives approach'd to weep
>   For men compell'd to slave at Sea.

There were all sights of Care & Toil;
   The Smith his ponderous Hammer heav'd,
The Labourer plow'd the thankless Soil,
   Porters their heavy Loads receiv'd,
Pale Weavers sat, of Air bereav'd,
   And sang the melancholy song,
And Watchmen, for a while reliev'd,
   Walk'd dolefully their Wards along.

I saw the Ships, & from the deck
   Men dropt into the rav'nous tide,
I saw the Ship itself a Wreck,
   And many strugling Wretches died;
   I saw the Fishers, how they plied
Their cold laborious Arts for bread,
   They tried & fail'd, & still they tried,
   By Misery cloath'd, by Meaness fed.

Men lame & blind were begging here,
   Where by them mov'd the heedless Throng,
Where dead Men's Bodies on the Bier
   By Men half dead were borne along.
   Bad Women sang the mocking Song
Of Love & Pleasure, when the face
   Bore every Mark of secret wrong
   And every Stain of foul Disgrace.

Poor jaundic'd Men at sick'ning Trades,
   I saw, in Palsies, half Alive,
Soon to depart, & now but Shades,
   And those yet fated to survive,
   Intent with idle Hopes to thrive,
All servile in their Thrift, & mean.   (224–69)

The crucial problem at this point is how the reader receives this "vision," one of Crabbe's strongest indictments of the hard lot of the labourer. I would submit that the hell described contains little if anything to warn the reader that it is not a representation of early nineteenth-century England.[8] Consequently, when the Gypsy-Queen changes the vision to one of luxurious Eastern splendour, where work is unnecessary and pleasure the norm, the man of course embraces the life of happiness. One should recall that the reader knows the man is mad, and therefore never doubts that the heavenly world of his vision is imaginary. The question is whether we condemn him for choosing an imaginary world of heavenly bliss rather than a real world of unremitting toil.

Then the unexpected occurs. Before the madman has finished his story—and up to this point the reader has been sympathetically absorbed in the narrative, held by the sheer persuasion of the verse—the guests rise suddenly in anger. It is startling to be reminded that the madman's voice is not that of the poem, but merely that of a character within the poem, and no doubt Crabbe would have had to revise the ending considerably for publication. Jacques irritably tells the man that he is deceiving himself, that his entire story has been a lie. He reveals, moreover, that the madman never worked in a mill, but is the son of a parish clerk. He became the servant of a rich lady upon whom he "dar'd to gaze with sinful View," and fell in love. When the affair proved impossible, he was driven mad, and the lady, out of pity, now provides for him. Needless to say, the ending comes as a great surprise. Although Crabbe has prepared us to accept that the madman has deluded himself about his present state of luxury, no intimation has been given that his entire story is false. The man's early life in the mill and his vision of the ignobility of most labouring jobs carries conviction.

Presumably Crabbe wished Jacques to represent the correct opinion, especially since the title of the poem supports Jacques's view. Yet as it stands, the ending makes Jacques appear unsympathetic. Since his speech, like the madman's, is presented in the first person, its effect on the reader depends similarly on the dramatic force with which its ideas are conveyed. That Jacques responds largely to abstract moral considerations, rather than the underlying human implications of the madman's history, reveals him to be somewhat shallow. If the man is harmlessly mad, Jacques has no reason to treat him insensitively, yet the tale so angers Jacques that he destroys the man's little flowers constructed of string and straw. While this concern for the man's immortal soul may be commendable, the attempt to bring him to a proper state of sin and fear of God seems perverse in this context. The threat to bind the man in a "strait Garment" in "Darkness" and to consign him "to silence! impotent & blind!" (418–20) is altogether out of proportion to his crime. Jacques threatens repressive measures more violent and blameworthy than anything the madman is said to have done.[9]

Had Crabbe wanted to show only the delusions of madness, he could have done so in a few lines. But as in "Sir Eustace Grey," he is genuinely concerned to present the madman's state of mind so as to develop the idea that madness is a psychological release from unbearable social or personal problems. Consequently, when Jacques condemns the man for his "real" actions and dismisses the story as a figment of imagination, he appears simple-minded; for the madman's recognition that he had to choose between two lives—one of servitude, the other, of independence—is by no means entirely illusory. Even if his story of working in a factory is discounted, one cannot deny that the boy must have had some premonition that his choice was narrow. As a labourer or a servant with no capital, no influence, and no representation of any kind, he was a victim of what Carlyle called the cash nexus. Even were he not actually born into a vast spinning mill, in one sense he was the victim of the great machine of industry. No one can blame him for believing that his future lay in marrying money when that was the way a great many people in trade and from the landed gentry saw their own future at this period.

In "The Insanity of Ambitious Love," Crabbe has presented two different views of ambition. In the first, the man portrays himself as a slave to the wheel of labour, and sees his alternative in the apparently luxurious life of his masters. The second view—presented by Jacques—is that the man goes mad because he is incapable of submitting to the ordinary difficulties and hardships to be found amongst all classes of men. For Jacques, the man fails because he has a romantic dream of perfection which bears no similarity to the real world, a dream which spoils him for the type of life demanded by the complexities of day-to-day existence. The point is that both views are potentially true. If the man could have married into the rich upper classes, he would not have had to work for a living. His vision is not false, but having failed to realize his dream, he now lives in madness rather than admit his failure. When Jacques orders the man to see that he is living a lie and that he must learn to overcome his pride the voice is one of repression, and the madness almost seems preferable to Jacques' version of reality.

The manner in which the utopian dream-vision of man's perfection rides roughshod over the practical considerations of man's fallen estate occurs relatively often in eighteenth-century literature. To some extent it is found in the fourth book of *Gulliver's Travels*, and it is certainly present in James Thomson's "The Castle of Indolence." In a way very similar to that of Crabbe in "The Insanity of Ambitious Love," Thomson begins with a description of the enchanted ground of the wizard Idleness, and, like Crabbe, for a time he seems overcome by his own descriptions of "this Ant-hill Earth" where men spend their lives in laborious tasks, searching for pleasures they "dare not taste" (i, XLIX). As a result, his presentation of the land where "Freedom reign'd" and everyone could "eat, drink, study, sleep, as it may fall" (i, XXXV) seems designed to recommend that man should eschew the limitations of the present for the potential of the future. One can see that both Crabbe and Thomson, when they looked around them at the lives of the labouring people, were overwhelmed by the feeling that man had lost his sense of proportion in the vast changes sweeping over England.[10] Thomson uses the image of an anthill; Crabbe speaks of a "vast Machine." The sense of total disorientation threatening age-old values caused both Thomson and Crabbe to doubt for a time the efficacy of reasoned self-control. Both were led to construct imaginatively an alternative world of luxury in which the individual allows himself to be ruled by his passions—a world that was ready to hand, since it already existed (at least from the point of view of the labourer) in the life of the gentry. In both poets the feeling is only momentary; they end by reaffirming the value of reason, self-control, and obedience to moral and social laws.

The problem remains, however, especially with Crabbe; for once the dichotomy between the two nations has been revealed or acknowledged, it becomes difficult to apply a moral standard to those who have attempted to leap the bounds. The moral values then seem too obviously a bulwark to maintain the class differences. As has been seen, the madman's tale angers Jacques (usually a sign of weakness), so that his values do not generate nearly as much conviction and energy as does the madman's vision of a world out of control. Moreover, the verse itself supports the madman. His use of strong, active verbs—"They comb'd, they wove, they span, they dyed"—gives a sense of the continuous toil of the workers. His lines, altogether stronger and more densely packed with emotive meaning than those of Jacques, give voice to the man's whole experience of life-denying labour. Jacques, on the contrary, has no way of representing the man's actual existence and is left with abstract comment.

Some of the poem's difficulties no doubt arise because Crabbe has described the madman as a victim of urban rather than rural problems. It is known that Crabbe believed the problems caused by the factories and crowded urban centres to be far greater than those of the countryside.[11] When Crabbe came to describe the madman as the victim of a depersonalized machine, the picture he conjured up was so horrific that the solutions were not at once apparent. Like Robert Owen, Crabbe realized that the new manufacturing system was creating not only new products, but a new type of person as well.[12] Notably, at the end of "The Insanity of Ambitious Love," Crabbe has Jacques claim that the madman is actually a son of the land, which suggests an attempt on Crabbe's part to repudiate the original picture of the man born into a "vast Machine." But a mere statement of this kind cannot destroy the central section of the poem in which we are given a personal vision in which the labourer, as grist for an indifferent mill, enacts the distance separating rich and poor. Crabbe's repulsion at the mechanical life of labour is so intensely realized that his own caution and disbelief in social alternatives can find no effective means of response. It will not do to *state* that the facts are otherwise, for we have been presented with the man's own experience, and experience is itself a fact.

Whereas in "The Insanity of Ambitious Love" the madman's first-person vision of a choice between relentless labour and luxurious ease was expressed so strongly that Crabbe found himself left with no effective means of comment or qualification, in "The Patron" (Tale v of *Tales*) he creates successfully a situation where a number of people enact in their own lives the split between those who work for a living and those who are ladies and gentlemen. The poem's narrative form allows a number of separate perspectives, permitting us to see the social and personal problems from different angles and in different shapes. The tale's complexity has meant that critics, searching for a single response to the problem of the individual and society, have tended to disagree about the tale's "meaning." Huchon, for instance, has commented that Crabbe wished to show how we must "recognise the frailty of our nature and no longer decline, in critical circumstances, the aid of religion."[13] Robert Chamberlain, on the other hand, claims that "the young literary hopeful deserves punishment for foolish behaviour . . ., [but] we sense in the poem an unjustified anger towards the somewhat inconsiderate but far from criminal noble patron."[14] Yet both these readings fail to do the poem justice. Nowhere does Crabbe suggest that the young poet "deserves punishment," nor does he show "unjustified anger" towards the patron. That the poem praises humility, as Huchon states, is certainly true, but it also suggests a totally different proposition, that the individual should trust himself by relying on his own strength of will. As will be seen shortly, the critics have fastened on one of Crabbe's portraits to the exclusion of others, thereby ignoring the manner in which the form of the poem holds together the constituent parts, demanding a response in terms of persons rather than abstractions.

The poem tells the story of an ambitious young man, John, a borough-bailiff's son who has great hopes of becoming a poet. At election time, John aids Lord Frederick Damer in his candidacy by writing squibs on his opponent. In return, Lord Frederick rewards John by inviting him for a prolonged visit to the family's country house. Praised, pampered, and spoiled, young John is overcome by the quality of life of the rich and the attentions the nobleman's sister bestows on him, until he begins to look forward to a reward enabling him to live in such surroundings. As a result, he soon finds his father's house, with its air of thrift, its cheap wine, and its "boil'd and roast," distasteful. But when the test comes, and John looks to Lord Frederick to place him in the church, the patron backs down. The frustration of John's ambition leads to a gradual decline, from which he emerges briefly into a religious happiness before his death.

The first thing to note is that the outline of the story, by itself, does not give any hint of Crabbe's intentions. Crabbe might easily have used the detail of the story either as a means to berate the aristocracy for failing to help John or as a means of showing the lower classes the dangers of attempting to rise above one's station. But both these views belong more to polemic than art; Crabbe encompasses, and at the same time dissolves, polemic as he deepens our understanding of the web of human relationships. At the beginning of the poem Crabbe establishes his presupposition that people in John's position, given a degree of prudence, can live a happy and prosperous life. John's father earns enough to keep his family in "decent state," and all of John's brothers are living in thriving circumstances. Since there is no suggestion that John has to live a hole-in-the-wall existence, the disjunction between the worker and the gentleman is diminished, as indeed it was to some extent by doctors, lawyers, merchants, and even artisans.[15]

At the same time, Crabbe shows that John differs from his brothers. As a young boy he is sickly, and lives apart from his family in the country where he develops his mind and his passion for poetry. It is no surprise that John feels "not a love for money-making arts." At the outset, two potential contradictories are established: first, anyone in John's station requires constant care to steer a path in "life's rough ocean"; second, John is naturally a literary and artistic person. Crabbe is careful never to suggest that John is a wastrel: when his father sends him to university, "John kept his terms at college unreproved." But John's nature drives him continually to look beyond his father's workaday life for satisfaction. In addition, Crabbe builds into John's personality a weakness that can later be used to explain his failure to bridge the social gulf:

> Yet in his walks, his closet, and his bed,
> All frugal cares and prudent counsels fled;
> And bounteous Fancy for his glowing mind
> Wrought various scenes, and all of glorious kind;
> Slaves of the *ring* and *lamp*! what need of you,
> When Fancy's self such magic deeds can do? (77–82)

As can be seen, John's hopes are dreams of beauty without any substantial content, the sort engendered by Aladdin's rings and lamps.

At the beginning, then, the dominant tone is a sense of foreboding that overshadows John's dreams of success. But Crabbe also creates a large degree of sympathy for John. When John writes his election squibs, Lord Frederick praises him as "the Burns of English race, the happier Chatterton." Moreover, Crabbe indicates that John's ambitions to become a man of letters are not wholly the result of vain imaginings. His poetry contains "weeds, but still proofs of vigour in the soil" (35). Moreover, when John helps Lord Frederick win his seat, Crabbe indicates that Lord Frederick is himself a political upstart, campaigning against an old, established family. That Lord Frederick wins with the help of John's father's influence in the borough suggests that John may also succeed. Not only does he have talents worth developing, Crabbe shows how social pressures work to convince him that talent is the great equalizing force between the two social classes. Lord Frederick and his family go out of their way to make him feel one of them. The patron's sister, Emma, even begins a flirtation. One should recall at this point that the madman in "The Insanity of Ambitious Love" went mad and was confined because of a similar love, although Jacques there refuses to say more than that the man gazed "with sinful View." In "The Patron" Crabbe has supplied a valid reason for John's love of Emma, for she encourages him. Thus John's over-confidence is fostered by a society where the foolishness and selfishness of the Lord Fredericks and Lady Emmas lead him to believe that the class structure is less rigid than it is.

At this point, many readers probably feel that what John requires is some solid practical advice to open his eyes to the actual state of the world. To some extent, Crabbe agrees, but he also recognizes how often advice in the abstract fails to touch the real needs of the individual. For instance, John's father writes a long letter filled with the sort of cautions that Crabbe learned when he was chaplain to the Duke of Rutland at Belvoir Castle. The irony is that in attempting to advise John about every possibility, John's father neglects to mention the very situation which brings about his son's downfall. As John comments: "It is, in truth, . . . / Correct in part, but what is *this* to me? (410–11). While John's father worries that his son may bring home a baggage of a serving maid, John dreams of meetings with the Lady Emma. Moreover, the Polonius-like advice of John's father, with its narrow, mercantile emphasis on the advantages accruing to self, is the very thing John is attempting to escape. The tragedy is that John expects Lord Frederick, the aristocrat, to possess a different set of values from those of the countinghouse.

And John has some reason to expect help from Lord Frederick, for when the latter returns to London he gives John an assurance that he will act as his patron. Crabbe brilliantly catches Lord Frederick's confusion in a situation where a specific promise is required (and given) because he feels himself embarrassed and compromised, not because he wants to help:

> Then came the noble friend—"And will my lord
> Vouchsafe no comfort? drop no soothing word?
> Yes, he must speak:" he speaks, "My good young friend,
> You know my views; upon my care depend;
> My hearty thanks to your good father pay,
> And be a student.—Harry, drive away." (458–63)

Again Crabbe presents the abstract situation in personal terms when he portrays John recognizing that he is being dropped, but refusing to believe what he can clearly see. The outcome—after months of waiting—is Lord Frederick's announcement that, since a place in the church is impossible, John will be sent to "busier scenes." The promise turns out to be worth little more than what John's father could have done.

Lord Frederick's letter is important, since it underlines how few were the options open to John. To elevate John to a position in society above that of the labourers, artisans, and tradespeople would have been a simple but decisive move: Lord Frederick could have found John a place in the church, bought him a commission in the army, or sent him to one of the Inns of Court to train as a lawyer. But good church places were taken by younger sons; commissions in the army were expensive; and lawyers needed influence to gain clients.[16] Because of the cost and scarcity of positions, one might conclude that Lord Frederick was not unwarranted in his decision to send John into business. Yet such a view ignores the crucial point. When John's father sent his son to college, he did so with the idea of educating him for the church—John "took his degree, and left the life he loved; / Not yet ordain'd" (58–59). Lord Frederick was acquainted with John's position at the time he promised to help him; his letter to John shows clearly that he understood John had expected his help in gaining a promotion in the church. Without the assistance of a patron, John would have had to content himself with the position of curate. As Crabbe pointed out in Letter III of *The Borough*, curates were generally miserably paid, and enjoyed none of the status for which their education qualified them.[17] John's father could give him the education but could not find him the parish. In refusing to help John into the position for which he was trained Lord Frederick consigns John's education to the flames, and bids him start afresh. When seen in this light, Lord Frederick's decision to send John into business appears at least partly culpable.

Naturally enough, after having his hopes raised so high, John finds it impossible to adapt to a life of business. Here Crabbe implicitly sympathizes with John, for he allows John's feelings to be expressed in indirect reported speech:

Thanks to the patron, but of coldest kind,
Express'd the sadness of the poet's mind;
Whose heavy hours were pass'd with busy men,
In the dull practice of th' official pen.   (581–84)

Crabbe's own voice has become the vehicle for John's attitudes, and although John's father still sees everything from his own point of view, and believes "the boy would learn to scramble and to climb," Crabbe's point is that John is really unfit for such a life. John's hours are "heavy" and his work "dull." Eventually his dislike of the work turns to hate, and he ends by becoming a failure. He leaves, so shamed in his own eyes that he falls into despair. Recovering briefly with the help of his family, John finds consolation in religion, becomes resigned to his fate, turns to heaven, and dies.

This use of the religious ending plays an important part in effecting a satisfactory conclusion; for Crabbe indicates that John was guilty of a spiritual sin as well as a wordly blunder in expecting Lord Frederick to provide for him with the sort of fulfilment that he eventually finds when he turns to God. It is only when John recognizes his own limitations and his need for God's assistance that he finds happiness. This conclusion reminds us of George Eliot's "solution" to Maggie Tulliver's ambitions. A peaceful end means exclusion from the social fabric, isolation, and death.

As he had done in "The Hall of Justice" Crabbe shifts the theme from an earthly to a spiritual level of interpretation, and once again the shift provides a less than satisfactory resolution. The difference in "The Patron" is that the poem goes on to investigate the insufficiency of the "religious solution." Huchon was of course correct in pointing out that John achieves happiness only when he conquers his pride and learns humility; nor do I disagree with his belief that Crabbe wished to show how necessary religion is to man. But the poem implies more than these simple statements, and thus offers a social perspective on "men must be humble." For instance, in his summing up Crabbe comments caustically on Lord Frederick and his sister Emma; he shows them both to be unsympathetic, with very little or no sense of responsibility for what has happened to John. Emma is rather pleased to find her beauty sufficient to drive a man to madness. And "my lord, to whom the poet's fate was told, / Was much affected, for a man so cold" (704–705). The poem implies that, to some degree, people such as John must learn humility because those in control of power are indifferent to the needs of the people they control and represent. It should not be forgotten that Lord Frederick is a member of parliament, and that Crabbe has taken pains to point out the part that John and his father played in gaining his election victory. Crabbe is here indicating that John has been humbled both spiritually and socially. He must learn humility because excessive pride is a failing, but he must also learn to be humble because the great of the land decree that he remain among "the humble." It is no coincidence that the lower classes are often called "humble people"—social rigidity ensures that they live in humility.

Moreover, in his comments at his son's funeral, John's father gives a new twist to the religious view that pride is a sin when he takes the perfectly logical but unexpected step of praising God for not sending him any other sons of genius:

> "There lies my boy," he cried, "of care bereft,
> And, Heav'n be praised, I've not a genius left:
> No one among ye, sons! is doom'd to live
> On high-raised hopes of what the great may give;
> None, with exalted views and fortunes mean,
> To die in anguish, or to live in spleen.
> Your pious brother soon escaped the strife
> Of such contention, but it cost his life;
> You then, my sons, upon yourselves depend,
> And in your own exertions find the friend." (718–27)

When John's father perceives that his son could be happy only if he were given an opportunity to use his education, and that such opportunities are rare, he concludes—realist that he is—that the world would be better off without educated lower-class people. At this point the reader is suddenly jarred to the realization that this is an endorsement of the view that the proper contribution of the poor is by means of labour alone. And if this were generally the case then a poem such as "The Patron," written by a poet like Crabbe, could not exist. John is resigned to leaving the world of man because he is entering the world of God; John's father, however, is resigned to his entering the world of God because he cannot enter the world of the rich.

In his logical manner, John's father draws the final conclusion that, since people such as John cannot rise above their station, no reason exists for bothering with the Lord Fredericks. If the social hierarchy does not benefit the poor man, then he should ignore it, and refuse to adapt himself to its conventions. Thus the resignation of John's father leads him to the conclusion that lower-class people should not affect to copy the upper classes. Such advocacy was, of course, in direct contradiction to the teaching of Christian moralists such as Wilberforce and Hannah More, who believed that it was dangerous to allow the poor to develop their own working-class ethos; for then they would ignore the teaching of the Christian religion, refuse to be resigned to their lot, and begin to claim equality. The church, Wilberforce believed, taught the wealthy to be benevolent, but more important, it taught the poor to be acquiescent:

> Softening the glare of wealth, and moderating the
> insolence of power, she renders the inequalities of the
> social state less galling to the lower orders, whom also she
> instructs, in their turn, to be diligent, humble, patient:
> reminding them that their more lowly path has been
> allotted to them by the hand of God; that it is their part
> faithfully to discharge its duties, and contentedly to bear
> its inconveniences; that the present state of things is very
> short; that the objects, about which worldly men conflict
> so eagerly, are not worth the contest; that the peace of
> mind, which Religion offers to all ranks indiscriminately,
> affords more true satisfaction than all the expensive
> pleasures which are beyond the poor man's reach.[18]

Crabbe gently explodes such apologetics with the figure of John's father, standing over his son's grave, seriously thanking God for not sending him any more geniuses. Unwittingly this businessman rebuts the argument of the Christian moralists when he calls upon his sons to ignore the benevolence of the upper classes and rely upon their own hard work. Had the lower classes complied, they would have deprived the gentry of any opportunity of influence. The attitude of John's father is not that of humility, but of ambition to succeed independently. It brings to mind that famous scene in *Bleak House* where Mr. Rouncewell, the Iron-master, meets Sir Leicester Dedlock, and by laying claim to values and knowledge that are outside Dedlock's perception, flattens the vertical hierarchy of conservative society.

In "The Patron" Crabbe does not attempt to state didactically any one particular solution to this problem of the individual in society, but maintains a number of conflicting views in tension with one another. John's Christian death is a personal solution to one man's personal problems. But such an answer does not meet the questions raised by the larger social problems of which John's life is an example. Nor does Crabbe suggest that an easy answer is possible for the large, complex social issues, but by means of John's father he advocates a social philosophy—"upon yourselves depend"—directly antithetical to John's personal resignation.

II

It is apparent that both "The Insanity of Ambitious Love" and "The Patron" contain a good deal of Crabbe's own experience, including his feelings of anger and shame occasioned by working at dull manual jobs—piling cheese and butter on the Slaughden quays—after having been educated for a better station.[19] Like the heroes of his poems, Crabbe had thrown over a relatively secure position (as apothecary in Aldborough) to search for a patron and the chance to make his name as a man of letters. Crabbe, of course, succeeded, but throughout his life he was haunted by dreams of how near he had come to complete failure in fulfilling his ambitions.[20] Also like his heroes, Crabbe knew the shame of near-defeat: he records the story of how, after sending his letter to Burke requesting help, he spent the night walking up and down Westminster Bridge. Imprisonment for debt was waiting had Burke, like Thurlow and Shelburne, refused to aid Crabbe. In addition, it will be remembered that in marrying Sarah Elmy, a lady considerably above him socially, Crabbe had done what he later showed his heroes in "The Patron" and "The Insanity of Ambitious Love" wishing to do, although in Crabbe's case there was no question of marrying for money, since Miss Elmy was living in reduced circumstances. His wife's later mental illness must also have given Crabbe cause to consider the wisdom of the marriage, even though the evidence suggests that Crabbe was a devoted husband and father.[21] The point is that in writing both "The Patron" and "The Insanity of Ambitious Love," Crabbe had as his model his own desperate attempt to leap the bounds of social class, and he builds into these tales his own feelings of weakness and inadequacy which had threatened to destroy his confidence, a confidence based on little more than a skimpy education and the belief that he could write poetry.

However, in "David Morris," another of the "new" poems from the John Murray manuscript collection, Crabbe creates a different curve of feeling, because David's strength of character leaves the gulf between the social classes as a reality which is to be overcome by personal effort, not to be dissolved by the imagination. There is, therefore, no factitious split in David's mind to mirror a real split in social class. Moreover, the question is not one of fickle Eros, but of talent and opportunity. In "David Morris," no fatal woman of higher station entices with the offer of an illusory paradise. Although at the end of the poem Crabbe introduces humility as a possible solution, the poem never centres on pride, which is personal by nature, but on aspiration, which depends on connection between the personal and something distinctly other. Thus "David Morris" presents a significant extension of the problems of ambition as presented in "The Insanity of Ambitious Love" and "The Patron."

In many ways, David, as a solitary figure of religious doubts, resembles the questioner of Wordsworth's *Excursion*, and indeed, the dialogue between David and the man of piety is generally similar to that of Wordsworth's poem. This is not surprising, for both Crabbe and Wordsworth were attempting to bring their "scientific" views of man—where he is to be studied as a natural phenomenon—into harmony with their Christian convictions.[22] More interesting still, both poems express a distinct unease with the religious answer even as they offer it. In "David Morris" Crabbe has created a character with much "natural" grace who confronts the problems of his life with an attitude of faithfulness that challenges the efficacy of the orthodox Christian dogma. David is finally led to commit suicide but the poem indicates that this act—usually believed to be irreligious—may have more of the substance of faith in it than the proposal of the Christian dogmatist —to live and suffer.

The story, told by an unnamed narrator, falls into two parts: the first section outlines the story of David's life, and the second narrates the argument on resignation that the narrator has with David shortly before his suicide. Quite clearly the two sections are related, with the first part providing the background to the argument. Yet David's story is not told so as to substantiate the narrator's argument in favour of resignation. Rather, David is developed sympathetically, thereby revealing the difficulties that a person of intelligence, with little economic means, will encounter. To this end, Crabbe makes David one of that large class of eighteenth-century fictional characters, the natural son of a rich lord and a peasant woman. At birth, David has one foot in the peerage and the other in the farmyard.

David's story begins when Kezia, "a Peasant's Daughter," comes from her village to serve at the home of a noble lady. The lady's son, young and unmarried, soon falls in love with Kezia, and she with him. Genuinely in love, the young man does not treat Kezia as a servant, plying her with false promises, but sets her up handsomely in "a quiet Seat" near the town. David, the child of this union, is given the chance to develop upper-class attitudes and expectations, the basis of which is later destroyed when the father's affection for Kezia dwindles and mother and child are forced to move to a small cottage where they live alone on a small annuity. This prepares the reader for the main section of the poem which shows the difficulties resulting from David's gentle upbringing when he tries to find a place for himself in society. For instance, when David goes to school, his sense of fair play is outraged by the boorishness of the village boys:

> Vulgar and rude were all, their chief Employ
> To play the Tyrant o'er the weaker Boy.   (196–97)

And quite rightly he refuses to endorse such behaviour. In itself this is a fairly typical situation, but Crabbe quickly proceeds to complicate the situation by showing David forced into taking sides against his mother. Because of feelings of guilt about her love affair, and her need for consolation, David's mother joins a dissenting religious group, whose stern and narrow rules shut her heart against her son. The preacher assures her of salvation if she will obey the rules of the sect; and this in turn becomes her answer to all David's problems. David, who has inherited his father's intelligence, quickly sees that the answers given by the false "prophet" have no validity in fact, and refuses to submit to his rule. Crabbe makes abundantly clear that he respects, and wishes his readers to respect, the way in which David refutes the abstractions of the fanatical preacher. David's initial distrust is justified later in the story when Crabbe depicts the preacher after his marriage to David's mother:

> He was no more the gentle Guide and Friend,
> Who to her Fears and Scruples would attend;
> His Cares of such domestic kind were closed,
> On whom an hundred Consciences reposed.   (349–52)

At the beginning at least, the portrait of David Morris gives the impression that Crabbe composed it with the sole intention of accurately mapping David's aspirations. This reflects Crabbe's tendency at this period to discover his themes in the lives of fully developed characters, rather than to choose characters illustrative of themes. For instance, when David writes to his father asking for help, Crabbe could have depicted the latter's reaction in black-and-white terms. Instead, Crabbe offers a subtle character portrait of David's father in which the usual stereotypes are disregarded. Although he refuses to consider the possibility of recognizing David as his son, the father is sufficiently impressed by David's clever letter to go to the unusual length of obtaining for him a place in the church. The simple solution would have been to make David accept the offer; instead, Crabbe ironically observes that what looks like a "good" offer on the part of the father hardly has the best interests of the church at heart. When David refuses the offer, saying that he cannot join the church, since he does not subscribe to all its creed, Crabbe illustrates the cynicism of the day in the surprised reaction of the lawyer: "What then? you can at least comply" (329). There is no attempt on Crabbe's part, however, to portray David as an exemplum of virtue; rather, David is seen to possess all the mixed motives of normal human beings—part moral, part pragmatic:

> Poor David briefly on the Subject mused,
> Then deeply sighed, but steadily refused,
> In part by Conscience led, yet thinking, too,
> There must be something that my Lord w^d do. (335–38)

Yet David's response is obviously praiseworthy. Even the lawyer is impressed by the young man's idealism, for he "unwilling from the Door retired, / And much condemned the Rashness he admired" (339–40). Considering the strong antilatitudinarian opinions prevalent when Crabbe wrote this poem, David's conscientious refusal of a church place is not to be despised.

Lacking any sort of position in or connection with society, David becomes very much an outsider cut off from the usual sustaining relationships. Thrown upon his own resources, he follows a path fairly typical of the distressed intellectual, in that he and a friend begin to question the conventional Christian interpretation of man's place in the world when they ask about the world's rationale, the meaning of life, and the existence of God:

> "What Good," they asked, "can rise
> From Man's Distresses, Wants and Miseries?
> How is it thus, that what we warmly love
> And fondly seek! should our Distruction prove?
> Is there a Power above, who feels it right
> To give the Wish, and mock the Appetite?
> . . . .
> Is he a Father? why his Children vex?
> Is he a Guide, why puzzle and perplex?
> A Friend! Why friendless do we then complain?
> A King, and Wretches groan beneath his Reign?
>
> (394-408)

David, it should be noted, is by no means the usual type of free-thinker that one finds in Crabbe's poetry—a man naturally inclined to immorality and viciousness. David's questions result from the discovery that his fundamentally loving nature is cut off from community. Moreover, David is an intellectual, even though an undisciplined one; his questions arise in the first place, not because he is an enemy of the church, but because he was too honest to debase himself (and the church) by hypocritically turning priest. How significant David's questions are meant to be, Crabbe never directly says. Although the narrator believes them to be the out-pourings of "nervous Men," they seem more like the eternal questions of the dispossessed. Curiously enough, the narrator him-self makes no attempt to rebut them; he contents himself by comparing them to Satan's questions in hell, and concludes that they are unhelpful:

> Such the fruitful themes
> Of nervous Men with melancholy Dreams,
> Who, when their Wants demand their utmost Care,
> Ask Why they want, and swell the Load they bear.
>
> (409-12)

Perhaps at the time Crabbe began his career in the 1780s, the narrator's attitude towards David would have been that of the majority of the population, but even then, many people were beginning to feel that such questions deserved an answer. Paley certainly thought so when he included his famous apology for social inequality in *Moral and Political Philosophy* (1785). While socialists such as Thomas Spence may have been laughed at as foolish Utopians, their "foolishness" caused them to spend a great deal of time in prison. And certainly by the second decade of the nineteenth century the narrator's refusal to take David seriously is no longer representative of contemporary attitudes to such questions. By this time the ways of God seemed once more in need of justification, thereby causing many people such as David to question the age-old theological answers. The narrator would have David resign himself to his misfortunes by making the best of a bad world, but this is to dismiss David's questions, not to answer them. Once the question of evil seriously arises, then a stage in the argument has been reached when the answer—one must be resigned—no longer satisfies. Moreover, the lack of metaphysical underpinning plays havoc with ideas of social justice, and David is led to ask economic questions of the sort asked previously in *The Village*:

> Why toils the Peasant, & why feasts the Lord?
> Why Flocks & Herds are feeding calmly round,
> And We in anxious Cares & Griefs abound?　　(433–35)

Yet such abstract questions are not the whole of David's lived experience. Made of sterner stuff than John of "The Patron," David finally decides to swallow his pride about his genteel background, acknowledge the limitations of the social system, and better his position by becoming a lowly customs officer. Unlike many of Crabbe's characters, David manages to learn, and to some extent benefit, from his experiences. This is an important turning point in the story, for it shows that David, although proud, is not without either humility or discipline. Yet at this crucial moment, Crabbe shows that David's early speculations are not entirely unjustified when all his hard work comes to nought:

> Still was he poor, and found his Efforts vain
> An higher Station by his Care to gain.
> Another gained it, though he laboured less;
> Interest, not Merit, there insured Success. (539–42)

Crabbe deliberately includes every conceivable option David might
have, and shows them all unworkable. Even the love of a woman is
denied him, since once again the fact of his birth intervenes:

> The untaught Fair
> Filled him with Scorn, th' accomplished with Dispair.
>   (529–30)

Only when David has attempted to better his life by his own
efforts, and has failed, does Crabbe finally complete the circle by
showing him falling into immorality. Even then, Crabbe attributes
David's decline to the effect of social pressures and David's own
loss of hope in self-improvement:

> He grew Remiss, His duties were declined,
> Indulged his Senses, & debased his Mind.
> He saw how Gain was made, and owned no Law
> That bad him shun the Evil Acts he saw;
> Then, overcome, he took a bolder View
> Of what he could, as others round him, do;
> If Conscience murmured, and his Spirits failed,
> These Wine inflamed, & over that prevailed. (545–52)

David is not a criminal by nature, but unable to find a place for
himself in society, he eventually ends with no allegiances, feeling
no obligations to obey any of society's laws. Finally he throws in
his lot with what he takes to be the blind, amoral forces of the
universe.

To this point, David's difficulties have been presented sympathetically, but as soon as the narrator begins to explain his own
part in David's life, he asserts that David's ambition was blameworthy, that he should have resigned himself to his station. This
of course ignores the point that David has no real class position.

The narrator's role is somewhat puzzling, since Crabbe introduces him as a person who is sympathetic to David as a result of having experienced many of David's troubles. Because the narrator is a spokesman for religion, one might expect Crabbe to endorse him rather than David. And in part, this is what happens, for as soon as the narrator learns of David's despondency, he attempts to convince him of "Man's true State." The surprise is that the poem does not support the narrator's position; at the end, the reader sympathizes more with David's refusals to bow to the *status quo* than with the narrator's insistence that all men must resign themselves to their station. It is possible to conclude that the poem is simply an artistic failure, that Crabbe failed to show the narrator's Christian apologetics supplying an answer to David's problem. Yet it is by no means clear that this was Crabbe's intention. At moments, the narrator's abstract insistence on dogma is startlingly similar to the fanaticism of David's stepfather. The ending of the poem, one of the most perceptive pieces Crabbe ever wrote, would suggest that Crabbe expressed his own sympathies and feelings in his characters, at the expense of orthodoxy, to a far greater degree than has been suspected.

Part of the reason why the narrator is so unpersuasive with both David and the reader is that his argument is couched in abstractions such as "Man's true State":

> I strove to soothe him, Chose him Books, and read,
> But his Desire and Love of Truth were fled.
> He neither granted nor denied the Proof
> Of Man's true State! but would reply: "Enough!
> It may be so! but all is dark to me.
> I've neither Power to argue, nor t' agree." (613–18)

David, interestingly enough, does not reject the narrator's belief; instead, he replies that, while "it may be so," he has no certain way of knowing, since he has experienced nothing that would give him evidence or touch his will. All remains "dark" to David, and such religious faith simply appears irrelevant. Yet David is not a vain and dogmatic atheist who rejects the narrator's arguments out of spite. Crabbe has already prepared the reader to see David as an intellectual who has read and studied the problems:

> His Books we knew not, but with us were found
> Some who conceived their Tenets were unsound;
> The Care he took that None those Books should find
> Were held as Proof of their pernicious Kind.
> His Sabbaths all to him were Days of Rest,
> He no Religion had, or none profest,
> Seldom at Church, he never found a Seat
> Where Congregations of Dissenters meet;
> Hence as an Atheist they the Man reviled,
> Who at their Censures and their Judgment smiled,
> For well he knew how they the Man condemn,
> The Wretch, who walks not in their Path with them.
>
> (28–39)

The comment glances not only at David's religion (and Crabbe is deliberately vague whether David is religious or not), but at the religion of all those people who condemn a man because he reads books or because he "walks not in their Path." Consequently, David appears far superior to the ordinary religious dogmatist.

Crabbe has also portrayed David as being at least the intellectual equal of the narrator himself. When David talked to the narrator about committing suicide, the narrator was so imperceptive that he did not comprehend David's seriousness: "He talked of Death, but, as it then appear'd, / There were in him no Symptoms to be feared" (623–24). The narrator thus answers David with the easy assurance that "Temperance & Care . . . will Health restore." David snaps back with a fine retort:

> "For what?", said he, "My comforts live no more,
> And when our Dwelling we no longer love,
> What Law on Earth forbids us to remove?"   (626–28)

The narrator, candidly admitting that he cannot answer these arguments, is forced to reply with what he knows to be a commonplace—"Who quits his Post is sure to meet Disgrace." Refusing to accept banalities, David asks, "Disgrace with Whom?" and with a masterly touch, finishes with a quotation from Spenser: "When weary Mortals die, / Let none ask How, or whence, or where, or Why" (631–34). Undoubtedly David has the best of the argument. In spite of the narrator's avowal that he has experienced the same problems as David, obviously he has not plumbed them to the same depths; for he cannot provide satisfactory answers. Crabbe's realization of the situation leaves no doubt that David has routed the narrator:

> Smiling he spoke, and earnest I replied:
> "The Poet's Verse is not the Sinner's Guide."
> And thus we parted—"Think not I forget",
> He said, "your Kindness, 'tis One pleasing Debt,
> And proves there's Love in Man."—My leave I took,
> And left poor David to his Bed and Book.   (635–40)

While the narrator's "earnestness" seems slightly comic, David's acceptance of the offer of human kindness expresses something of "natural" grace.

It might be thought that Crabbe would not agree with David's statement that no one knows what happens after death. But not necessarily. In the figure of David, Crabbe was projecting some of his own doubts. Writing to Miss Elizabeth Charter in July 1816, Crabbe said: "When thoughts of the fate of those near to me enter my Mind, I confess I banish them as quickly as I can, leaving this mysterious Subject as unrevealed and inexplicable. God is good I say and think no more, that is I dare not think."[23] Unlike the poem's narrator, Crabbe was never anxious in his own life to engage in theological debate. In a letter written the year before his death, Crabbe cautioned his son George on the dangers of theological argument, and explained his own procedure: "I would not, in the State of my Mind—so soon confused by Argument as it really is— enter into a conversational—Debate with any & especially any zealous Contender for his own Opinions—my Way is to study the Point—whatever it may be,—by myself & such Books as I would consult & even then I leave off as soon as I feel in any degree confused."²⁴ And about his own convictions, Crabbe wrote: "Conscious that I never shall arrive at the very Truth & that there will remain Difficulty in some Questions & Uncertainty in some points more or less important I rest quietly in those Facts which Reason assents to unforced and as I believe, unbiassed & these are sufficient to keep my Mind at Peace."²⁵ It is hardly surprising, then, to find in a poem such as "David Morris," where the central character claims to be uncertain about man's destiny and the narrator is weak in argument, that neither appears to win an outright victory. As happens with many great artists, Crabbe's own sympathies have become divided between two characters, and in their conflict, Crabbe acts out the disquiet in his own mind.²⁶

Not only does the narrator fail to convince David, but David's insistence on remaining true to his own lights forces the narrator to reconsider his own position and to reiterate his own struggles with the problem of doubt. Yet when the narrator was unable to help or convince David, it is unlikely that a soliloquy of after-thoughts will be any more convincing to the reader:

> Yet thought I much, for I before had grieved
> For what I doubted, nay, for what believed,
> For my Belief was clouded, and my Doubt
> Made cold, Belief, Devotion undevout,
> And kept me with perturbed & anxious Mind,
> Seeking for Rest, but not with Hope to find,
> Till One dear Friend, the Friend of all his Race,
> Led me to see the Truth, & to embrace.   (641–48)

Certainly the narrator believes sincerely that his own views are correct and David's wrong; he is too ingenuous to be guilty of hypocrisy. But one questions whether he was convinced of the soundness of his views by force of argument or because of his will to believe. All the narrator can do to help David is to leave him at a time when he needs help, and rush off to find the "One dear Friend, the Friend of all his Race," who had helped to dispel his own doubts. The phrase, "One dear Friend," contains a possible reference to Christ, but the "Friend" in this case is clearly a neighbour.

Consequently, this dependence reflects tellingly on the Christian answer to David's problem. The narrator's faith seems to be not so much in God as in the "One dear Friend," and this in turn suggests a faith in reason or the power of human argument. Moreover, he appears more interested in the abstract problem than in David's personal predicament, and appears to see, not David's problem, but in David a reflection of his own. One is left with the suspicion that, had the "One dear Friend" arrived in time to speak to David, he would have been able to accomplish little.

Disregarding for the moment the narrator's qualifications as a teacher of Christian doctrine, it is still difficult to see how his religious answer could serve as an adequate solution to David's problems. Part of the reason is that Crabbe has juxtaposed the narrator's advocacy of resignation with David's own resigned attitude to death. The greatness of Crabbe's depiction lies in the manner in which he shows David, after years of effort in the attempt to gain happiness, quietly deciding that further attempts at success would be futile. For David, the advice to give up his own clear-sighted vision of the world is defeatist; David prefers to end his life rather than to live a failure. The narrator believes that the only type of resignation is that of obedience to the church. But David's calm, philosophical death reveals another type of resignation, that of acting responsibly, where the idea of "responsibility" entails responding to the situation as given. As Hume pointed out in his essay on suicide, if man does not know how God wishes him to live, there is no *a priori* way of knowing whether God intends him to commit suicide or not.

Another reason why the narrator's religious arguments do not seem altogether convincing is that they are similar to those of David's mother, which Crabbe had already shown to be superficial. When David went to his mother for advice and help, "She in her Zeal conjured him to repent, / Told him that Heaven alone deserv'd his Care" (450–51). The word "Zeal" reveals that Crabbe felt this reply to be narrow and puritanical. Yet at the end of the poem the narrator advises David to do exactly the same thing—overcome his pride and look to Heaven—an answer which again fails to meet David's needs.

The narrator's replies to David embody the same type of reasoning as was used by Job's comforters. Finding that David has failed, the narrator concludes that David must have offended God by committing the sin of pride. One has the feeling that this conclusion could be applied to everyone, even if pride were not evident. In David's case, Crabbe has taken especial care to show David's ambition to be well founded. David is endowed with excellent qualities: ambition, a fine intellect, sensitivity to beauty, and the will to work. Yet because of his birth he is unable to create a place for himself in society. The narrator has no positive solution to offer; all he can affirm is that a belief in God's wrath will frighten people into submission. This "solution" was widely believed in the late eighteenth and early nineteenth centuries; William Paley, one of the chief exponents of orthodoxy, had made fear of God the foundation of his system of morals. Yet in "David Morris" Crabbe shows clearly that fear of God is no longer a sufficient deterrent, since it does not prevent David from committing suicide.

In the character of David, Crabbe has created an individual who embodies the doubts of the time, doubts that the narrator cannot meet adequately because he answers with abstract beliefs rather than with faith. As his letters reveal, Crabbe himself was troubled by such confrontations and uncertain as to the direction the church should take in meeting the new questions being raised by scientists and social reformers. In early poems such as "The Hall of Justice" (1807), Crabbe managed to avoid resolving his overt social questions by dissolving them in the religious terminology of his conclusions. Such a technique could work effectively only when the central character was himself penitent, a situation in which questions of worldly wrongs are eclipsed by the individual's spiritual fulfilment. In "David Morris," however, the gulf between the social classes is never conjured away. The most forceful part of the poem is the rendering of David's own problems and the incontrovertible fact that his difficulties and anguish result from his struggles to give his ambition scope. That the poem itself does not entirely succeed seems almost immaterial when the rendering of David's own presence is so definitively maintained. Throughout his life, Crabbe had been intent on showing the gulf between true and false ways of seeing the world. In "David Morris," he indicates that David's attentiveness to the world around gives him strength, and perhaps even grace itself, in the face of which the orthodox religious dogma is shown to be inadequate. Indeed, Crabbe seems to have been moving towards a view of the world in which religious faith becomes faithfulness, a step with enormous implications for breaking down the old categories by which humanity—social and individual—is contained.

Chapter 5
Enough, my lord, do hares and pheasants cost

I

It has been commonly asserted that in his later poems Crabbe cannot be considered primarily a social critic. Howard Mills, for instance, has commented that "by 1812 'Crabbe the Social Critic' is a misleading approach."[1] In a sense this is correct. As was seen in *The Borough* and *Tales*, Crabbe was becoming increasingly interested in the possibilities of employing verse in the creation of detailed and intricate character portraits. Far from suggesting that he has lost interest in social issues, his movement towards more and more detailed character studies can be seen as the outgrowth of the earlier poems where perception was shown to be highly contingent on the percipient. It becomes clear that, not only does awareness of social issues grow out of personal experience, but that narrowness of individual perception tends in aggregate to lead to social problems. Certainly Crabbe was interested in presenting character in terms of psychological processes, but he maintained his basic premise that because men exist in society, individuals and their beliefs cannot be considered as distinct from action in the physical, social world. In this way the question of social abuses versus social harmony is necessarily seen as an integral function of the interplay between man's perception and his actions. In his later poetry, Crabbe no longer tends to take specific social issues as his subject, but incorporates the social within a larger vision of man, where, paradoxically, the world is defined by the limits of man's perception.

In discussing *Tales of the Hall*, which I consider to be in many ways the finest of Crabbe's poems, I shall begin with one particular book—"Smugglers and Poachers"—from the twenty-two books constituting the complete poem. The final chapter will deal with *Tales of the Hall* as a whole. "Smugglers and Poachers" is of particular interest in view of what has been said above about Crabbe's growing awareness of the connection between the social and the personal, because, although designed to criticize the game laws of the early nineteenth century, the criticism grows out of Crabbe's characterization of the two brothers, James and Robert— keeper and poacher. Crabbe's delight in portraying the complex motives which lead the two brothers to choose opposing ways of life is apparent, but the portrayal is more than merely delightful. It has human and social relevance because the brothers' ways of life define the age-old injustices arising from outmoded legislation. A number of social historians, including the Hammonds and Chester Kirby, have quoted from the poem approvingly, and have employed it as quasi-evidence of the human problems caused by the game laws.[2]

"Smugglers and Poachers" has added interest as a social document, since Crabbe's son mentions that the subject was first suggested to Crabbe by Sir Samuel Romilly, the great criminal law reformer.[3] Crabbe first met Romilly in June 1818,[4] and seems to have been immediately attracted by Romilly's humanitarianism. Either at this meeting or shortly afterwards, Romilly suggested to Crabbe that he write a poem about game laws. At this period Romilly was endeavouring to gather support for his campaign to reform the game laws by bringing their inhumanity to the attention of the public. What had particularly angered Romilly was the piece of game-law legislation that had slipped unnoticed through the House at the end of the session of 1816. Under the guise of an amendment to the Rogue and Vagabond Act, a bill had been passed allowing magistrates summarily to punish night-poachers with a seven-year transportation sentence for a first offence. Romilly remarked: "The Act professed in the preamble to be made against persons who went armed by night, and committed acts of violence and murders; but, in its enacting part, it punished, with transportation for seven years, any person who should be found by night in any open ground, having in his possession any net or engine for the purpose of taking or destroying any hare, rabbit, or other game. . . ."[5] In the following year Romilly was able to have this bill partially repealed, so as to allow the accused poacher at least the chance of a trial before jury. But the country gentlemen, while preaching charity and patience, would have their pound of flesh; the punishment of seven years' transportation remained.

Shortly after this legislation, and only a few months after his first meeting with Crabbe, Romilly committed suicide, apparently distraught at the sudden death of his wife. On hearing the news, Crabbe composed a poem in Romilly's memory—appropriately enough, on a blank leaf of the manuscript of "Smugglers and Poachers." This poem, never meant for publication, gives some indication of the respect Crabbe felt for Sir Samuel and of his desire to write a poem ("Smugglers and Poachers") following his advice. In it, he says:

> Yes! I was proud to speak of thee, as one
> Who had approved the little I had done,
> And taught me what I should do!—Thou wouldst raise
> My doubting spirit by a smile of praise,
> And words of comfort! great was thy delight
> Fear to expel, and ardour to excite,
> To wrest th' oppressor's arm, and do the injured right.[6]

In writing "Smugglers and Poachers" at Romilly's request, Crabbe was guided by his principles; it was meant to be a contribution to justice—"to wrest th' oppressor's arm, and do the injured right."

When Romilly suggested in 1818 that Crabbe write a poem on the game laws, he was not asking Crabbe to take up some unknown or ultra-radical cause. From about 1815 onwards, reform of the game laws had become a topic of "serious general attention,"[7] so that when "Smugglers and Poachers" appeared in 1819 Crabbe could feel assured he was addressing his poem to a large audience already acquainted with the major issues of game-law reform.

Whether his reader were a liberal townsman in favour of reform or a Tory squire, both would know that poaching had become a problem of national concern. In the previous five years more than a dozen pamphlets had been published on the subject of the game laws, most of them advocating reform, and of course much about the game laws would be common knowledge since "no other subject caused so much litigation and brought so many cases into the courts in the eighteenth century as did the game laws."[8] Although Crabbe was by no means the first writer to take up the subject of the conflict between the poacher and the squire, he was one of the first poets to deal with the problem. If the anonymous pamphlet, *Poetical Remarks on the Game Laws* (1797), which is not very poetical, is excepted, I know of no other poem, earlier than Crabbe's, which deals in depth with the unsatisfactory nature of the game laws. Sir Walter Scott's poem "The Poacher" (1811) deals with poaching, but Scott's poacher is feckless, shifty, and antisocial. Scott's poem will be mentioned again, for it is in professed imitation of Crabbe's early style, and will provide an excellent comparison with "Smugglers and Poachers."

Why was there such a sudden outpouring of interest in the game laws after 1815, and what were the reasons that convinced Crabbe of the need for changes? This chapter is no place for a full-scale discussion of the game laws; nor would such a discussion be possible, for the English game laws, unlike those of France, are a subject still largely unworked by historians. But a few significant facts should be mentioned to set the background and to allow a better understanding of Crabbe's poem.[9]

After about 1815 it became generally recognized that the game-law legislation, which had worked more or less efficiently a century before, was no longer effective. Although Sydney Smith might be considered a controversial *Edinburgh Review* Whig, few men would have disagreed with him when in 1819 he opened his essay on the game laws with the remark: "The evil of the Game Laws, in their present state, has long been felt, and of late years has certainly rather increased than diminished. We believe that they cannot long remain in their present state."[10] After all, Sydney Smith was only echoing what Blackstone, that eminent conservative, had pointed out half a century earlier.[11] Even Sir William Elford, an aristocrat who believed that hunters should be allowed to pursue game over another man's property, agreed that the feudal game laws of the seventeenth century were no longer applicable to the new commercial Britain. In his pamphlet *A Few Cursory Remarks on the Obnoxious Parts of the Game Laws*, he exclaimed that "all experience has shewn that the injustice of the system, is at least equalled by its inadequacy to the intended end."[12]

In their origin, the game laws were closely associated with the barons' struggle to wrest power from the king. Just as the barons obtained special concessions in land, so they obtained privileges to hunt game. Game, however, is more difficult to define than property, and the question was never settled how anyone could own as property *ferae naturae*, which were by definition wild and thus not containable within boundaries. For all intents and purposes the game laws in Crabbe's time were essentially those codified in 1671, when a system of "qualification" was established.[13] Under this system no one actually owned the wild game, but certain people were given the privilege of hunting it. By this act the only persons allowed to hunt game (fox-hunting was in a separate category) were those who had an income from land and tenements of more than £100 per year and those with leases of ninety-nine years or more, the income of which was at least £150. Eldest sons of men who ranked as esquires or higher were also qualified. A curious anomaly was that while these eldest sons were qualified, their fathers were not, unless they also held the income above mentioned.

This system of qualification, based solely on social privilege, worked fairly well for approximately a hundred years. So long as the country gentlemen remained the most important social force in the kingdom, and so long as the rest of society was geared to serve their interests (generally speaking, this was until the eighteenth century), few social or moral reasons existed to cause farmers and workers to question the privileges bestowed by the game laws. The qualification system did not put an end to poaching but until about the time of the Napoleonic Wars the poacher was considered little more than a social nuisance. If apprehended, he would be taken before a justice of the peace, fined a few unpayable shillings, or given a few days in jail.

As early as the second half of the eighteenth century, however, voices of dissatisfaction began to be heard. The farmers had the most to be discontent with, since the game lived off their crops, and they could only wait until a "qualified person" came at his leisure to shoot. Either that, or they could risk breaking the law and turn poacher by hunting or trapping the game themselves. As always, the farmers were poorly organized so that their complaints were not often heard.[14]

Still, opposition to the game laws was increasing, and had the exigencies of the Napoleonic Wars not silenced all effective opposition for some twenty years, the game laws might well have erupted into a national issue sooner than they did. When peace was finally achieved in 1815, and Wellington returned to England to shoot his pheasants, the problems caused by the game laws (along with many other domestic issues) were immediately brought to the public's attention. Moreover, by 1815 new methods of hunting game had been introduced, methods which increased the difficulties of enforcing the laws. As a result of large-scale enclosures, and the consequent necessity of preserving game, the country gentlemen had begun to create game preservation areas for their private use. The special preserves made shooting more certain, but they involved considerable expense in stocking the preserve and in maintaining keepers to care for and protect the game. Unfortunately for the squire, this concentration of game made the work of the poacher easier as well. In one night, with his nets and snares, he might make off with several dozen pheasants.

The most significant reason for the breakdown of the game laws actually had little to do with the squires or the poachers, but was to be found in the tastes of the new monied classes of the large towns and cities. The country people of quality, still the leaders of taste, had set the example of making game a compulsory dish for all fashionable suppers. Naturally enough, the new monied classes of the city desired to follow this lead, so that for important occasions, large dinners, and even ordinary suppers in inns, game became a necessary dish. At Christmas and the Lord Mayor's banquet, game was on the menu, whether illegal or not. The Select Committee on the game laws (1823) noted in their report "that the practice of purchasing Game is not confined to any one class of the community, but is habitual to persons of every class who have not the means of being sufficiently supplied with that article from their own manors or land."[15] As the new class of prosperous merchants and industrialists whose money came from sources other than the land increased, so the demand for game increased also.[16] Evelina may have disliked to see the tradespeople aping the habits of their betters, but if Lord Orville ate game for supper, then so would the Branghton family—game which in both cases might come from Lord Orville's estate.

In order that a growing section of the urban population might satisfy its demand for game, game had to appear daily in the butcher shops. But the game laws proclaimed illegal the sale of game by any person, qualified or not (although until 1818 it was legal for a qualified person to buy game!). The forces of economics do not follow the wishes of a minority sector of the community; a large demand for a certain item calls into operation the suppliers. The innkeepers and gentlemen of the city were determined to have their game for supper, and as the only way they could buy it was through the poacher-coachman-poulterer ring, the demand for game in the cities created a large-scale business in the transportation of game from the country. This thriving trade created a demand for poachers. The Select Committee of 1823, noted "that although in some instances, persons legally in possession of Game, dispose of it by sale, yet that the great supply of the market is in the hands of the poachers, who are, by this nearly exclusive trade, encouraged in the greatest degree to the continuance of their depredations."[17] As the number of poachers increased to meet the demand for game, so did the squires increase the number of armed gamekeepers until England found herself with two opposing armies—the keepers and the poachers.

This metaphor of "two opposing armies" is by no means an exaggeration as one might at first think. The historian A. J. Peacock mentions that the "press of the time contains hundreds of accounts of pitched battles at night."[18] And Robert Haldane Bradshaw in his evidence to the Select Committee commented, "I can command a little army, who assist my keepers, and go out at nights."[19] When the squires found that the trade in game was being openly conducted by poulterers and hawkers in the towns and cities, their natural reaction was to increase the punishment against poaching. In 1800 a law was passed making gang poaching punishable by two years' imprisonment and a whipping;[20] two years later the punishment for deer stealing was increased to seven years' transportation.[21] In 1803, Parliament once again obliged the country gentlemen by passing Lord Ellenborough's Act, making it possible to sentence to death anyone resisting arrest. But the harshness of these laws had little effect in reducing the number of poaching offences. If anything, they made the poachers more violent than ever, so that blood was spilt on both sides.

When the Napoleonic Wars ended, and the silence which had reigned over domestic issues for some twenty years was finally broken, men were horrified when they looked about them at the blood and misery caused by the game laws. The immediate consequence was the formation in 1816 of Colonel Wood's Select Committee to take into consideration the laws relating to game. But even as this committee was meeting, a new law was passed in Parliament making it possible for a magistrate to sentence a poacher summarily on his first offence to seven years' transportation. The severity of this new law at a time when liberal thinkers were expecting positive reforms was what induced Romilly to take up game-law reform. Although Romilly succeeded in introducing a minor amendment in the following year, and influenced people such as Crabbe to advocate less severe game laws, game-law reform was not instituted until 1831.

II

As was noted at the beginning of this chapter, Crabbe couches his social criticism in a story about individuals, in this case the story of James, Robert, and Rachel. As a result, it becomes important that he realize his principal characters—and especially the poacher—in terms of attitudes and character traits that relate to the community situation of which the game laws are a part. If the poacher is sympathetically portrayed, then inevitably the game laws are made to appear unjust; but if the artist chooses to present the poacher as a species of vermin, encroaching on the property of honest and benevolent gentlemen, then punishments of sizeable fines, transportation, and even death, may not seem out of place. Crabbe endorses neither stereotype. Although his presentation of Robert is sympathetic, and resembles Fielding's characterization of Tom Jones, Crabbe by no means suggests that Robert is wholly the victim of an unjust legal system. Crabbe is not interested so much in attaching blame to individuals or governments as he is in displaying how an entire community can be undermined when it continues to pay lip-service to rigid moral and legal systems, the values of which no longer effectively serve as motives. Incidentally, it is worth remarking that, given this sort of depiction, solutions to social problems will not be easy, for a change in individual goals— if the change is to be precisely stated, and not simply a vague longing—must have its origin in changed circumstances. It is impossible for a person to have an aim that he does not know exists.

For Crabbe to have made his poacher a wealthy farmer's son or a dishonest gamekeeper would have diminished the class conflict inherent in the game-law situation,[22] and would have lost him the opportunity of developing the colour and vitality of the lower-class rogue. Therefore he begins by describing Robert as a pauper-ward of the parish. Paupers such as Robert and his brother James could expect little more from the parish than the means of subsistence. If no work were available for these wards, often the case in the late eighteenth and early nineteenth centuries, then they were set to repair the roads at about three shillings and sixpence per week.[23]

Since the flourishing trade in illicit game made it easy for the poacher to sell pheasants from the local manor at a shilling or more apiece, it was no wonder that many of England's rural poor turned to poaching to supplement their meagre income.

While Crabbe carefully describes the impoverished background of his poacher, he does not appear to wish to defend the extreme thesis that a poor background is the ultimate cause of Robert's poaching. To ensure that the reader does not mistakenly draw this conclusion, Crabbe employs a stock eighteenth-century device— that of two brothers with antithetical personalities—and gives Robert a foil in James. If Robert brings to mind Tom Jones, then James clearly bears similarities to Blifil. Cautious and somewhat narrow, James, like Blifil, inspires respect and not love in the villagers. Yet the distinction between the two brothers is not so clear-cut as in *Tom Jones* or in Thomas Day's *Sandford and Merton* (1783–89). The brothers' personalities tend to merge in the beginning; only as the boys grow older do they take different paths. In their separate ways each brother has marked ability, but this remains undeveloped since the social pressures of the game laws exploit their weaknesses rather than their strengths. Through the voices and actions of the two brothers—in the beginning they are indistinguishable—Crabbe develops a sense of the ways in which the game laws break down the bonds of human affection and loyalty.

Robert and James begin with the same opportunities, or rather lack of them; yet when Robert turns to "sundry kinds of trade"— not all legal—James takes up a respectable and secure position of service at Nether Hall. Beginning as an assistant, James soon rises to the important position of head gamekeeper. It should be noted that nothing in the early character of James suggests his later vindictiveness. Only in comparison to his brother Robert, and Robert is the epitome of the open-hearted man, does James seem to lack any of the virtues. Taken by himself, James at first appears to be an excellent man of the community who earns an important post at the manor by means of his own efforts. Yet compared with his brother Robert, and Crabbe proffers the comparison as often as possible, James appears narrow.

This narrowness is apparent when James first goes to Nether Hall to be employed as an assistant to the gamekeeper, possibly one of many; while the law said that only one head gamekeeper could be licensed to shoot game, it said nothing about the number of his assistants.[24] When the post of chief gamekeeper falls open, James is appointed. On the surface everything about this move seems legal and fair, but does Crabbe not hint that James treated his chief unfairly? The following four-line description contains a subtle suggestion that James may have had a hand in removing the game-keeper from his position:

> He with the keeper took his daily round,
> A rival grew, and some unkindness found;
> But his superior farm'd! the place was void,
> And James guns, dogs, and dignity enjoy'd. (60–63)

The crux here is the half line "But his superior farm'd." It was in the squire's interest to have gamekeepers of unquestioned loyalty. If the squire allowed one of his tenants to be keeper, then this tenant-farmer might destroy the game or frighten it away. The anonymous country gentleman who wrote *Thoughts on the Expediency of Legalizing the Sale of Game* pointed out that the farmer's interests were opposed to those of the squire and his gamekeeper: "It is now decidedly the interest of every farmer, to destroy the breed of game on his land, as it eats up his corn and invites trespassers upon his farm, and he has no compensation for these annoyances; he is frequently, therefore, in league with the poacher."[25] Moreover, in strictly legal terms the gamekeeper could not be a farmer, since he had to be a servant of the owner of the land.[26] The lord of the manor would have been breaking the law had he kept a gamekeeper who was also a farmer.

Crabbe states that at the time James began to rival the keeper, and the keeper became unkind to him, the squire suddenly became aware that his keeper was farming. Who informed the squire? Crabbe never says directly that James had any part in the affair, but the juxtaposition of the keeper's unkindness to James with his dismissal leaves the impression that James is not faultless. No doubt even if James did inform against the keeper, he has done nothing legally wrong, and perhaps nothing morally wrong, since to employ a gamekeeper-farmer was illegal. But when James's behaviour is compared with that of a more open-hearted young man—Tom Jones, and his treatment of Black George—James's meanness becomes evident. The passage is the first indication that James's success is not the result of his hard work alone, but of deceit. Robert, one feels, would never have stooped to such deceit; consequently he might not have risen by "honest means."

Robert's virtues and vices are of the same order as those of any eighteenth-century gentleman; indeed, except for his mean birth, Robert very much resembles a gentleman. Pictured as a type of British empire-builder, Robert wrests his living, not from the spices of the East, but from the game preserves of the squire. Had Robert been the son of a man of means, his ambition would have been accepted as a matter of course. But he is not. Hence, through no fault of his own, Robert has little choice of avenues, other than illicit ones, for pursuing the independence appropriate to his nature, and mistrusts the authority of a society which tells him to subordinate that nature simply because he was born to a low station. Significantly enough, Robert does not choose the usual resort of the distressed gentleman, the highway, but the less vicious crimes of smuggling and poaching. The suggestion is that in the context of England's social conditions, Robert's actions are natural enough.

In his characterization of Robert, Crabbe consciously broke with the Tory tradition of presenting the poacher as a member of a low order of humanity. The squires had a vested interested in caricaturing poachers as mean, rascally fellows, far beyond hope of redemption. For instance, in Hannah More's *Black Giles the Poacher*, one of the Cheap Repository Tracts (1795–98), Giles is presented as a person who will stoop to anything—even to robbing the Widow Brown of her apples! Mary Leadbeater in *Cottage Dialogues Among the Irish Peasantry* (1811) and Rev. Legh Richmond in his three famous tales of village life (1809–14) had also presented the rural workers as limited persons with little or no ambition and no spirit.[27] While commending the lower classes for industry, sobriety, frugality, they reserved the highest praise for those who refused aid from the poor relief. Cowper, who felt that in most cases poverty was "self-inflicted woe; / Th' effect of laziness or sottish waste," described the poacher as the dregs of humanity:

> 'Tis quenchless thirst
> Of ruinous ebriety that prompts
> His ev'ry action, and imbrutes the man.
>
> *(The Task* IV. 459–61)

He called for "a law to noose the villain's neck." Unlike these authors who believed that obedience was the sum of all lower-class virtues, Crabbe realized that no man—whether of the upper or lower class—was evil because he wished to live "by his wits" (in Hannah More's *Black Giles the Poacher* such a philosophy is bitterly condemned).

In part, the gentry probably believed many of their own stories about the perfidy of the poacher, but much of this distortion of the character of the poacher was a justification for the severe penalties and spring guns. One has only to read the evidence given before the Select Committees to realize that Crabbe's presentation of Robert, with the emphasis on Robert's fine qualities of boldness and courage, typifies many of the poachers of this time. Potter Macqueen's description of the poachers in the Bedford gaol shows that many were young men of good reputation:

> In January, 1829, there were 96 prisoners for trial in Bedford gaol, of whom 76 were able-bodied men, in the prime of life, and, chiefly, of general good character, who were driven to crime by sheer want, and who would have been valuable subjects had they been placed in a situation where, by the exercise of their health and strength, they could have earned a subsistence. There were in this number 18 poachers awaiting trial for the capital offence of using arms in self-defence when attacked by game-keepers; Of these 18 men, one only was not a parish pauper, and he was the agent of the

> London poulterers, who, passing under the apparent
> vocation of a rat-catcher, paid these poor creatures more
> in one night than they could obtain from the overseer
> for a week's labour.[28]

Macqueen makes two interesting points here: first, that many of
the poachers were decent young men; and second, that they were
driven to poaching because of the bad economic conditions. Although Crabbe clearly wishes to describe Robert in the best light
possible, he plays down Macqueen's second point that poverty
leads to poaching.

Since art usually celebrates the instinctive and the spontaneous,
it is not difficult to see why most works of literature treat the
poacher sympathetically. When Wordsworth, in a well-known
passage, tells how he went night-poaching as a boy, the reader
obviously delights in these adventures:

> Ere I had told
> Ten birth-days, when among the mountain slopes
> Frost, and the breath of frosty wind, had snapped
> The last autumnal crocus, 'twas my joy
> With store of springes o'er my shoulder hung
> To range the open heights where woodcocks run
> Along the smooth green turf. Through half the night,
> Scudding away from snare to snare, I plied
> That anxious visitation. . . .[29]

No one asks if Wordsworth were qualified or not. Working within
the same tradition, while not wholly endorsing it, Crabbe finds
little difficulty in gaining sympathy for his poacher. Although
Robert was more than "ten birth-days," and what is excusable in
a young boy is often punishable in a man, much of the assent given
to the young Wordsworth is due Robert as well.

Scholars have often felt that the Crabbe of *Tales* and *Tales of the
Hall* turned away from the liberalism of his youth, but his presentation of Robert gives reason for altering this view. On the other
hand, Crabbe by no means sides wholly with Robert; he appreciates

that the two brothers represent opposing but valid philosophies of life. James is an honest but dull man who lacks imagination:

> James talk'd of honest gains and scorn of debt,
> Of virtuous labour, of a sober life,
> And what with credit would support a wife. (75–77)

Robert replies to these domestic values with all the fire and energy of a William Blake advocating reform:

> But Robert answer'd—"How can men advise
> Who to a master let their tongue and eyes?
> Whose words are not their own? whose foot and hand
> Run at a nod, or act upon command?
> Who cannot eat or drink, discourse or play,
> Without requesting others that they may.
>   Debt you would shun; but what advice to give,
> Who owe your service every hour you live!
> Let a bell sound, and from your friends you run,
> Although the darling of your heart were one;
> But, if the bondage fits you, I resign
> You to your lot—I am content with mine!" (78–89)

At first sight James's philosophy—that he must work hard, save his money, and eventually marry a good wife who will help with the household accounts—may seem reasonable and practical. Yet a double standard has crept in imperceptibly, for among the upper classes anyone who lived such a life would have been despised. And since Robert's own life embodies many upper-class values, the reader is able to appreciate James's narrowness, and see that in the type of life James advocates, the only possible virtue is "virtuous labour." The danger for James is that he will come to resemble the mother of David Morris who, when she lost her follies, "lost her feelings, too."[30]

It appears quite natural that Robert with his strong feelings and his "quicker parts" should turn to all types of employment that offer adventure. As the title of the poem indicates, Crabbe deals with two crimes—smuggling and poaching. Whereas in the first half of the poem both smuggling and poaching are mentioned, in the second half Crabbe shifts the focus to concentrate wholly on poaching. Working with these two crimes, Crabbe gains a number of effects. First, by minimizing Robert's poaching in the first half, Crabbe is able to set up the circumstances whereby a conflict between the two brothers is seen to develop over a length of time, allowing space for the two brothers to grow into mortal enemies. By the time James actually swears to apprehend his brother for poaching, Crabbe has set the scene and portrayed the different personalities of Robert, James, and Rachel. Second, in describing Robert as both a smuggler and a poacher, Crabbe complies with the norm of his time. The two crimes were seen to be complementary. It was generally believed that a man who was a smuggler would also be a poacher, if circumstance permitted, and this is borne out in the testimony before the Select Committees on game. Furthermore, by depicting Robert as both smuggler and poacher, Crabbe indicates that the social attitudes relevant to the game laws apply in all sorts of situations, such as smuggling. Consequently, particular abuses such as the game laws are themselves rooted in a general social situation which is both caused by and reflected in the set of attitudes commonly held by the community. Although the game laws are a problem, and in need of reform, the introduction of smuggling points out the ways in which poaching is related to other issues, and suggests that lasting changes in the game laws may require an understanding of the more deep-seated and general problems. Robert is not an idealized figure of social repression, but an active participant in a social drama that involves the entire community. In short, Crabbe's depiction of both crimes makes poaching seem less serious, for when the community accepts even smuggling with its reasonable laws, then James's belief in the evil of poaching appears reactionary since the laws against poaching were seen to be quite unreasonable.

One of the most telling arguments ranged against the game laws at this time, and one which Crabbe introduces, was that wild animals were not property in any strict sense. If this assertion were accepted, then it followed that a poacher was not really stealing when he snared a few woodcocks. When asked by Lord Wharncliffe if he did not think he committed an offence when he sold game, Mr. R. S., a small shopkeeper, replied, "God made Game, and I considered it every man's right." When pressed further, he replied that "in regard of God" he did not commit any crime, although "in regard of man" he did.[31] The Select Committee of 1823 had found the sale of game to be so widespread and open throughout the kingdom that it concluded: "A breach of these particular laws appears not to be considered as any moral offence whatever."[32] Crabbe introduces this argument through Rachel, the simple but virtuous village maiden:

> Of guilt she thought not—she had often heard
> They bought and sold, and nothing wrong appear'd;
> Her father's maxim this; she understood
> There was some ill—but he, she knew, was good;
> It was a traffic—but was done by night—
> If wrong, how trade? why secrecy, if right?
> But Robert's conscience, she believed, was pure—
> And that he read his Bible she was sure.   (176–83)

Crabbe pokes fun at Rachel's simple test of the truth, that Robert read his Bible, but on the other hand Rachel's attitude is symptomatic of that of a great many villagers. To the village community, the law was something alien and strange; they lived, not so much by what lawyers and judges decreed, as by what had become common custom over the centuries.[33] It was difficult to persuade the villager who had been brought up in the belief that poaching and smuggling were trades men winked at, but did not absolutely condemn, to accept the new laws that the squires were implementing to save their game preserves.

As the servant of the squire, James refuses to accept the poacher's argument that game belongs to all men:

James, better taught, in confidence declared
His grief for what his guilty brother dared:
He sigh'd to think how near he was akin
To one seduced by godless men to sin;
Who, being always of the law in dread,
To other crimes were by the danger led,
And crimes with like excuse—The smuggler cries,
"What guilt is his who pays for what he buys?"
The poacher questions, with perverted mind,
"Were not the gifts of heaven for all design'd?"
This cries, "I sin not—take not till I pay;"—
That, "My own hand brought down my proper prey."—
And while to such fond arguments they cling,
How fear they God? how honour they the king?
Such men associate, and each other aid,
Till all are guilty, rash, and desperate made;
Till to some lawless deed the wretches fly,
And in the act, or for the acting, die.   (184–201)

Crabbe, it should be noted, does not himself introduce these arguments from natural law; nor does he permit Robert to proclaim them. Rather he gives them to James. Crabbe has introduced the argument in such a way that one can either believe or disbelieve it to the extent that one sympathizes with James. James of course is "better taught," but all this means is that he has acquired the squire's principles, and is willing to uphold the *status quo*. Edward Christian, also "better taught," had claimed that morality, religion, and law all stated game was property,[34] but the common man did not believe this, and time has proved him to be correct. Moreover, because the game laws were based on the principle of qualification, and did not imply ownership, Christian's statement was in fact legally suspect. Blackstone, at that time the greatest authority on law, maintained that "the sole right of taking and destroying game belongs exclusively to the king."[35] It would seem that the poor man's argument that game was not property had some validity in a legal sense. To make matters even more difficult, Roman law, to which English law so often looked for example, stated that wild animals belonged to the person who could catch them, even upon another's land. James may have believed that the smugglers and poachers were entirely in the wrong, but as the Select Committees on game discovered, this represented a minority opinion.

The most powerful of all the arguments used by the game-law reformers, and certainly the most persuasive, was that the existing laws actually encouraged men to become poachers. The anonymous author of *Three Letters on the Game Laws* pointed out: "It is not because the poacher kills the game, that the poulterer buys it, and that I dress it; but it is because the Aldermen, the Directors, the Lord Mayor, the Squires, the Lords, and the Justices, *will have it,* that I dress it, that the poulterer buys it, and that the poor poacher kills it."[36] As Crabbe observes, the townspeople know full well that the game they buy has been poached:

> The well-known shops received a large supply,
> That they who could not kill at least might buy. (265–66)

Yet instead of prosecuting the "well-known shops" the squires waged war against the elusive poachers. Robert, because he is adventurous and despises hypocrisy, is soon led into smuggling and poaching when he sees respectable people countenancing the so-called criminal:

> He saw connected with th' adventurous crew
> Those whom he judged were sober men and true;
> He found that some, who should the trade prevent,
> Gave it by purchase their encouragement;
> He found that contracts could be made with those
> Who had their pay these dealers to oppose;
> And the good ladies whom at church he saw,
> With looks devout, of reverence and awe,
> Could change their feelings as they change their place,
> And, whispering, deal for spicery and lace:
> And thus the craft and avarice of these
> Urged on the youth, and gave his conscience ease.

> (160–71)

The result of this disclosure that Robert forms only one link in a long chain of economic connections further weakens any moral censure of his crimes. Furthermore, as Robert does not "sin" against God's laws but is guilty only in relation to man's laws, and since men do not want to maintain these laws, Robert becomes in one sense a hero. Nor does Robert need to be ashamed of himself; as Sydney Smith pointed out, "At present, no one has the slightest shame at violating a law which every body feels to be absurd and unjust."37

Crabbe's open-minded portrayal of Robert was bound to annoy many of his Tory readers, and among this number was the reviewer for *The Christian Observer* who observed: "We are sorry indeed to find, that Robert the Poacher, during his nightly and nefarious trade, 'read his Bible'." The reviewer continued, "We entirely doubt the fact; and we quote in our support the approved saying of an old divine, that 'either men will leave off sinning, or they will leave off praying'."38 Aside from missing the irony which Crabbe in this passage directed at Rachel's simple-mindedness, the reviewer has also missed Crabbe's point that the common people (indeed most of the population of England) did not believe poaching to be a sin against God.

Hatchard, who had been Crabbe's publisher, saw the review and sent a copy to Crabbe. Fortunately Crabbe's reply to Hatchard is still extant:

> This Gentleman will pardon me, I hope, when I assure
> him that Smugglers pray and read their Bible: I do not
> mean by Smugglers, noctur[n]al Ruffians, who if they
> did not smuggle would rob, even in their Sense of the
> Word, but Men and *Women* engaged in the Buying and
> selling Goods which have not paid the legal Duties.
> These people look upon this as half of [an] adventurous
> but not criminal, not immoral Nature. I knew at one
> period of my Life two Villages, and I am convinced,
> nay I am *almost* certain, that *if* I except the Minister
> and 2 or 3 of the more opulent Farmers' Wives, there

was not an Inhabitant in either who did not deal in
this Trade, and this Gentleman will not surely judge
so hardly as to suppose, the instructed people of
two populous Villages to be without piety or prayer.
In truth, they are taught that illicit traffic is
hazardous but not forbidden by their Religion.[39]

Crabbe admits that some smugglers and poachers are driven into
"desperate measures" and in these cases he concedes that they
probably cease to be God-fearing men. But he concludes: "When
my Smuggler turned poacher he probably used to read, to pray,
and as far as he could, to think—but I do not mean to dispute the
Sentiment as a general one."[40] The last part of this comment is
particularly interesting, for it points up one of the central features
of Crabbe's art, that he built his scenes from particular incidents
which are handled with such a degree of attention and intensity
that they stand on their own, independent of general moral and
social truths. As a result the particular contains inferences about
truths, but as D. H. Burden has observed, the particulars are not
"easily susceptible to generalization."[41]

III

To gain some perspective on Crabbe's position, it may help to
compare briefly "Smugglers and Poachers" with a poem written
a few years earlier by Sir Walter Scott. Scott's "The Poacher"
(1811) is of especial interest and value to a study of Crabbe's poem,
not only because it is about poachers, but because it is written in
imitation of Crabbe's style.[42] Scott wrote to James Ballantyne,
"Understand I have no idea of parody but of serious anticipation
if I can accomplish it—The subject of Crabbe is 'The Poacher' a
character in his line but which he has never touched."[43] Huchon
finds Scott's poem "almost unreadable" and believes it to be "very
like parody,"[44] but this is an exaggeration. With its emphasis on
retribution and the inevitable punishment of the guilty man, the

poem definitely captures something of Crabbe's early style in "The Parish Register." Lockhart claims that Crabbe, when he first read the poem, said, "This man, whoever he is, can do all that I can, and *something more.*"[45]

"The Poacher" begins very much in the style of *The Borough*, with one person telling another something of his village. But Scott immediately introduces a political theme when the villager informs the visitor that he is wrong to believe that the laws work to the disadvantage of the ordinary people:

> Like his, I ween, thy comprehensive mind
> Holds laws as mouse-traps baited for mankind:
> Thine eye, applausive, each sly vermin sees,
> That baulks the snare, yet battens on the cheese;
> Thine ear has heard, with scorn instead of awe,
> Our buckskinn'd justices expound the law,
> Wire-draw the acts that fix for wires the pain,
> And for the netted partridge noose the swain;
> And thy vindictive arm would fain have broke
> The last light fetter of the feudal yoke,
> To give the denizens of wood and wild,
> Nature's free race, to each her free-born child.[46]

Scott leaves no doubt that he dislikes the poacher because he is a criminal, and that he believes the "grave stranger," a Radical, to be completely mistaken in his ideas about the injustice of the law. The two protagonists, therefore, are opposed by Scott, the narrator. The conception of the situation is also completely abstract, so that when the "stranger" argues for the "rights of man," Scott counters with the example of the French Revolution:

> But mad *Citoyen*, meek *Monsieur* again,
> With some few added links resumes his chain.

Tories such as Scott were particularly concerned that Radicals in England would attempt to emulate the French example with regard to the game laws, since after the revolution anyone in France was allowed to hunt game. Thomas Paine's argument—"The French constitution says, There shall be no game laws; that the farmer on whose lands wild game shall be found (for it is by the produce of his lands they are fed) shall have a right to what he can take: That there shall be no monopolies of any kind"[47]—had struck fear into the hearts of many of the upper class who regarded the law as a means to uphold their privileges.[48]

Since Scott does not bother to develop his poacher as part of the social context, there is little sense of the poacher's personality, and in the end the poem becomes a conflict between ideas. Although Scott asks the stranger to accompany him and witness for himself the effects of the doctrine of the rights of man on the poacher, Edward Mansell, there is little sense of this being a particular situation. In the beginning Edward Mansell is "the lightest heart / That ever play'd on holiday his part!" But in true Crabbe fashion (and here Scott shows that he had studied the early Crabbe of "The Parish Register"), Edward has one flaw which leads to his downfall. Edward "loved a gun." But the whys and wherefores are left totally unexplored, and Scott nowhere suggests the significance of loving a gun. As a result, Scott merely *tells* how Edward soon falls in with a crowd of hardened criminals, turns to more serious crimes, and ends with murder as he attempts to escape from a gamekeeper— the very future that Crabbe has James predict for Robert. After this murder Edward is transformed into the scum of society, "Black Ned," and Scott says to those who would defend the poacher:

> No, scoffer, no! Attend, and mark with awe,
> There is no wicket in the gate of law!

Such a description would suggest that the game laws were above reproach and occasioned no controversy at all.

Although Edward Mansell's end resembles that of Abel Keene, Jachin, and Peter Grimes, the omission of one important quality of Crabbe's presentation leaves "The Poacher" in the ranks of second-rate social criticism. By keeping his artist's eye on the subject, Crabbe reveals moral complexities usually unnoticed.

Peter Grimes, for instance, poached as a young man, but Crabbe does not repudiate Peter on this account. On the contrary, the reader feels that the crueller Peter becomes, the more he fascinates Crabbe. At the end of Book 1 of "The Parish Register," Crabbe introduces a carousing, free-thinking poacher, but far from condemning the man, Crabbe portrays his crimes and blasphemies with tremendous gusto. The interest in and even sympathy for the criminal, qualities evident in all of Crabbe's work, differentiate his portrayal of the poacher in "Smugglers and Poachers" from that of Scott's in "The Poacher." As soon as Edward Mansell begins breaking the law, any empathy between Scott and Edward is destroyed. For Scott, Edward Mansell is only a name or a "sign" to refute the theory of the rights of man. Crabbe occasionally mentioned the rights of man,[49] but even though he believed it to be a highly dangerous idea since it was ahistorical, he never set out to write a poem which didactically demonstrated the bad effects of such a theory.

Written to demonstrate a single idea, "The Poacher" does not explore any of the social reasons that lead to poaching, and therefore its texture remains thin. Moreover, it is this way because Scott, unlike Crabbe, is never able to make the situation human, and thus capable of being dealt with. It is possible to do something with people; ideas remain fixed. For instance, in his description of Peter Grimes's cruelty to his apprentice boys, Crabbe becomes so interested in attempting to understand Peter that he is able to explain something of the social background which gave birth to such cruelty. Whereas most of Crabbe's characters reflect their environment, in Scott's poem the metamorphosis from Edward Mansell to Black Ned is blamed on Edward's own vicious will and the agency of such extraneous demons as Tom Paine. Where Scott seems to have no feeling for the social forces involved in poaching, Crabbe erects a case for Robert in which the blame is distributed. In creating a story involving the complex social relations leading to poaching, Crabbe does not begin by refuting a highly abstract theory, but by exploring a concrete case of poaching. In this way the inferences are contained in the situation itself.

VI

"Smugglers and Poachers" has two points of climax, one minor and one major, both centring on James's capture of Robert for poaching. In both cases, Crabbe is able to vindicate Robert to a large extent by his presentation of an issue which would have been fatal to Scott's picture of the poacher as the villain of society. That issue is the law itself and its justice.

For instance, when James begins to pursue his brother, Crabbe shows him motivated as much by jealousy as by justice. Although James had known for some time that his brother had been breaking the law, the news does not particularly affect him until he falls in love with Rachel. His enmity towards his brother and his passion for bringing him to "justice" date from the time he finds that Rachel and Robert are in love. Moreover, when Crabbe depicts the two brothers vying for Rachel's love, the reader's sympathies are naturally with Robert since James begins by abusing his brother. James's rhetoric reminds one of the devious and underhanded tricks of Blifil:

> James talk'd of pity in a softer tone,
> To Rachel speaking, and with her alone:
> "He knew full well," he said, "to what must come
> His wretched brother, what would be his doom."
> Thus he her bosom fenced with dread about;
> But love he could not with his skill drive out.
> Still, he effected something—and that skill
> Made the love wretched, though it could not kill;
> And Robert fail'd, though much he tried, to prove
> He had no guilt—She granted he had love.   (223–32)

Robert, on the other hand, refuses to act treacherously through innuendo, and speaks his mind openly: "Robert, more generous of the two, avow'd / His scorn, defiance, and contempt aloud." While imputing the crime of poaching to Robert, Crabbe skilfully convicts James of something worse—a lack of generous love.

When one brother is a keeper and the other a poacher, the outcome of the quarrel is predictable. After Rachel has rejected James and declared her love for Robert, James soon begins to pursue the poachers:

> Thus they proceeded, till a winter came,
> When the stern keeper told of stolen game.
> Throughout the woods the poaching dogs had been;
> And from him nothing should the robbers screen,
> From him and law—he would all hazards run,
> Nor spare a poacher, were his brother one—
> Love, favour, interest, tie of blood should fail,
> Till vengeance bore him bleeding to the jail. (233-40)

When James says that nothing will hide the poachers "from him and law" the emphasis is on the word "him," with the phrase "and law" added as an afterthought. A good gamekeeper, of course, should be conscientious and vigilant in his duties, but James has reduced the conflict between himself and the poachers to a personal feud. Although James tries to hide his personal motives under the guise of duty, when he vows not to spare any of the poachers, even "were his brother one," the word "vengeance" reveals his true purpose. James has identified the poachers with his brother Robert. Nor is he content simply to arrest his brother; he wants to take him "bleeding to the jail." Since the poachers take blood, James remains unsatisfied until he also draws blood. James appears to be hunting down the poachers on the Old Testament formula of an "eye for an eye." Unfortunately, what drives James is the passion of his own blood, not righteous retribution for the spilled blood of the game.

Crabbe's depiction of James as a type of rural constable does not exaggerate conditions. Acts of Parliament had already given the gamekeeper authority to deal with suspicious persons.[50] Moreover, gamekeepers could search the houses of persons suspected of possessing game illegally, and seize firearms and dogs from those they believed were unqualified to keep them.[51] Nor were they absolutely required to obtain warrants for such actions. The gamekeeper, as well as the squire, was often the "little Nimrod" of the parish.

After James's open avowal of the necessity of revenge, it is evident that Crabbe is setting up a situation where much of the blame must rest with the forces of law and order. James again applies to Rachel, telling her that she must give up Robert because of his wickedness. But Rachel cannot be persuaded, with the result that when the poachers begin serious depredations, James renews his hunt for them in earnest:

> James was enraged, enraged his lord, and both
> Confirm'd their threatening with a vengeful oath;
> Fresh aid was sought—and nightly on the lands
> Walk'd on their watch the strong determined bands:
> Pardon was offer'd, and a promised pay
> To him who would the desperate gang betray. (267–72)

While sympathizing with the squire over the loss of his game, at the same time one recognizes that the violent rage of the lord and his gamekeeper is out of keeping.

In the growing feud between Robert and James—"James was enraged, enraged his lord"—Crabbe points out how easily the issue of poaching could turn into a blood feud between two sections of the community. Sydney Smith noted that "the very mention of hares and partridges in the country, too often puts an end to common humanity and common sense."[52] When the landed interest found it impracticable to enforce the laws forbidding the sale of game, they were left no option but to hit out at the surface symptom, the poacher. The result was a fierce and highly personal battle between the squire and the poacher, with the squire transferring all his rage against economic forces he could not understand to the vulnerable and always suspect parish poor. This is not to say that the squire had no right to protect his game, but to recognize that the frenzy, hysteria, and personal rancour associated with the subject often destroyed even a semblance of justice. As Crabbe points out, the squire's desire for revenge against the poacher was in large part a cause of the increase in violence.[53]

After Robert has been captured and sent to gaol, the poem might seem to be at an end, for Robert the poacher has received his just desert. That the poem continues makes clear, if it were not so already, that Crabbe is not writing a moral fable. Once one sees the necessary relation between individual needs and social norms, it is no longer satisfying either in artistic or social terms to present punishment as a solution. The unity of social criticism and characterization makes itself felt at this point in the very noticeable way that the poem continues when it could well have stopped, and by so doing draws attention to the reciprocal relationship of man and society.

In introducing the theme of justice from *Measure for Measure*, Crabbe shows convincingly that authority often used the harsh game laws as a tool to forward its own interests. Robert, it appears, has been charged with a capital offence, although Crabbe is not explicit about the exact nature of the charge. Possibly Robert is held under the Black Act of 1723 for deer-stealing at night while disguised; more likely, he is held under Lord Ellenborough's Act of 1803 whereby persons who presented a gun or tried to stab or cut "with Intent to obstruct, resist, or prevent the lawful Apprehension and Detainer of the Person or Persons so stabbing or cutting . . . or any of his, her, or their Accomplices for any Offences for which he, she, or they may respectively be liable by Law to be apprehended, imprisoned, or detained," should suffer death as a felon.[54] This law meant that the most hardened highwayman in the country might receive only a jail sentence, while a poacher could be hanged for resisting arrest. At any rate Crabbe points out that Robert seems certain to die if his brother James testifies against him. James reveals his true colours when he pretends complete indifference, declaring that he can do nothing but allow the law to run its course. He maintains that if the law calls him to testify against his brother then he will be forced to obey, and his brother must die. Yet he skilfully points out that if he is not called, the court will be forced to free Robert because of lack of evidence.

Crabbe's point is that James is willing to save his brother's life, but at a price:

James knew his power—his feelings were not nice—
Mercy he sold, and she must pay the price.   (317–18)

James tells Rachel he will have his lord dismiss the action if Rachel
will give up Robert and promise to marry him. The parallel theme
occurs in *Measure for Measure* when Angelo promises Isabella
mercy for her brother Claudio if she will become his mistress. Just
as Angelo found himself unequal to the temptations of power, so
James finds himself willing to sell mercy and bribe the girl he
desires. Like Claudio, Robert proves too weak for the test and asks
Rachel to save his life by marrying James.

While this *Measure for Measure* theme is interesting for the insight it gives into the brothers' personalities, Crabbe's use of it has
important social ramifications. As has been shown, Crabbe was
careful to point out the personal, vindictive causes of the feud
between the poacher and the gamekeeper. Now he proceeds to
demonstrate how the law can be bent arbitrarily to serve the
purposes of James and his master. Crabbe is here raising several
points often touched on by the game-law reformers. By law, a man
is presumed innocent until proved guilty. Unfortunately, as a result
of the uneven administration of the law from county to county—
partly owing to the fact that justices of the peace were for the most
part large landowners who resided in the country—this was often
theory rather than practice. In Robert's case everyone accepts that
he has no chance, that the judge will sentence him to hang. However, Robert's conviction would have been by no means certain had
he been tried by a jury picked impartially.[55] As the Select Committees on the game laws discovered, the farmers were by no means
opposed to the poachers; often a jury of farmers refused to find a
poacher guilty. In several cases they even refused to convict a
poacher who had shot and killed a keeper.[56]

The lord who holds the power of life and death over Robert is
certainly arbitrary, since he willingly hands over the case to his
trusty gamekeeper. James, halfway between the landlord and the
worker, was in an excellent situation to mediate between the two.
But James is a stern and revengeful keeper. In effect, Robert finds

the law being administered by his brother, and the result, as has been seen, is not justice, but the thwarting of justice for personal ends. A man charged with poaching could be convicted on the evidence of one man before a single judge. As Chester Kirby has pointed out, it was not unknown at this time for squires to judge cases of poaching in which they themselves were the injured party.[57]

As noted earlier, one of the reasons why Robert rebelled against society was his distrust of authority. Although Robert's independence finally leads him afoul of the law and legitimately makes him liable to punishment, the blatant disregard for due process in the law substantiates his original mistrust. What Crabbe brings out through James—"mercy he sold"—is that, because of the administration of the law, justice is denied Robert. In the England of 1819, Robert's belief, that as a poor man he could obtain neither freedom nor justice, is not entirely unwarranted.

As an example of the relations between the squires and the people, it is interesting to note that when Crabbe was made a justice of the peace in Wiltshire, one of his first tasks was to support his fellow magistrate, W. L. Bowles, in an appeal to the king to soften the penalty imposed by the local squires on a poor woman for stealing. The woman had been fined £40 and sentenced to six months' imprisonment for stealing some cups and saucers valued at four shillings and sixpence. When the squires were informed that they did not have the authority to fine the woman, they recalled her and changed the sentence to six months' solitary confinement.[58] Presumably such cases were the exception, but it was generally recognized that squires could be extremely arbitrary and capricious in their sentences, especially when the man before them was someone whom they found particularly objectionable, some rebel spirit who wished to see conditions changed.

Crabbe further complicates the issue by having Robert escape from prison after Rachel has married James. Not knowing of James's promise to free Robert, the poachers make a daring raid on the prison. And Crabbe adds yet another twist of irony, for "in truth, a purposed mercy smooth'd their way, / But that they knew not—all triumphant they" (437-38). Allowing Robert to escape, instead of dropping the charges—is that mercy? or self-interest? Naturally enough, when Robert finds himself freed from prison, but with a capital charge still hanging over him, he becomes desperate.[59] After Robert returns to the forest, the war between the two brothers escalates until they face each other with two armies.

Since most of the community sympathized with the poacher,[60] James once again has to muster his men and information by devious means:

> James knew they met, for he had spies about,
> Grave, sober men, whom none presumed to doubt;
> For, if suspected, they had soon been tried
> Where fears are evidence, and doubts decide.   (487–90)

In order to pursue the poachers James has found it necessary to corrupt the entire community and destroy the due process of law. E. P. Thompson has observed, "The Employment of spies and of *agents provocateurs* after the Wars was the signal for a genuine outburst of indignation in which very many who were bitterly opposed to manhood suffrage took part."[61] That James had destroyed all semblance of law—"where fears are evidence"—is perhaps Crabbe's strongest indictment against him. Moreover, such descriptions of James as a sort of secret policeman correspond well with what is known of the general character of the gamekeeper. One of the results of the Act of 1671 had been to transform the gamekeepers into an extension of the police force.[62] Because they worked for the squire, gamekeepers such as James had no interest in maintaining harmony in the parish, as did the constables, but only in serving the squire by ruthlessly hunting down all trespassers. Most of the community fear James, because they are aware of his influence over the law, a law where "doubts decide."

Such tactics on the part of the landowners were directly responsible for the great game battles that threatened to divide England into two opposing camps of rich and poor. As Crabbe builds towards his climax of the battle between Robert and James, he manages to suggest much of the climate of suspicion that James has caused. For instance, in his description of the informer who tells James of the poachers' meeting in the forest, Crabbe says:

> But in this night a sure informer came:
> "They were assembled who attack'd his game;
> Who more than once had through the park made way,
> And slain the dappled breed, or vow'd to slay;"
> The trembling spy had heard the solemn vow,
> And need and vengeance both inspired them now.
>
> (499–504)

By "dappled breed" the spy of course means "deer," the point being that the slaying of deer was a more serious offence than the poaching of game birds. While the status of game remained in dispute, most people recognized that deer (not usually classed as game) were property. Does the spy inform James that Robert and his gang are deer slayers? If so, they are in fact committing a serious crime. In the words of this "sure informer," they have "slain the dappled breed, or vow'd to slay." The word "sure" becomes ironic when it is seen that the informer is quite uncertain of his facts— have they slain the deer? or merely vowed to? In lieu of better evidence, the intention is accepted as proof of the deed itself.

In pointing out that the squire has armed his gamekeepers, Crabbe again indicates that much of the responsibility for the game battles rests with the country gentlemen:

> There was a call below, when James awoke,
> Rose from his bed, and arms to aid him took,
> Not all defensive!—there his helpers stood,
> Arm'd like himself, and hastening to the wood.   (509–12)

A few years after the publication of "Smugglers and Poachers" a judge in Lancashire ruled that a squire who armed his servants was to be held responsible for their actions.[63] This precedent horrified the country gentlemen, since it recognized that poachers could not be shot with impunity as vermin. The squire and James feel that poaching is a serious enough crime to warrant murder; they "would shoot the man who shot a hare" (527). And it is this attitude,

Crabbe reveals, which leads to the double shooting in which brother kills brother.

In the figure of Rachel, Crabbe introduces an element of pathos which heightens the problem while at the same time helping to make it human. When Rachel arrives on the scene after the fatal shooting, she finds Robert close to death. Immediately she kneels to help him and is stricken with grief as he dies in her arms. The keepers return with lights at this moment, so that Rachel's weeping is suddenly cut off by their excited but prosaic explanations to the lord of the manor. The keepers, aghast to find Rachel weeping for a common poacher, primly warn her to stay away from her mortal enemy. In this scene Crabbe contrasts Rachel's impulsive, human reaction with the impersonalized response of the gamekeepers. Only when the keepers see that the two dead men were brothers do they realize the full extent of the evils of the game war:

> Now, more attentive, on the dead they gazed,
> And they were brothers: sorrowing and amazed,
> On all a momentary silence came,
> A common softness, and a moral shame. (596–99)

That it takes such violence to bring the keepers to a sense of shame, an awareness of the human dimension, emphasizes the pervasive corrupting quality of the game laws. Although Crabbe says the shame is felt by "all," in fact there is one telling exeception: for the first and only time the squire speaks—"Seized you the poachers?" Unaffected by the sight of the two dead brothers, he wants to know only whether the other poachers were captured. His servants rise above the situation (and their master) to answer him:

> They fled,
> And we pursued not—one of them was dead,
> And one of us; they hurried through the wood,
> Two lives were gone, and we no more pursued.
> Two lives of men, of valiant brothers lost!
> Enough, my lord, do hares and pheasants cost! (600–605)

And in this reply rests Crabbe's own conclusion; the protection of game is not worth the lives of men. An abstract idea of justice can be inhumane. Yet this conclusion is not couched in terms of abstractions. The squire's facile question reveals the extent to which he has become isolated from the community, and since he is the representative of the law, Crabbe is able to show in concrete human terms the extent to which the game laws have become divorced from the actual situations they are supposed to regulate. Crabbe is practising what he is preaching: his ideas have now found objective modes of expression. There is no need for him overtly to condemn the squire; the irony of the squire's isolation is self-evident.

The poem however does not end with the dramatic twin deaths of the brothers and the reproach to the squire, for Crabbe adds a coda in which he explains the reaction of the rest of the community to the battle. Again one is questioned by the form of the poem, and by now it should be apparent that such questionings are by no means irrelevant to an appreciation of Crabbe's art. After the game-keepers say to the lord of the manor, "Enough, my lord, do hares and pheasants cost!" Crabbe adds:

> So many thought, and there is found a heart
> To dwell upon the deaths on either part;
> Since this their morals have been more correct,
> The cruel spirit in the place is check'd;
> His lordship holds not in such sacred care,
> Nor takes such dreadful vengeance for a hare;
> The smugglers fear, the poacher stands in awe
> Of Heaven's own act, and reverences the law;
> There was, there is a terror in the place
> That operates on man's offending race.   (606–15)

Not only does Crabbe appear to hold out bright hopes for the future; the village also seems to have benefited from the death of the two brothers. Peace has been restored, or if not peace, then at least a truce.

In part, the coda can be seen as the manifestation of Crabbe's belief that life is not composed of a series of dramatic flourishes, or as his presentation of the ways in which the social fabric of life must continue, squire and villager coping with the aftermath of civil war. If any of Crabbe's Tory readers had begun to have doubts about Crabbe's own political credentials, then the following passage, promising order and peace, would have reassured them:

> Such acts will stamp their moral on the soul,
> And while the bad they threaten and control,
> Will to the pious and the humble say,
> Yours is the right, the safe, the certain way,
> 'Tis wisdom to be good, 'tis virtue to obey. (616–20)

Not only does the passage show no hostility, but as it progresses, it becomes more and more conservative and simplistic, and thereby seems to ignore most of what Crabbe had to say in the poem; for "Smugglers and Poachers" reveals that no simple answer can be given to the question of whether the keeper or the poacher is to blame. Thus the platitude, "'Tis wisdom to be good, 'tis virtue to obey," seems wholly inapplicable as an answer. From what has been observed in previous poems, it is perhaps legitimate to feel that Crabbe has added this section in order to prevent the confirmed Tories and sentimentalists from taking umbrage at his daring to attack the squirearchy as well as the poachers.

While plausible in themselves, none of these explanations has taken into account Crabbe's use of dramatic form, in terms of both characterization and structure. Although Crabbe has made it appear as though he is speaking, and in fact he ends a verse paragraph with the platitude, he begins the following verse paragraph with the crucial words:

> So Rachel thinks, the pure, the good, the meek,
> Whose outward acts the inward purpose speak. (621–22)

The phrase "So Rachel thinks" parallels the earlier phrase "So many thought" which follows the line "Enough, my lord, do hares and pheasants cost!" The village girl who believed Robert to be free from guilt because she was sure he read his Bible may be sympathetically portrayed, but she is not Crabbe's mouthpiece.

Critics have too often fallen into the error of accepting whatever is said in the poems, no matter by whom or in what context, as Crabbe's own statement of belief. [64] Yet in this case what the poem says is clearly at variance with what Rachel says. In the context of the poem's portrayal of the intricacies of the game-law situation, Rachel's pious warning appears ironic. Of course it is "wisdom to be good," but as "Smugglers and Poachers" manifests, to know what is good is by no means easy—especially when people are "Taught that illicit traffic is hazardous but not forbidden by their Religion." [65]

Since at this point the person who is the victim of the game laws, and who might therefore be expected to have most insight into the problem, has in fact only platitudes in which to express her sorrow, the poem's ending indicates nothing has basically changed in the attitudes that create and permit such specific evils as the game laws. The poem reveals that as a result of the violence, people are now aware for the first time of the evil that they have been submitting to, yet it also suggests that they still have no grasp of the general situation, nor any understanding of the roots of the specific problem. So that even if, as Rachel's naive comments indicate, she and the community have now the best will in the world to make the changes, the poem suggests nothing that would safeguard them in the future. All that has saved them is violence. And it looks as though all that will save them in the future is violence. Crabbe's exposition indicates that even relatively minor social changes, if they are to be effective and lasting, require an understanding of the relation between the individual's responses and the society that conditions them. "Smugglers and Poachers" ends with the melancholy implication that such an understanding is still far to seek.

Chapter 6
We cannot all the lovely vase restore

I

In "Smugglers and Poachers" Crabbe was clearly dealing with the specific issue of the game laws, even though he developed the topic through his portrayal of individuals. In most of the other books of *Tales of the Hall*, and certainly in the frame story of George and Richard, specific social issues tend to assume far less importance, as Crabbe attempts an ever more searching analysis of moral and social attitudes in his portraits of individuals. For this reason, terms such as "social critic" and "social criticism" have limited usefulness with regard to *Tales of the Hall*, since they inaccurately describe the range of Crabbe's concerns. One of the implications of the term "social criticism" is that the critic will show how conditions in a society can be improved to benefit its members and to bring about greater justice. Often the hidden assumption is that while man is moral his social institutions are immoral and in need of change. Yet such an assumption ignores the important part that individuals play in creating their societies. This is not merely to say that men receive the institutions they deserve, although there is some truth in this, but that man himself must recognize that his own individual desires require educating so that he may benefit from and maintain the freedoms that society can guarantee him as a citizen. Therefore the social critic, who teaches man his rights, has to be complemented by the educator or moralist, who teaches man his responsibilities.[1] When either half of this reciprocal relationship between the individual's rights and his social responsibilities is obscured, extremist social critics and moralists develop systems, not in terms of the interaction between individuals and their society, but from such single immutable sources as God's will, natural law, the world process, etc.

Since this discussion of the development of Crabbe's poetry has reached the point at which his interest in character portrayal is apparent, it is now appropriate to call him "moralist" in a way that previously could have been misleading. Whereas earlier it was evident what sort of moralist Crabbe was not—one whose aim is to teach mankind to embrace an abstract system of principles—it should now be clear that he can be called a moralist in the tradition of Sir Thomas More, Swift, and Johnson, writers who invited their readers to see themselves more clearly, and thus to bring their actions into accord with their own legitimate needs and aspirations. Although either "social critic" or "moralist" is of itself insufficient to describe Crabbe's approach, the two terms taken together serve as signposts to the major perspectives from which he wrote and from which he can be read. Like many other nineteenth-century writers who were interested in depicting particular individuals in social relationships, Crabbe found it necessary to describe the manner in which any individual's social and moral outlook is altered by his own bias.

In *Tales of the Hall*, Crabbe more than ever before indicates in his character portraits that individuals understand little about the motives which lead them to action. Such an emphasis inevitably shifts the focus away from specific social issues, for, if actions are the result of temperament, habit, and prejudice, then to understand the way men function in society one has to study, not the institutions, but the psychological causes that lead men to build these institutions. The institutions and laws are themselves the rationalizations of time, class, and self-interest. Since the time of Locke, philosophers had accepted that a study of man must begin with a study of the mind. In *Tales of the Hall* Crabbe sets out to do exactly this, and quickly discovers what David Hume had shown seventy-five years earlier, that "Reason is, and ought only to be the slave of the passions."[2] Although Hume meant that feelings always govern conduct, he also believed that the means to reach the ends determined by feeling could efficiently be chosen with the help of reason. What Crabbe wishes to show is that the subtlety of the mind often deludes man into believing that reason is helping to select the means, when in fact the individual is guided only by his passions—sometimes the best, more often the worst.

As will be seen shortly, much of *Tales of the Hall* is devoted to a probing of the question of motivation, often with the negative conclusion that individuals cannot know themselves. Yet these various tales are told within the frame story of the brothers George and Richard. When the brothers tell their own life stories, and the stories of acquaintances, they do so in order to learn more about one another and to resolve their personal and social differences. Unlike the narrator of "The Parish Register" whose viewpoint adds little to the individual stories, the narrators of *Tales of the Hall* are themselves changed as a result of what they see and hear. The frame story of George and Richard is significant, not only because it supplies the reason for the individual tales, but because the individual tales alter the brothers' perceptions, and therefore modify the frame story itself. In the story of the brothers we witness something that has only been hinted at in the earlier poems: the individual can begin to discern his motives through experience, and as a result of this personal growth, he has an effect on the people and society around. As will be seen shortly, Crabbe's emphasis on seeing clearly (a quality evident from the time of *The Village*) by no means falls on the act of introspection alone. What the brothers learn about each other is as important as their individual attempts to "know thyself." Because of their differing social and religious views, George and Richard could have become enemies, but instead of challenging one another in terms of their beliefs, they learn to see how their public ideas on morality, society, and religion are dependent on personality. This clarity of vision creates understanding and allows appropriate action. Before dealing more fully with this matter, I propose to comment on the scenes in which Crabbe explores the ways in which psychological problems both create and reflect social problems.

To this end, the subject of love was ideally to his purpose.[3] He treats love in many different modes—between men and women, between brothers, between sisters. Yet these human relationships offer considerations much more largely revealing than the purely personal. For instance, the connection between marriage and the social questions of morals, property, and position is obvious, and especially important in a time such as Crabbe's when the class structure is being subjected to the pressures of change. Moreover, the expression of love relationships is conditioned by time and place, and the forms of such relationships are themselves influential in creating the social modes and categories through which individuals perceive the world. This can be seen especially easily in the connections between love and charity, synonymous in theory, but often poles apart in fact. As witnessed by literary conventions of the time, charity is the social manifestation of true personal love or love-worthiness, but a close examination may well reveal less than ideal motives in both. Such revealing examinations mark Crabbe's portrayal of love relationships as the meeting-ground of personal and social forces.

An interesting instance of his treatment of this theme occurs in Book XI when he shows young Rupert attempting to woo a middle-aged maid by impressing her with his virtues. Rupert's speech, taken out of context, could almost be accepted as straightforward panegyric, of the eighteenth-century type discussed in Chapter 1 in relation to such writers as Akenside and Armstrong:

> The humble good of happy swains to share,
> And from the cottage drive distress and care;
> To the dear infants make some pleasures known,
> And teach, he gravely said, the virtues to his own.

(XI. 958–61)

But Crabbe offers ample evidence to indicate that he is treating Rupert's idealism satirically. The phrase "he gravely said" casts doubts on Rupert's sincerity, and Crabbe also compares him ironically to Sir Charles Grandison. Certainly the rest of the story reveals Rupert to have no deep concern for the poor; he mentions them because they may bring a tear of sympathy from the spinster and because he feels the idea of children will help his suit. The point is not that Crabbe disliked Rupert's ideals, but that he wished to show how often ideals such as Rupert's are grounded in self-interest.

Crabbe's tone here is subtle and difficult to describe. The effect is certainly not to make the reader detest or hate Rupert for the callous way he uses charity and the poor. Rather, the tone permits one to smile at Rupert's self-deceit and his attempts to deceive others, and derives in part from the gradual discovery that none of the characters is idealistic. The spinster herself earlier used Rupert's techniques for her own ends when she retired with a friend to a rural village, determined to win the esteem of her neighbours by deliberately setting out to gain a reputation for benevolence:

> We were the ladies of the place, and found
> Protection and respect the country round;
> We gave, and largely, for we wish'd to live
> In good repute—for this 'tis good to give.　(XI. 735–38)

In this case the motive is hardly charitable. The spinster wishes respect, and one of the ways to gain this respect is by appearing charitable. Yet the matter-of-fact tone of the last line surprises, and since there is no authorial comment, the reader is led to wonder whether such motivation, ordinarily considered to be only "partially" charitable, is all there is of charity.[4]

The manner in which Crabbe often juxtaposes the act of benevolence with the personal motive leaves the reader with the uncomfortable feeling that such a link is always to be found. As Kant indicated, such a link can never be disproved. In Book XVII, the widow's second husband, once he has achieved affluence and success, wishes to play the role of public benefactor:

> As wealth increased, ambition now began
> To swell the soul of the aspiring man.
>
> . . . .
>
> He would, moreover, on the Bench debate
> On sundry questions—when a magistrate;
> Would talk of all that to the state belongs,
> The rich man's duties, and the poor man's wrongs;
> He would with favourites of the people rank,
> And him the weak and the oppress'd should thank.
>
> (XVII. 291–304)

In the mind of such a person, public duty and charity are not only ends in themselves, but also useful tools to increase one's reputation or to help in playing an expected social role. And Crabbe's presentation makes this appear quite unremarkable, an expected fact of human nature.

Novelists at this period were fond of showing that their heroines possessed a keen social sensibility by portraying them dispensing alms in the homes of cottagers. Even Jane Austen, who usually excludes the poor from her novels, portrays Emma paying "a charitable visit . . . to a poor sick family, who lived a little way out of Highbury."[5] And John Moore shows his hero Mordaunt falling in love with Miss Clifford the first time he sees her coming from a charitable visit to a cottage.[6] In Book XIV Crabbe employs a similar situation, but then has Henry cast doubts on Emma's reason for her visits to poor cottagers when he says:

> Well, I know, you feel
> For suffering men, and would their sufferings heal,
> But when at certain huts you chose to call,
> At certain seasons, was compassion all?
> I there beheld thee, to the wretched dear
> As angels to expiring saints appear
> When whispering hope—I saw an infant press'd
> And hush'd to slumber on my Emma's breast!
> Hush'd be each rude suggestion!—Well I know,
> With a free hand your bounty you bestow,

And to these objects frequent comforts send;
But still they see not now their pitying friend.

(XIV. 296–307)

As this passage reveals, Emma's motives for her visits were only partly charitable, Crabbe suggesting that she herself was unclear about her other motives.

Women of this day were often recommended to devote their time and talents to the poor. Hannah More and her evangelical friends saw such an effort among women as something good in itself. Wilberforce once remarked, "There is no class of persons whose condition has been more improved within my recollection than that of unmarried women. Formerly there seemed to be nothing useful in which they could be naturally busy, but now they may always find an object in attending to the poor."[7] Crabbe's interest in the subtleties of motivation enabled him to see that in many such cases the poor were actually welcomed because they helped lonely women fill up their time or provided them with a substitute for frustrated or unrequited love. Book XVII contains a typical example of charity from such an impulse. While waiting for her lover to return, Ellen retreats to her native village to perform good works among the poor:

And Ellen to her native village fled,
With native feeling—there she oped her door,
Her heart, her purse, and comforted the poor,
The sick, the sad—and there she pass'd her days,
Deserving much, but never seeking praise:

. . . .

Nor turn'd from any, save when Love pursued;
For, though to love disposed, to kindness prone,
She thought of Cecil, and she lived alone. (XVIII. 233–44)

Crabbe does not condemn such charity, since the end may be good. Nor does he condemn the motives, but he does show that in many such acts of charity there exist motives that altruists and idealists tend to ignore. In the case of Ellen, his opinion that her good deeds result from her kind nature is particularly apparent. But the last line of the above-quoted passage indicates that Ellen's charity is in part a way of keeping off unwanted lovers.[8] In fact Ellen knows her own mind so little that when Cecil finally returns, she turns him away, and then immediately regrets the decision, "Her thoughts were guardless, and beyond her power" (XVIII. 303). Where Wilberforce looked at the good which had accrued from Hannah More's charitable work, and concluded, "This is truly magnificent, the really sublime in character,"[9] Crabbe was moved to probe below the surface and reveal the complex of motives leading to the good actions.

Where the Evangelicals often mutilated the spirit of charity was in believing that when the rich gave the money, the poor incurred an obligation. Crabbe, however, believed that when a rich man decided to extend help the debt was contracted on both sides. It will be recalled that in Letter III of *The Borough* the curate remarked that when relief is properly given "All painful sense of obligation dies" (III. 313). Crabbe's portrayal of this theme—at length with George and Richard, the principal narrators of *Tales of the Hall*—is presented in miniature in Book III with Hector Blane and his protégé, Charles. A rich man, Sir Hector decides to patronize "a widow's son." But Sir Hector helps the boy for his own peculiar reasons—"He tried the luxury of doing good" (III. 139).[10] When Charles proves to be only a little above average in his studies, Sir Hector is not at first deterred. However, at the conclusion of Charles's studies, when Sir Hector perceives that the community is no longer offering praise for his charity, but is waiting to see how he will meet the remainder of his obligations by providing for the boy, Sir Hector's attitude changes:

> The deed was pleasant while the praise was new,
> But none the progress would with wonder view.
> It was a debt contracted; he who pays
> A debt is just, but must not look for praise:
> The deed that once had fame must still proceed,
> Though fame no more proclaims "how great the deed!"

> The boy is taken from his mother's side,
> And he who took him must be now his guide.
> But this, alas! instead of bringing fame,
> A tax, a trouble, to my lord became. (III. 168–77)

No longer feeling himself praised, Sir Hector chooses the least expensive alternative and decides to send Charles to sea. But to his surprise, Charles, who wishes to be an artist, refuses the offer. When Sir Hector washes his hands of his protégé, Charles determines to attempt his own fortune. In this he fails, and dies a pauper.

The point to the story is not that Charles is a great artist badly treated, nor that Sir Hector should have maintained Charles in unlimited patronage, but that far more is involved in charity than a sum of money changing hands. Crabbe wants to know why Sir Hector gave the money and what effect this money will have on the attitudes of Charles. He also wants to know to what extent Sir Hector is truly attentive to the situation before him. As the outcome of the story indicates, Sir Hector has not really acted responsibly, since he has allowed an abstract ideal of charity to prevent him from seeing the individual case of Charles.

In his own life Crabbe was renowned for his generosity to the poor,[11] and indeed Joanna Baillie felt Crabbe was too charitable since he gave both to the worthy and the unworthy poor.[12] Yet Crabbe was a much better analyst of his own motives. In a letter to Miss Elizabeth Charter, he remarked:

> A poor Woman called at my Door, since I have been
> Conversing with you, and gained her Purpose
> by naming Taunton as her Home [where Miss Charter
> lived]: so it is that Motives insinuate themselves into
> our Minds and we oftentimes impute that to our
> Resolution or our prudence which was caused by some
> kind thought dropt among our other Cogitations
> and overruling them all.[13]

In another letter to the same correspondent he commented: "For Heaven's sake do not think me over attentive to my Duty. . . . I am not exemplary and half my virtue is unavailing Desire."[14] Many of his actions, Crabbe recognized, were influenced by motives he barely perceived.

Quite clearly the cumulative effect of Crabbe's psychological analyses of "charitable" actions is to call into question the degree to which individuals can be said to know themselves and to be in control of their actions. In Book I, where presumably Crabbe is the narrator, he says, "We cannot nature by our wishes rule, / Nor at our will her warm emotions cool" (I. 340–41). In describing Harry Bland, George says, "His mind approves the virtue he forsakes, / And yet forsakes her" (III. 433–34). George, and the reader too, cannot help sympathizing with a person such as Harry, who knows what is right, approves it, and yet finds he cannot follow it. Similarly, Richard at first thinks his older brother to be a distinguished representative of the cool, calm upper class. But he discovers that George is as human as himself:

> Then, thou too, Brother, couldst of weakness tell;
> Thou, too, hast found the wishes that rebel
> Against the sovereign reason.   (VII. 41–43)

In "Delay has Danger," Henry is in part the victim of his own subconscious desires. "'Tis thus our secret passions work their way, / And the poor victims know not they obey" (XIII. 370–71). And Jacques, the rector, notes that the commonplace—"the passions, insolent and strong, / Bear our weak minds their rapid course along" (XII. 63–64)—has enormous implications for the study of human nature. Some of these implications of course were being worked out by the Romantic poets in ways very different from those of Crabbe, although Wordsworth in a hostile analysis in *The Prelude* of his own Godwinian phase had commented that the "passions had the privilege to work, / And never hear the sound of their own names" (X. 813–14).[15]

Crabbe stresses, as the Romantics rarely do, not only the influence of feelings, but of habits as well.[16] As he says of the differences in emotion and imagination between George, the conservative, and Richard, the liberal: "We saw the differences by their habits made" (II. 30). George remarks that he became resigned to a life of commerce when "The force of habit held me to the oar" (VII. 800). Jacques similarly comments about himself: "Small daily actions into habits grew" (X. 482). Another instance occurs when George wants to forgive Rosabella her life of promiscuity, and Rosabella desires to renounce such a life—if for no other reason than to win George's protection. Despite George's encouragement and her own good intentions, she fails, for as George says, "she did not know / How deeply rooted evil habits grow" (VII. 694–95).

In his description of man's lack of control over himself Crabbe may well have had in mind Christ's plea—"Father, forgive them; for they know not what they do"—since he says:

> Let mortal frailty judge how mortals frail
> Thus in their strongest resolutions fail,
> And, though we blame, our pity will prevail.
>
> (XVI. 903–905)

Certainly if man is not in control of himself, one wonders to what extent the individual is responsible for his actions. The question can even arise as to whether man has any right to pass sentence on his fellow man. Farmer Ellis asserts that man does not have the right: "Tell me not, sir, of rights, and wrongs, or powers! / I felt it written—Vengeance is not ours!" (XII. 848–49). *Tales of the Hall* can be seen as an exploration of ethics in human relationships developed by means of a series of variations on the theme of love. The characters are confronted with situations in which not only do *they* have great difficulty in choosing correctly, but the *reader* also becomes aware that formal, theoretical moral truths are of little use in judging such situations. For example, the story of Henry and Emma tells of the *natural* death of love. The emphasis is no longer upon the mistakes of individuals but upon the inevitable development of forces within a given situation. If one asks whether Belwood, in Book XV, was wrong to run off with the schoolteacher's daughter, the answer is not at once apparent. Belwood did what seemed natural and logical in the given situation. Can one blame

Ruth for committing suicide? Perhaps not, when one considers the alternative choices. In Book XII, Henry leaves his fiancée at the request of his father to visit a noble lord. While at the hall, he falls into a situation where he is forced to marry the orphan Frances. Yet it would be a very strict and austere judge who would feel Henry was wrong to meet Frances. Nor are the lord and the steward to blame for attempting to bring Henry and Frances together. Henry could have avoided the situation in the first place by refusing to leave Cecilia, but such an action would have meant disobeying his father. Crabbe has placed Henry in a complex situation where blame and responsibility are difficult to apportion, and where actions are not clear-cut and devoid of history but the result of a long process of accretion.

Nevertheless, Crabbe is unwilling to give everyone *carte blanche* freedom to use this argument: it may be that moral truths are difficult to apply to complex psychological situations, but this does not mean that all answers are equally invalid. In Book XI when Frederick claims that truth is impossible to find, the spinster asks disarmingly: "If truth be hidden, why art thou so sure?" (XI. 724). As will be seen shortly, Crabbe suggests that such situations can be understood, or at least partially understood, and then, while decisions will never be clear-cut and easy, man can make the best choice possible under the circumstances.

In attempting to analyse the various love stories, one rapidly comes to the conclusion that Crabbe has deliberately created situations where it can be seen that happiness or fulfilment is not inevitably linked to prudence, intelligence, health, moderation, etc. For instance in Book XIII, "Delay Has Danger," the title is in direct contradiction to Malthusian principles of prudence. In all Crabbe's previous tales he had suggested that young people would be well advised to wait a number of years before marrying. Yet in this tale, delay does bring danger.[17] Similarly, when the reviewer for *The Monthly Review* lashed out at the "ale-house politics" of "William Bailey," what he disliked was the compromise-ending in which Frances is rewarded with William's love. He believed that Lord Robert's seduction of Frances had left her unworthy of William.

In effect, he wished to see William treat Frances as Farmer Ellis refused to treat his unfaithful wife. But Crabbe observes that William and Frances can and do live happily together in spite of Frances' love affair with Lord Robert. William and Frances enjoy married life because neither of them sets impossible moral standards.[18]

In Book x, Jacques tells a story of his youth that illustrates well the irrelevance of generalized moral axioms. In order to gain his father's permission to marry the daughter of their political opponent, Jacques attempts to convince his father that Whigs and Tories need not quarrel:

> First I began my father's heart to move,
> By boldly saying "We are born to love;"
> My father answer'd, with an air of ease,
> "Well! very well! be loving if you please!
> Except a man insults us or offends,
> In my opinion we should all be friends."   (x. 176–81)

Such generalities, while true, never really help in any crucial decision:

> This gain'd me nothing; little would accrue
> From clearing points so useless though so true.
>   (x. 182–83)

Jacques's conclusion is indicative of the point that *Tales of the Hall* makes in its entirety, that general moral principles—men should love one another, it is wrong to lie, one should be honest—are of little use in all but the most simple situations where there is no conflict of duty.

Robert Chamberlain has argued that Crabbe was essentially a conservative moralist: "Crabbe continued to support the established, long-familiar code whose roots lay ultimately in the medieval scorn of the world."[19] But this is to underestimate the depth of Crabbe's exploration of moral themes (and the medieval Church's sense of social responsibility). In *Tales of the Hall* people such as Farmer Ellis have to rediscover both for themselves and for the gentry that man cannot live by a few simple rules, nor on a morality founded on individualism. Certainly *Tales of the Hall* suggests that the problem of sorting out right from wrong may in the last analysis be irrelevant. In Book III, George asks:

> How is it, men, when they in judgment sit
> On the same fault, now censure, now acquit?
> Is it not thus, that *here* we view the sin,
> And *there* the powerful cause that drew us in?
>
> (III. 396–99)

What Crabbe has done is to supply the reader with a great deal of information about these powerful causes, thereby showing how difficult it is to make moral decisions. Henry Fielding, in something of the same dilemma as Crabbe about valid guides to conduct, relied on man's good nature, but Fielding's idea of the good-natured man actually applied to few. Tom Jones is hardly a paradigm. Indeed, Mrs. Miller says he is "infinitely too good to live in this world" (XVIII. xi). Christianity of course has traditionally claimed a source of knowledge outside the Book of Nature. Crabbe does not discuss the role that the Scriptures can play in helping man to make decisions, but he introduces two tales in which supernatural signs play an important role.

Interest in the supernatural was still at a high pitch in the early nineteenth century, and not a few people entertained the idea, as a last resort, that perhaps the Divine Will employed ghosts to direct man.[20] As if to underline the extent of man's solitude, in both cases in which Crabbe introduces the supernatural this element proves to be completely ineffectual in providing answers. In Book XVI, "Lady Barbara; or, the Ghost," Crabbe gives a serious account of a ghost story,[21] and one that is of especial interest for its unusually free characterization of religion. Lady Barbara and her brother Richard have been brought up by their father to be free-thinkers. But at the time their father dies, they still have found no absolute truths, and their ideas remain unsettled:

Free, sad discourse was ours; we often sigh'd
To think we could not in some truths confide.
Our father's final words gave no content;
We found not what his self-reliance meant. (XVI. 488–91)

In attempting to give them some religious instruction, their relatives present so many different accounts of the "truth" that Lady Barbara and her brother agree that the only certain way to learn the truth is for the one who dies first to return and instruct the other.

Years later, on the night of Richard's death, Lady Barbara sees a "vision," which, while it remains vague about religious matters, cautions Lady Barbara that she needs guidance in her personal life. Predicting that her husband will soon die, the ghost warns that she must never remarry. Sure enough, her husband dies, and some years later Lady Barbara faces the decision whether or not to remarry. Her would-be lover, a youth to whom she gave a mother's care, finally overcomes her scruples, and against the advice of the ghost she remarries. The outcome is predictable. The boy-lover proves a bad husband, fulfilling the ghost's prediction of a miserable life. Crabbe's last comment is just:

... One moral let us draw,
Be it a ghost or not the lady saw.
    If our discretion tells us how to live,
We need no ghost a helping hand to give;
But, if discretion cannot us restrain,
It then appears a ghost would come in vain. (XVI. 963–68)

Signs sent by God would serve no purpose, since man has to interpret the signs, and he will naturally interpret them as he wishes. The second ghost story, not nearly so fully developed as the first, merely adds to the irony. In "The Cathedral Walk" a rather "spiritual" young girl, searching for the ghost of her beloved, mistakes a grave-robber for the ghost. Ironically enough, even the grave-robber does not find what he is looking for.

In the end, Crabbe paints something of what might now be called an existential picture of man—man alone with the abyss—where neither spiritual signs nor moral formulae can serve as adequate guides to life's complexities. If a man cannot see the realities of his own life, no amount of received wisdom is going to help him. In this sense, possibly the most disturbing feature of Crabbe's description is man's lack of control over his most deeply felt and important responses. The existentialist at least posits freedom of will; Crabbe at times suggests, "That which is done is that we're born to do" (XIX. 484). When Emma rebukes Henry for no longer loving her, Henry replies: "It is the fault of nature, not of me" (XIV. 153). He repeats this sentiment when he says: "'tis in vain / The course of love and nature to restrain" (XIV. 204–205). In Book III Jacques asserts that while education can check "the progress of each idle shoot," in the end the man is "what you saw the boy would be" (III. 102–107). As Crabbe indicates, most people live out their lives under the illusion that they are moved by personal, social, and religious ideals which in practice have little effect on the natural bent of their lives. Each of the characters in "Gretna Green" thinks he acts in the best interests of the others, but Crabbe reveals that Belwood wishes to gain his freedom, Clara acts out of simple-minded vanity, Mrs. Sidmere wishes social position, and Dr. Sidmere covets wealth and power.

Although Crabbe perceives how easy it is to despair in the face of ubiquitous self-deception, he does not permit his readers to shirk the business of assessment. Since the self is a mysterious entity in Crabbe's view, with action and choice seeming to occur with little or no reflection, then it becomes most important for the individual to discipline himself by attending closely to the world around. Such a discipline, Crabbe suggests, will create appropriate decisions at crucial moments based, not on fantasy, but on a perception of the "real." Like Jane Austen, Crabbe stresses the necessity of clear perceptions at all times so that the emotions can be directed to real objects and not projections of the mind. But where Jane Austen, with her single narrative viewpoint, suggests the possibility of discovering the truth, Crabbe's constantly shifting viewpoint calls such a possibility into question and gives him closer links to later nineteenth-century novelists such as the Brontës, Thackeray, and Dickens with their perception of how deeply rooted the moral is in the psychological, and how even truth itself includes some measure of illusion.

Although Crabbe has chosen tales of love to illustrate the extent to which man is at the mercy of social and psychological forces, he clearly felt his diagnosis applied to all aspects of human life. In a letter to Mary Leadbeater, he commented: "With respect to our religious associations and fellowship, there is much, I believe, that does not depend upon our own will or our own conviction. We are born with such convictions, and are led, guided, and governed by circumstances and situations over which the will has no control."[22] What *Tales of the Hall* does so effectively is to demonstrate the extent to which man is governed by circumstances and situations that limit, not only his actions, but his aspirations. When he retires to Binning, George comments: "Yet much is lost, and not yet much is found" (VII. 819). As *Tales of the Hall* indicates, the first step towards finding positive answers is a devotion to truth; for the individual, this involves learning the degree to which he is beyond his own control.

II

In many modern instances where authors have described the layer upon layer of motives leading to a particular action, one of the depressing conclusions has been that the individual appears incapable of volition and change. Because the individual can never know all the causes of his action, he can never hope to change his deep-seated patterns. As was seen in the earlier discussion of "Smugglers and Poachers," Crabbe is well aware of the difficulty in effecting meaningful and lasting changes, yet *Tales of the Hall* as a whole does tend to treat this problem optimistically, if for no other reason than that the devotion to truth evidenced by many of the characters, especially George and Richard, permits them new perceptions. Certainly Crabbe is quick to satirize those characters who fall back upon an early and easy pessimism embodied in "whatever is, is right." In Book XVII he describes the lovely but superficial widow who is unable to think for herself—except in the matter of obtaining husbands. After the death of her last husband, Crabbe gives the following description:

> The widow'd lady to her cot retired,
> And there she lives delighted and admired.
> Civil to all, compliant and polite,
> Disposed to think, "whatever is, is right,"
> She wears the widow's weeds, she gives the widow's mite.
> At home awhile, she in the autumn finds
> The sea an object for reflecting minds,
> And change for tender spirits; there she reads,
> And weeps in comfort in her graceful weeds.
>
> (XVII. 521–29)

If one can weep in comfort it is perhaps easy to believe that "whatever is, is right."

Crabbe again satirizes this belief in the essential rightness of all things when George finally meets Rosabella, his mysterious lady. Seeing George dismayed by her life of less than exemplary virtue, Rosabella attempts to hide her faults in specious philosophy:

> Come, my dear friend, discard that look of care,
> All things were made to be, as all things are;
> All to seek pleasure as the end design'd,
> The only good in matter or in mind.   (VII. 593–96)

Pope's famous dictum has been coupled with the utilitarianism of Bentham to produce a comfortable philosophy allowing Rosabella to pursue her every inclination while attributing the results to fate.

Although *Tales of the Hall* permits a tempered optimism, this does not mean that Crabbe abandoned his Realist scepticism towards Idealist theories of the perfectibility of man. Such idealism remained for him a generally disruptive influence on social life. In his acceptance of the Augustan premise that "the bliss of Man . . . /

Is not to act or think beyond mankind,"[23] Crabbe's social values are clearly those of a long line of eighteenth-century moralists who attacked the Idealist philosophy of life as a search for visionary and often unobtainable absolutes. Indeed, in his principal character and narrator, George, Crabbe goes to considerable effort to show the failure of the experiment with romantic values. George, for instance, begins life as a youth who was "pleased in lonely ways to tread" (VII. 66), one for whom "the lover's frenzy ruled the poet's pen" (VII. 63). In many ways George resembles a character such as Scythrop in Peacock's *Nightmare Abbey*.[24] Certainly his description of his youth as a solitary, diseased misanthrope has obvious romantic overtones which bring to mind the confessions of a Wordsworth or a Byron:

> The mind's disease, with all its strength, stole on,
>
> . . . .
>
> I thought I was not of my species one,
> But unconnected, injured and undone!   (VII. 430–43)

Crabbe obviously distrusted this romantic emphasis on the imagination, and was disinclined to believe that man's general well-being was linked to the imagination. Shelley's statement that the imagination is "the great instrument of moral good"[25] would have been satirized sharply by Crabbe since he felt no assurance that man's imaginative constructs had any inner, purposive logic. For instance, when George is swayed by "the power of fancy," he is merely obeying every random "impulse of the mind" (XX. 7–8). Whereas for Shelley the imagination gives man hopes of reaching "the eternal, the infinite, and the one,"[26] for Crabbe experience brings an end to "lofty hopes that grasp'd too much" (X. 609) because the imagination does not necessarily extend man's social sense but often leads him on illusory personal quests.

George's conservatism in his later years of course grows out of these experiences in which he learns to distrust the transforming power of man's imagination. Because Richard, George's younger brother, is of a more open, trusting, and loving nature than George, one might expect him to have greater optimism in man's nature, and in part this is the case. But Crabbe shows that Richard also must learn to distinguish between utopian imaginings, which blind him to actual social circumstances, and a realistic vision of the possibilities available for improvement. For instance, when he first learns of Matilda's love for him, he delights in a Wordsworthian sense of joy, and says:

> All thought, yet thinking nothing—all delight
> In every thing, but nothing in my sight!
> Nothing I mark or learn, but am possess'd
> Of joys I cannot paint, and I am bless'd
> In all that I conceive—whatever is, is best.
> Ready to aid all beings, I would go
> The world around to succour human wo;
> Yet am so largely happy, that it seems
> There are no woes, and sorrows are but dreams.
>
> (VI. 353–61)

In this instance Richard's love for a fellow human being has obviously distorted his vision, so that he has to be restored to the world where suffering and sorrow are always present:

> Such was the blessing that I sought for pain,
> In some degree to be myself again;
> And when we met a shepherd old and lame,
> Cold and diseased, it seem'd my blood to tame;
> And I was thankful for the moral sight,
> That soberized the vast and wild delight.   (VI. 382–87)

This meeting with the shepherd is reminiscent of that with the leech-gatherer in "Resolution and Independence." While Wordsworth saw in his old man a reason for hope, for Richard the old shepherd is a salutary warning that man's concern lies with the particular and the tangible, not with the abstract and the ideal.

Yet this emphasis on what is the case here and now does not lead Crabbe to cynicism or philistinism, although he clearly saw the danger of this happening. George, for example, after having been driven to melancholy and even madness by his hopeless pursuit of a visionary woman—symbol of all man's spiritual ideals—is helped by a "thrifty uncle" who tempts George with the philosophy of the utilitarian-philistine:

> He, when inform'd how men of taste could write,
> Look'd on his ledger with supreme delight;
> Then would he laugh, and, with insulting joy,
> Tell me aloud, "that's poetry, my boy." (VII. 391–94)

In renouncing romantic ideals, George swings to the opposite extreme by attempting to find happiness in worldly success. Although he finds some measure of satisfaction in the poetry of the countinghouse, he retains a lingering belief that there would be more to life if he could recover Rosabella. When this eventually happens, he finds her a "fallen woman," attempts a decent life with her, and fails. She dies shortly after returning to her former licentiousness. At this point, late in life, George recognizes how destructive has been his shallow desire for worldly success:

> 'Twas in that chamber, Richard, I began
> To think more deeply of the end of man:
> Was it to jostle all his fellows by,
> To run before them, and say, "here am I,
> Fall down, and worship?"—Was it, life throughout,
> With circumspection keen to hunt about,
> As spaniels for their game, where might be found
> Abundance more for coffers that abound?
> Or was it life's enjoyments to prefer,
> Like this poor girl, and then to die like her? (VII. 750–59)

The problem then is to find a goal that will take the individual beyond both the work ethic and the pleasure principle, and yet still remain free of extravagant individualism.

The most popular eighteenth-century solution to this problem— and the one George embraces for a time—was to find a country retreat where the Horatian pleasures could be enjoyed. Unlike his literary predecessors, however, George discovers that the pleasures of the country are insufficient to appease his mental hunger, and he confesses:

> But, where th' affections have been deeply tried,
> With other food that mind must be supplied:
> 'Tis not in trees or medals to impart
> The powerful medicine for an aching heart;
> . . . .
> Man takes his body to a country seat,
> But minds, dear Richard, have their own retreat;
> Oft when the feet are pacing o'er the green
> The mind is gone where never grass was seen. (IV. 112–21)

George is not unlike many of Crabbe's earlier characters. Indeed, the MS draft shows that Crabbe had originally conceived George to be rather like Gwyn, "the gentleman farmer" (Tale III of *Tales*), but George differs in having enough intelligence to accept the discovery that romantic ideals are illusory, and enough self-command to prevent his falling prey to worldliness or someone else's personality.

Although Crabbe often presents man's condition in the world as essentially solitary, he does not allow this to become a reason for hypochondria or misanthropy. George may have no *raison d'être*, but he persists in searching for one, and makes social obligations serve as a stop-gap measure. Like Samuel Johnson, George may often feel melancholic, and may even indulge the feeling for a time,[27] but always he returns to the conviction that man must find a way of utilizing his talents, however small. In part, one can see that Crabbe remains within the medieval, catholic tradition emphasizing man's collective responsibilities. The poem's resolution, with George finally escaping from his disease of introspection, to live within Richard's family, indicates that Crabbe is posing Christ's paradox—that to gain life, the individual must first lose it. The danger is that people such as George will come to consider any striving after an earthly ideal to be a waste of time, and therefore (perhaps a little like St. Paul) will give their sanction to all those obligations demanded by the state, however unjust. But as will be seen, Crabbe includes the portrait of Richard for exactly this reason—to challenge George's conservative sense of social responsibility.

In many of the stories, Crabbe portrays individuals who mirror aspects of George's attempt to live a solitary, retired life. For instance, in "The Cathedral Walk" Crabbe shows how a young woman, at the death of her lover, projects all her personal grief on the world at large:

> Then had I grief's proud thoughts, and said, in tone
> Of exultation, "World, I am alone!
> I care not for thee, thou art vile and base,
> And I shall leave thee for a nobler place."   (xx. 259–62)

In later years, she recognizes that her own attitude has helped "to make this odious world so sad a one" (xx. 268). In "The Maid's Story" much the same sentiment is voiced. When the maid begins to take stock of her life, she is at first pleased because she harms no one, but then is startled to find that her seemingly praiseworthy life is entirely negative, since she does not contribute anything to society. She then recalls another woman, Elizabeth Fry, whose virtues were positive rather than negative, and whose life was a "fight / With powers of darkness" (xi. 647–48). But Crabbe points out that to work for others is by no means as easy as it looks. First, the motives of those offering help are seldom pure, and second, the people being helped are often in no condition to bear the additional weight of charity. In describing the plight of the sisters cheated out of their competence by the dishonest bank manager, George comments:

> 'Tis true, the rapid turns of fortune's wheel
> Make even the virtuous and the humble feel:
> They for a time must suffer, and but few
> Can bear their sorrows and our pity too.   (viii. 39–42)

Thus the emphasis falls not upon an abstract principle—help the poor—but upon learning to see the poor as individuals whose needs are many, not the least of them being friendship. And friendship, of course, differs greatly from pity; for pity generally incorporates the assumption of superiority. As William Blake said, "Pity would be no more / If we did not make somebody Poor."[28]

While social responsibility or fellowship is certainly necessary to man's life, it is hardly sufficient. Few people find that the concept of duty is enough in itself to supply the *raison d'être* or even the energy for a full life. Religion has traditionally been the source of spiritual energy and goals, in that it offers a transcendent Good— God—that informs all temporal goals. But as might be expected from Crabbe's depiction of the clergyman-narrator in "The Parish Register," the main spokesman for religion in *Tales of the Hall*— Jacques—relegates the various types of religious individualism which stress the search for union with the Godhead to the counsels of perfection, and emphasizes instead the *religious* aspects of man's responsibility to his fellow men. Although his parishioners think Jacques misguided in his continual insistence on good works— " 'Heathens,' they said, 'can tell us right from wrong, / But to a Christian higher points belong' " (xiv. 23–24)—and nickname him the "*Moral Preacher*" (Crabbe's italics), Crabbe indicates that in large part he agrees with Jacques's emphasis on morality. From what his son says in the *Life*, Crabbe seems to have resembled Jacques.[29] While Crabbe complained that "men more imbued with a sense of the terrors of the Lord and less with his mercies, succeeded better" as pastors,[30] he obviously felt that his own function was to act as a guide in the duties of this life.

Even though Jacques suggests that responsible action can better man's condition, he also retains a strong Pauline sense that man must learn to live with his fallen nature, that suffering is a brute fact that cannot be dismissed and often cannot be mitigated. In this, of course he is simply echoing Article IX of the Church of England which states that without grace, man is doomed to a life of misery. At one point George asserts that man can do nothing but accept sorrow, and hope that his fortitude will be rewarded in the next world:

> Heaven would not all this wo for man intend
> If man's existence with his wo should end;
> Heaven would not pain, and grief, and anguish give,
> If man was not by discipline to live;
> And for that brighter, better world prepare. (VII. 781–85)

Yet this extreme view results from George's meditations at the deathbed of Rosabella, and soon proves transitory. Even though such stoicism is orthodox, *Tales of the Hall* seems to suggest that the discipline achieved by undergoing suffering brings rewards not only in the next world, but in this one as well, since the discipline allows individuals to participate more fully in human relationships and the life of the community.

In view of what has been said, it should be clear that religion does not play the degenerate role of a spiritual balm to man's worldly ills. The emphasis throughout *Tales of the Hall* is not on divine love, but on human love. In fact the secular orientation of the poem as a whole led John Wilson to comment: "There is, however, one point on which we cannot agree with Mr Crabbe, and on which we feel that we may, without arrogance, affirm that he is wrong. He has not made that use of religion in poetry which a poet, a philosopher, and a Christian such as he is, might—and ought to have made." Wilson felt that Crabbe's picture of man and society was imperfect because it failed to stress "the influence of religion on the whole structure of society and life."[31] Obviously Wilson is here referring to the effect of religion's abstract moral code of duties, and he is quite correct that in *Tales of the Hall*, these duties are rarely offered either as convincing motives to action or even as regulative influences on society. At most, the belief in a life hereafter is offered to the fatigued as consolation when the limited possibilities for happiness in this world have been exhausted.

A particularly good example of Crabbe's choice of secular and pragmatic goals rather than religious absolutes is displayed in Book XIV, "The Natural Death of Love." In this story, which tells of the slow loss of romantic love between Henry and Emma, Crabbe shows that the same standards used to measure social and material progress can be applied to individuals. Emma, when she discovers that the first bout of romantic love in her marriage to Henry has passed, becomes terribly upset, attempts to make Henry the guilty party, and accuses him of deception. Henry, however, takes a much more attentive view of the situation, and suggests that even though the first enthusiasm has gone, much can be emended. He then offers a surprising comparison between England's progress in economic prosperity and the state of a marriage, and suggests that they attempt the same plan in their own lives which has proved so successful in the country at large:

> There was a time when this heaven-guarded isle,
> Whose valleys flourish—nay, whose mountains smile—
> Was steril, wild, deform'd, and beings rude
> Creatures scarce wilder than themselves pursued.
> The sea was heard around a waste to howl;
> The night-wolf answer'd to the whooting owl;
> Amd all was wretched—Yet who now surveys
> The land, withholds his wonder and his praise?
> Come, let us try and make our moral view
> Improve like this—this have we power to do.
>
> (XIV. 393–402)

No mention is made here of marriage as a sacred institution or of the vows and obligations of the partners; instead Crabbe suggests that marriage, which begins with the untamed passions of romantic love, must be cultivated and improved over time, just as England itself had progressed from its dark times of barbarism. Crabbe of course shared with most people of his time a profound distaste for the time of the Civil War when religious strife had created chaos in the land, a feeling which is summed up in F. M. Eden's comment:

> From reviewing the aera of freedom which has
> practically existed since the Revolution, I should
> venture to assert, *a priori*, that the exercise of civil and
> religious liberty must, from the very nature of things,

have been attended with a proportionate acquisition of
social comforts; and that, not only the aggregate body
of the nation must have advanced to wealth and
independence, but that the portion of the community,
which consists of those who are emphatically called the
labouring classes, must have considerably bettered it's
condition in the course of the present century.[32]

In the story of Henry and Emma, Crabbe suggests that individuals
must progress beyond their first impulses of passion, which are
self-oriented, to build relationships which are based on mutual
recognition and which permit growth and change as situations
alter. Moreover, improvements in either social conditions or an
individual's "moral view" must stem from an awareness of the
existing problems. In the original MS version, Emma had said, "It
seems from fairy land we come / To this of truth!" The land of
truth, Emma finds, is "bleak and cold, / And all is dark and dull."[33]
Whereas in *The Village* Crabbe leaves one with the sense that it is
impossible to escape the darkness, except by means of a transcendent leap, *Tales of the Hall* modifies this considerably, since the
darkness is not entirely "other" but also a product of unperceptive
and uncritical intelligence. To perceive the extent to which man
both creates and is created by his external world is to introduce the
possibility of change.

III

The difficulty in achieving a balance between the position of the
social critic and that of the moralist—one reforming society and the
other, man—has been noted earlier. Part of the problem lies in
creating a tone of voice and a point of view that will permit the
author to express his feelings about the injustices of society and the
clouded perceptions of individuals without losing the intricate
connections between the two. In "William Bailey," Book XIX of
Tales of the Hall, Crabbe achieves a voice of narration that allows

him to adopt both roles, or rather to tell his story so that it can be seen in terms of either role. Because in "William Bailey" Crabbe's emphasis is on the emotions of the individual as they are excited by events in society his criticism has a personal rather than a social orientation, and this prevents the reader from seeing the story only as a model of the English social system emphasizing the injustice of class and the bad effects of paternal benevolence.

The story is briefly told. William and Fanny, two young lovers, are separated when Fanny goes on a visit to her aunt, the head housekeeper of a noble lord. While there, Fanny is seduced by the baron's son, runs away with him, and is eventually forsaken. Some years later, William meets Fanny again, and the two are happily married. However, this skeletal outline reveals little of the story's real interest. For instance, through his particularised portrait of the spinster aunt, Crabbe reveals the general dangers which result from a complacent acceptance of the established order. This spinster aunt has been with the family for such a long time that she feels herself a part of the establishment, and has become a devoted admirer of her master's efficient household where all the servants have their correct places and everyone receives his due reward:

> Now that good dame had in the castle dwelt
> So long that she for all its people felt;
> She kept her sundry keys, and ruled o'er all,
> Female and male, domestics in the hall;
> By her lord trusted, worthy of her trust;
> Proud but obedient, bountiful but just.
> She praised her lucky stars, that in her place
> She never found neglect, nor felt disgrace;
> To do her duty was her soul's delight,
> This her inferiors would to theirs excite,
> This her superiors notice and requite;
> To either class she gave the praises due,
> And still more grateful as more favour'd grew.
> Her lord and lady were of peerless worth,
> In power unmatch'd, in glory and in birth;

And such the virtue of the noble race,
It reach'd the meanest servant in the place.
All, from the chief attendant on my lord
To the groom's helper, had her civil word;
From Miss Montregor, who the ladies taught,
To the rude lad who in the garden wrought;
From the first favourite to the meanest drudge,
Were no such women, heaven should be her judge;
Whatever stains were theirs, let them reside
In that pure place, and they were mundified;
The sun of favour on their vileness shone,
And all their faults like morning mists were gone.

(XIX. 234–60)

In a military-minded way, the spinster has so fallen in love with the efficiency of the household that she is incapable of seeing anything but superficial external appearances. Because she has a good position, and the household flourishes, the aunt believes that the establishment is above criticism.

However, Crabbe submits the noble family to a test when the aunt invites her niece Fanny, a village beauty, to visit her at the hall, a visit which reveals some unexpected implications of the principle of subordination. When Fanny's beauty catches the eye of the baron's son, and he seduces her into running away with him for a gay adventure, Crabbe points out that the aunt, had she not been blinded by her false estimation of the family, could have seen Fanny's danger in time to warn her. The social ramifications are fully revealed when Crabbe introduces Fanny's father. A bold yeoman unawed by rank, Fanny's father is righteously angry when he seeks out his sister, Fanny's aunt:

Moved by his grief, the father sought the place,
Ask'd for his girl, and talk'd of her disgrace;
Spoke of the villain, on whose cursed head
He pray'd that vengeance might be amply shed.

(XIX. 398–401)

Even though he presents his sister with the facts, she still refuses to admit the baron's son capable of such a vile deed. She would rather ignore the incident than criticize the perfect establishment. She exclaims:

> The Lord be good! and O! the pains that come
> In limb and body—Brother, get you home!
> Your voice runs through me—every angry word,
> If he should hear it, would offend my lord.   (XIX. 413-16)

The pun on the word "lord" serves to underline Crabbe's point that the spinster aunt has substituted unthinking obedience to a system for genuine moral feelings. Like many apologists for the class system she has equated God's order with the existing order.[34]

Crabbe's portrayal of the meeting between the baron and Fanny's father demonstrates that the poor had little means of redress from the wealthy. The scene is carefully presented to bring out the baron's belief that he is a being of superior order who need not account for his actions:

> My lord appear'd, perhaps by pity moved,
> And kindly said he no such things approved;
> Nay, he was angry with the foolish boy,
> Who might his pleasures at his ease enjoy;
> The thing was wrong—he hoped the farm did well—
> The angry father doom'd the farm to hell;
> He then desired to see the villain-son,
> Though my lord warn'd him such excess to shun;
> Told him he pardon'd, though he blamed such rage,
> And bade him think upon his state and age.
> "Think! yes, my lord! but thinking drives me mad—
> Give me my child!—Where is she to be had?
> I'm old and poor, but I with both can feel,
> And so shall he that could a daughter steal!"
> . . . .
> My lord replied—"I'm sorry, from my soul!
> But boys are boys, and there is no control."—

> "So, for your great ones Justice slumbers, then!
> If men are poor they must not feel as men—
> Will your son marry?"—"Marry!" said my lord,
> "Your daughter?—marry—no, upon my word!"
> "What then, our stations differ!—but your son
> Thought not of that—his crime has made them one,
> In guilt united—She shall be his wife,
> Or I th' avenger that will take his life!" (XIX. 421–50)

The baron's reaction to the accusation is one of pity. For him the question of justice does not arise since Fanny is a member of the lower orders.[35] The passage brings out clearly the injustices inherent in a situation where the rich act as if they were the masters of the poor. Paternalism and philanthropy may work well enough at times, but they are only second-best. Justice is required; not pity.

The baron, who believes that Fanny's father is wrong in daring to accuse him of injustice, advises him in the same way a clergyman might advise one of his flock; indeed, the baron believes himself to be in the same sort of relation to the poor as God is to man:

> "Old man, I pity and forgive you; rest
> In hope and comfort—be not so distress'd;
> Things that seem bad oft happen for the best.
> The girl has done no more than thousands do,
> Nor has the boy—they laugh at me and you."—
> "And this my vengeance—curse him!"—"Nay, forbear;
> I spare your frenzy, in compassion spare."
>
> (XIX. 451–57)

The incident, which ends with the baron acting out the role of a compassionate, paternalistic overlord, effectively reduces the vengeance of Fanny's father to impotent curses.

While presenting this scene between the baron and Fanny's father with what appears to be high seriousness and a genuine concern for the lot of the poor, Crabbe deliberately refuses to draw the social conclusions implicit in the argument, and even leaves the reader wondering if the baron's worldly view of the matter does not contain some sound wisdom. After all, Fanny is old enough to know better. Crabbe leaves the story of the parents at this ambiguous point, and proceeds with the stories of William and Fanny. One of the results of Fanny's seduction is that William, her former lover, falls into the company of Radicals. In the work of a socially committed writer, William—a poor country boy—would have attempted to take revenge for the loss of his Fanny to the nobility by overthrowing the class system through revolutionary action. But Crabbe has William reject the Radicals. Indeed, at the end of the poem the high passions and the even higher ideals of the parents are dispelled when William ends his journey after meeting Fanny, now the virtuous keeper of a respectable public house, appropriately named "The Fleece."

William and Fanny may be star-crossed lovers kept apart by the machinations of a wicked aristocracy, but their marriage as keepers of the Fleece is anything but exalted. The general image of the publican is that of a person with no strong opinions of his own, but willing to listen and agree to the ideas of anyone who stops for refreshment,[36] and in this respect William and Fanny are the ideal innkeepers:

> This pair, our host and hostess of the Fleece,
> Command some wealth, and smile at its increase;
> Saving and civil, cautious and discreet,
> All sects and parties in their mansion meet;
> There from their chapels teachers go to share
> The creature-comforts—mockery grins not there;
> There meet the wardens at their annual feast,
> With annual pun—"the parish must be fleeced";
> There traders find a parlour cleanly swept
> For their reception, and in order kept;
> And there the sons of labour, poor, but free,
> Sit and enjoy their hour of liberty.   (XIX. 716–27)

The attitude in this passage is almost Pickwickian. Misfortune, although acknowledged, never lasts, and is completely overshadowed by the presence of contentment.

The entire passage, however, is undercut with irony. The chapel preachers can frequent the Fleece without fear of mockery, because the owners have no wish to lose their trade, and thus do not "mock" the preachers' pretended abstinence. The use of the euphemism "creature-comforts" instead of the blunt word "ale" underlines the falseness of their position. The churchwardens at their annual feast are probably only too correct in their pun. The penultimate line, with its rather pompous "sons of labour" contrasts oddly with the earlier description of the poor whom William had met on the road. The workers are said to be "poor, but free"; only in the following line do we see how free they are. Their hour in the inn is "their hour of liberty," the implication being that the remainder of the time they are captives.

The reviewer for *The Monthly Review* complained that the ending to "William Bailey" was gross:

> The story of "*William Bailey*" is not, we think, so good
> in its moral effect as the great majority of Mr. Crabbe's
> productions. Here is a virtuous attachment broken off
> by the subsequent immodesty of the female; and, not
> contented with destroying all the *romance* of love, by
> representing, after the lapse of years, the offending
> beauty as the fat landlady at "*The Fleece*," the poet
> makes the poor tame contented lover reunite himself to
> his worthless mistress, and actually become her deserving
> and happy husband! These may be *ale-house politics*:
> but certainly we see neither poetic justice nor manly
> feeling in the composition.[37]

But the reviewer, like many of Crabbe's critics, seems to have completely missed the large element of humour in the story. At the beginning of the tale Crabbe portrays both Frances and William with a good deal of the comic about them. About William, Crabbe says, "His placid looks an easy mind confess'd; / His smile content, and seldom more, convey'd" (XIX. 132–33). At the end of the tale Crabbe seems to be saying that "ale-house politics" are suitable for alehouse keepers.[38] What misled the reviewer for *The Monthly*

Review into feeling that Crabbe has given the tale a dubious moral ending was his failure to see how Crabbe very often combines the serious and the humorous within a single story. Jeffrey noted that "'William Bailey' . . . is curiously and characteristically compounded of pathos and pleasantry,—affecting incidents, and keen and sarcastic remarks."[39] The point is that in a tale such as "William Bailey," Fanny and William are never allowed to become tragic victims; the social criticism is unable to dominate the poem since it arises out of situations in which the characters themselves live out their lives in the comedy of day-to-day existence. Crabbe's emphasis is not on the "customs and laws, and institutions of society," but as *Blackwood's* commented so perceptively, on the "passions" of individuals as they are "excited and exacerbated" by the social conditions.[40] Whereas in the first half of the tale Crabbe is the critic of social conditions who points out the injustices of the class system, in the second half he is the moralist who describes individuals reconciling themselves to these conditions and achieving happiness in spite of them. It is rare to find a poet such as Crabbe with enough vision, detachment, and humour to create characters who—although the victims of social injustice—possess the comic potential to triumph over their circumstances.

IV

I wish now to turn from individual stories of *Tales of the Hall* to a discussion of the frame story—the meeting between Richard and George—for it is from the portrayal of the brothers' personal and social problems that *Tales of the Hall* derives much of its unity and cohesiveness. This is not only because the brothers' meeting is the occasion that calls into being the individual stories, but also because the stories are told in part to resolve the problems between the brothers. Thus, it is in the frame story that Crabbe offers solutions—private though they may be—to the doubts raised throughout the poem about the extent of man's knowledge of his motivation, about the clarity of his perceptions, and about his ability to participate in community.

One of the reasons why the portrayal of the brothers George and Richard has such immediacy and strength of detail, and is therefore able to inform the other stories, is that Crabbe divides his own ambivalent opinions and feelings between them. In addition, the depiction of the two brothers has its source in the events of Crabbe's life at this time. The integrity of form and content in Crabbe's poems always seems to benefit when the setting or structure arises out of his personal experience. In December 1816, Crabbe arranged for his younger son John and John's wife Anna to come and live with him at the rectory in Trowbridge.[41] In a letter to Miss Elizabeth Charter, Crabbe described them in much the same way that he portrayed Richard and Matilda in *Tales of the Hall*: "My Son is an affectionate Husband and I think the young pair have never been parted for more than a few hours since they married."[42] Like George in *Tales of the Hall*, Crabbe hated to live alone, and for some years after the death of his wife he considered remarrying. His own state of mind as described to Miss Charter— "My foolish heart at this Time and in spite of Reason and Experience, wants Kindness, Sympathy, Affection"[43]—obviously resembles that depicted in the lonely old bachelor, George. For a time it looked as though Crabbe might marry Miss Charlotte Ridout,[44] but in the end he decided against marriage at his age, and like George in *Tales of the Hall*, settled down comfortably with his family. The interesting point, however, is that Crabbe chose not to transpose this situation entirely to *Tales of the Hall*, thereby giving George, the older brother, his own beliefs, but to alter the situation so as to divide his personality among a number of people. In so doing, he created a narrative structure in which several characters share aspects of his own beliefs.

Both Richard, especially in the details of his youth by the sea, and Jacques, in his religious beliefs, bear similarities to Crabbe. And indeed the point is not to attempt to identify Crabbe with any one character, but to observe his sympathetic involvement with totally different characters, and his ability to give an understanding of the reasons why they hold their different points of view.[45] This refusal to identify wholly with any one point of view, central to *Tales of the Hall,* quickly becomes evident in the rhetorical structure Crabbe employs to set up his frame story at the beginning of the poem. He creates a type of political allegory,[46] in which George, the rich elder brother retired to Binning Hall, is described in Tory terminology while Richard, the poor relation, is given Whig sympathies. Since Crabbe's eldest son has stated that in later life Crabbe slowly abandoned his "popular or liberal opinions" as he imbibed "aristocratic and Tory leanings,"[47] and since the relation between the two brothers of *Tales of the Hall* is similar to that of Crabbe to his son John, one might naturally assume that the older brother of *Tales of the Hall* represents Crabbe's own position. Yet this is only partially correct, since Crabbe never allows the brothers merely to represent political ideas; rather the political ideas inform the two brothers, helping to describe and define their different personalities. In this way neither brother can be altogether right, since the political opinions of each result naturally and inevitably from background and temperament.

It may be helpful to pause here for a moment to explore briefly Crabbe's own political position, not because *Tales of the Hall* is obscure, but because in the past it has often been read in the light of what was thought to be Crabbe's position, and this has resulted in over-simplification. The first thing to observe is that Crabbe was not a highly political individual; his son mentions that he had no particular interests in politics. Yet it was impossible for a man in Crabbe's position not to develop some political attitudes, however vague. Crabbe held three votes,[48] and since he was often called upon to use them, presumably he was forced to make political decisions. Crabbe's son, it will be remembered, felt that Crabbe forsook his early liberal opinions to become something of a Tory in his old age, and certainly several of Crabbe's acquaintances, Lockhart included, believed that Crabbe was a strong Tory. In a letter to John Wilson Croker of 26 January, 1835, suggesting that Crabbe's son should be given some sort of government place, Lockhart warned Croker that Crabbe's son, "unlike his father," was "a bit of a Whig."[49] Yet other evidence is not so clear. Although Crabbe seconded Croker's nomination in an election at Aldborough in 1826, this seems to have been a spur-of-the-moment action. Croker asked him as a friend to do so, and Crabbe complied, "in very few words."[50] In 1816 at a Trowbridge election, however, Crabbe supported John Benett of Pyt House, nominally a Whig.

Although Crabbe appears to have become temperamentally conservative as he grew older, he never rejected attempts to introduce democratic measures. Two years before publication of *Tales of the Hall*, in the midst of reform propaganda and the East Anglia bread riots, he expressed in a letter to Miss Elizabeth Charter his belief in the country's general sanity: "You ask my opinion of the Times. I cannot give a satisfactory one but I dread no Insurrections, no Hunts, no Cobbetts; and I hope cheerfully, and I have comfort in the Benevolence and morality of the country in general."[51] Crabbe seems to have kept himself detached not only from political parties but from political questions as well. As late as 1831 he was unable to make up his mind about the greatest issue of the day, parliamentary reform. He wrote to his son George:

> In Government, in Religion[,] In many things that
> intimately relate to Man's Happiness, Man is not able
> to decide what is to be wished or preferred: I[t?] would
> be most distressing to me to be called upon to decide on
> the Questions of Church Property, Parliamentary
> Reform, or what Kind of Government is best suited to
> the Welfare etc. of this Country; but I may rest
> contented: these Matters will not be determined in my
> Time—nor in Yours—at least so I think but they may
> be agitated at least so I—fear?[52]

Nor were Crabbe's fears of agitation groundless; while staying with his friends the Hoares at Clifton in October 1831, he witnessed the Bristol riots.

However, in a curiously detached and farsighted manner, he saw that the actual contents of the Reform Bill would not be cause for great jubilation or alarm to either party: "With some it is ruin; with others it is renovation; neither my hopes or fears are very strong; the lower class of our brethren can be but little affected by the bill, whatever they may be by the effects of it, and of those effects who has foresight enough to determine?"[54] The historian E. L. Woodward has confirmed Crabbe's opinion of the bill in his statement that neither Whigs nor Tories had any understanding "that the greatest changes resulting from the reform bill would take place outside parliament and in the sphere of administration."[55] Unlike Tories such as Croker, Crabbe never seems to have been frightened by the idea of a reformed parliament.[56]

In October 1831, two weeks after the House of Lords had thrown the country into consternation by rejecting the second bill,[57] Crabbe wrote cheerfully to his son George that he felt the Whig ministers would manage to reconcile the opposition to the reforms: "I believe there is a fund of good sense as well as moral feeling in the people of this country; and if ministers proceed steadily, give up some points, and be firm in essentials, there will be a union of sentiment on this great subject of reform by and by; at least, the good and well-meaning will drop their minor differences and be united."[58] Staunch Tories such as Lockhart and Croker would have been sadly disillusioned in their belief in Crabbe's Toryism had they known of his easy acceptance of the Reform Bill.

Huchon has deduced from this last letter that Crabbe was both in favour of the Reform Bill and that he remained a "Liberal up to his last moments."[59] However, when Crabbe wrote his letter of 24 October, the mood of the people was dangerous; meetings supporting the government were taking place throughout the country. It was clear to all that the bill had the genuine support of most of the country, and that continued conflict was likely to produce civil war. The evidence would suggest that Crabbe held no strong opinions on the subject of parliamentary reform,[60] but once the passage of the bill became inevitable, he wished to see compromise among right-thinking politicians so that Earl Grey would be assured of a majority in the House of Lords.

It is probably true that, as Lockhart believed, Crabbe's son was more of a liberal than Crabbe himself. In one of Crabbe's manuscript sermons in the John Murray archive, someone has changed in pencil Crabbe's original sentiments:

> They submit and bear as Christians whatsoever is
> necessarily connected with that State of Life to which
> it has pleased God to call them. They are as the
> Disciples of their Saviour Humble in Station, humble in
> Heart, Mind. And yet with this Humility, they know that
> with the greatest & most wealthy of their Fellow Sinners,
> they shall stand at the Judgment Seat of Christ. . . .

In the first sentence the words "submit and" have been deleted. The entire second sentence has been deleted and replaced by: "Knowing that Religion does not forbid them bettering that State could they do so by Lawful Means."[61] What seems to have happened here is that when Crabbe's son decided to use the sermon, he introduced changes to make it agreeable to his own democratic feelings.[62] Crabbe's sermons, it may be noted, were always orthodox in their teaching of humility.

Crabbe, however, seems to defy the attempts of critics to pigeonhole his beliefs. While in London in 1818, he witnessed the hotly contested Westminster election in which the Tory Sir Murray Maxwell was challenged by the Radical Sir Francis Burdett and the liberal reformer Sir Samuel Romilly. Crabbe commented: "I was in Covent Garden during most part of the Contest, but was perfectly quiet and walked through the great Collection of people as calmly and undisturbed as if they had known how insignificant and indifferent I was; yet not so entirely, I had a secret wish or two for my Friend Sir Sam: Romilly who does me the Honour of both saying and doing very kind Things."[63] Crabbe seems to have been one of those independent country gentlemen who gave their allegiances to the candidate rather than the party. In a letter of 1827 he remarked that he "felt considerable respect" for both sides, and wished to see time and good feeling soften "the spirit of animosity that now reigns among them."[64]

In *Tales of the Hall* Crabbe expresses his characteristic social ambivalence, not in terms of one character who represents all the tensions, but in terms of a number of characters, with each being allotted one point of view—a primary fictional device of the nineteenth-century novel. With such a structure, the poem clearly cannot become an argument for any one ideal. This does not mean that *Tales of the Hall* cannot advocate social changes. However, the need for and possibility of such changes are seen, not in abstract political terms, but in terms of individual attitudes and convictions arising from background and experience.

The presentation of George and Richard in terms of their differences in social background is especially interesting, because at the beginning it looks as though these differences might be divisive, but by the end of the poem this proves not to be the case. As will be seen, the brothers are not presented as mere stereotypes; over a period of time they come to recognize the irrational basis for their beliefs, and this permits meaningful change.

Of the two brothers, Richard, who has lived an adventurous life at sea among men who naturally saw their enemy as the established order, is predisposed towards a Whig view of history. George is a disappointed lover who has spent his life in commerce, and he favours the Tories. Crabbe indicates that even heredity has a part in forming a person's opinions. Richard and George, it will be recalled, are only half-brothers. When George's father died his mother married an Irishman. Throughout the poem Crabbe alludes to Richard's Irish blood as a possible reason for his spontaneous compassion for his fellow men.

As has been noted earlier, George's religious beliefs are formed late in life after many years as a successful businessman, and after his hopes for romantic love with all its associations of an individual discipline through Eros have been disillusioned. Quite naturally he distrusts individual responses and looks to the firm structure of institutions for support and guidance. In religion George is definitely a churchman, although by no means a fanatic:

> GEORGE loved to think; but, as he late began
> To muse on all the grander thoughts of man,
> He took a solemn and a serious view
> Of his religion, and he found it true;
> Firmly, yet meekly, he his mind applied
> To this great subject, and was satisfied.   (I. 126–31)

George does not believe everything the rector preaches, but finding himself in agreement with the fundamentals, he accepts the Established Church as the institution most closely approximating the truth:

> The church he view'd as liberal minds will view,
> And there he fix'd his principles and pew.   (I. 138–39)

In politics as in religion George finds that the existing institutions are best.[65] He dislikes the thought of government by the majority, and believes that "the public good" must be in "private care." Naturally he recoils from the Jacobins or any of the workers' movements demanding a revolution in the government of England:

> George loved the cause of freedom, but reproved
> All who with wild and boyish ardour loved:
> Those who believed they never could be free,
> Except when fighting for their liberty
> . . . .
> For, public blessings firmly to secure,
> We must a lessening of the good endure.   (I. 146–55)

While pointing out that George believes his conservatism to be reasonable, not blind and reactionary, Crabbe also pokes fun at George's desire to be thought a liberal conservative. After describing George's attitude to the political needs of the nation, Crabbe says:

> The constitution was the ark that he
> Join'd to support with zeal and sanctity;
> Nor would expose it, as th' accursed son
> His father's weakness, to be gazed upon.   (I. 168–71)

The verb "expose" carries a double meaning. Knowing that the constitution has weak points, George refuses to bring it into the open where its exposure would allow people to see these weaknesses. It is indeed a weak constitution that cannot bear discussion. This passage, like the previous one in which George fixed his "principles and pew," contains a good deal of irony which should alert the reader that George is by no means entirely Crabbe's mouthpiece.

As has been observed earlier in this chapter, Crabbe believed that habit played as important a role as reason in forming men's beliefs in politics and religion. Although George thinks he has superior reasons for choosing one church over another—"He saw— he thought he saw—how weakness, pride, / And habit, draw seceding crowds aside" (I. 140–41)—the emphasis lies on the phrase "he thought he saw." George may believe he is uninfluenced by habits in his choice of religion, but the reader easily sees that his temperament as much as his reason influenced him. In a letter to a friend, Crabbe commented that people often gave their assent to religious principles for causes "independent of any merit of their own."[66]

Richard, as Jeffrey notes, is in many ways the opposite, or rather the complement, of George, being "more open, social and talkative —a happy husband and father, with a tendency to Whiggism, and some notion of reform."[67] In religion Richard is not altogether a sectarian, but his openness does contain a strong mixture of sectarian views:

> By nature generous, open, daring, free,
> The vice he hated was hypocrisy.
> Religious notions, in her latter years,
> His mother gave, admonish'd by her fears;
> To these he added, as he chanced to read
> A pious work or learn a christian creed.
> He heard the preacher by the highway side,
> The church's teacher, and the meeting's guide;
> And, mixing all their matters in his brain,

> Distill'd a something he could ill explain;
> But still it served him for his daily use,
> And kept his lively passions from abuse;
> For he believed, and held in reverence high,
> The truth so dear to man—"not all shall die." (I. 220–33)

Crabbe's own position as a vicar of the Church of England, and the satiric references to the enthusiasm of Dissenters in his early poems,[68] should not blinker one to the fact that Richard is presented as a sympathetic character. In politics, indeed in all public affairs, Richard hates arbitrary authority, and strongly advocates freedom and liberty. Naturally enough, Jeffrey and others of his time saw him as a Whig:

> He spake of freedom as a nation's cause,
> And loved, like George, our liberty and laws;
> But had more youthful ardour to be free,
> And stronger fears for injured liberty.
> With him, on various questions that arose,
> The monarch's servants were the people's foes;
> And, though he fought with all a Briton's zeal,
> He felt for France as Freedom's children feel;
> Went far with her in what she thought reform,
> And hail'd the revolutionary storm. (I. 240–49)

Quite clearly, Richard's forced self-reliance in his youth has given him faith in the individual's own abilities to shape afresh the direction of his life, and this predisposes him to support new political solutions.

This is not the entire story, however, since in his depiction of Richard, Crabbe does not create the strong Whig that he might have done. Although at the beginning, Richard's dislike of the king's power and his zeal for revolutionary France make him appear almost a Radical, his radicalism is given a sudden twist when unexpectedly he refuses to apply his principles to England:

> Yet would not here, where there was least to win,
> And most to lose, the doubtful work begin;
> But look'd on change with some religious fear,
> And cried, with filial dread, "Ah! come not here."
>
> (I. 250–53)

Jeffrey mentioned that Richard had "some notion of reform," and although the general picture of Richard's optimism supports this idea, Crabbe has actually shown Richard to fear reform in England almost as much as does George—for he "look'd on change with some religious fear." While Richard is certainly the forward-looking, optimistic sort of person to whom ideas for reform would appeal, his interest proves to be solely theoretical since he will not "the doubtful work begin." He appears to be a gentleman's idea of a "decent" democrat.

In fact Crabbe may well be describing the period of his own youth in Richard's zeal for the early years of the French Revolution.[69] The emphasis upon opposition to the "monarch's servants" recalls the reforming idiom of the 1780s rather than that of the first decades of the nineteenth century, and brings to mind such events as Dunning's famous resolution carried in committee in the House of Commons, "that the influence of the Crown has increased, is increasing and ought to be diminished."[70] Later, in Book XXII, Crabbe again uses this reforming idiom to characterize the difference between a Whig and a Tory squire (XXII. 164–67). Certainly in 1819 the power of the monarch was no longer the reformer's principal objection, so that Crabbe is probably thinking of a late eighteenth- rather than an early nineteenth-century setting for the frame-story.

Although Crabbe obviously meant George and Richard, with their differences in religion and politics, to represent opposing philosophies of life, it is important to notice that he continually qualifies their beliefs so that serious arguments do not arise. Originally Crabbe had intended the differences between the two brothers to be much greater than they now appear. This can be seen especially in Book IV when Richard and George, who are out walking, hear a shot. In the original manuscript version, George is provoked to a vehement condemnation of poachers:

> "That gun itself, that breaks upon the ear,
> Has something suited to the dying year."
> "The dying partridge!" cried, with much disdain,
> Th' offended 'Squire—"Our laws are made in vain:
> The country, Richard, would not be amiss,
> But for these plagues, and villanies like this."[71]

But in the final version George merely comments innocuously on the pleasures of his model farm. Possibly Crabbe omitted George's diatribe against poachers as being out of keeping with the theme of "Smugglers and Poachers." Had the passage been retained, George would have appeared so reactionary that readers would have drawn a comparison between him and the squire of "Smugglers and Poachers" who set the lives of partridges above the lives of men.

An even more important alteration of this type occurs a few lines further on. At line 88 in the published version, George asks Richard to observe the breeding improvements in his flock of sheep. After doing so Richard candidly asks whether such agricultural interests actually give pleasure, and George replies honestly that although worthwhile, they do not bring him much joy. Here the discussion ends. However, in the original manuscript, the passage is quite different, for when Richard first asks the question, George pretends that his flock gives him great satisfaction, and only when Richard repeats his question does George admit to being uninterested in sheep. George then melodramatically demands what, if anything, can hold man's interest. Richard replies:

> "Suppose," said he, "we look about the green,
> In younder cots some objects may be seen,
> T' excite our pity, or relieve our spleen."[72]

Richard is here obviously suggesting that philanthropy will give George an interest, but surprisingly, this suggestion angers George, and an argument ensues:

"Oh! they are thieves and blockheads," George replied,
"Unjust, ungrateful, and unsatisfied;
To grasp at all, their study, thought, and care,
All would be thieves and plunderers, if they dare;
His envious nature not a clown conceals,
But bluntly shows the insolence he feels."
    "And whence," said Richard, "should the vice proceed,
But from their want of knowledge, and their need?
Let them know more, or let them better feel,
And I'll engage they'll neither threat nor steal."
    "Brother," said George, "your pity makes you blind
To all that's vile and odious in mankind;
'Tis true your notions may appear divine,
But for their justice—let us go and dine."[73]

Richard's question has spurred George on to show some of his true
Tory colours, so that when he denounces the poor as "thieves and
blockheads" he appears in a most unsympathetic light. What
particularly angers him is that the poor refuse to show proper
respect and gratitude when given charity.

Thus, in the manuscript version, George's rather theoretical and
melodramatic question about the tragic fate of man soon becomes
a bitter discussion of practicalities, in which Richard gives his
brother some projects to "fix the mind of man." Whereas Richard
obviously believes that one can find completely self-justifying
projects to better social conditions, George follows much more in
the tradition of Samuel Johnson in his belief in the vanity of all
human wishes. That Crabbe deleted this incident in which genuine
disagreement occurs between the brothers is significant, for in so
doing he modified both George's view—that the poor were
naturally evil—and Richard's view—that they were naturally good.
Obviously erroneous, both views lead to action which is unworkable: Richard's pity leads to Godwinian perfectionism while
George's anger leads to houses of correction.[74]

    In softening the quarrel between Richard and George so that they
could later live together as men of good will, Crabbe doubtlessly

created a less interesting confrontation and denied himself the
sort of fireworks to be found in the vituperative battles between
Blackwood's and *The Edinburgh Review*. But Crabbe himself had
come to believe that such ideological battles were superficial if they
did not take into account the historical situation and the direction
of change already in process within the country. The following
letter is particularly interesting for what it shows of Crabbe's
awareness that effectiveness in political action depended upon the
individual's ability to understand and modify the direction of
change inherent in the state's own growth:

> With respect to the parties themselves, Whig and Tory,
> I can but think, two dispassionate, sensible men, who
> have seen, read, and observed, will approximate in their
> sentiments more and more; and if they confer together,
> and argue,—not to convince each other, but for pure
> information, and with a simple desire for the truth,—the
> ultimate difference will be small indeed. The Tory, for
> instance, would allow that, but for the Revolution in
> this country, and the noble stand against the arbitrary
> steps of the house of Stuart, the kingdom would have
> been in danger of becoming what France once was;
> and the Whig must also grant, that there is at least an
> equal danger in an unsettled, undefined democracy;
> the ever-changing laws of a popular government. Every
> state is at times on the inclination to change: either the
> monarchical or the popular interest will predominate;
> and in the former case, I conceive, the well-meaning
> Tory will incline to Whiggism,—in the latter, the honest
> Whig will take the part of declining monarchy. [75]

This sense of an evolutionary form of government may well owe
something to the ideas of Burke, although Crabbe gives the notion
his own cast of mind when he suggests that the movement is more
cyclical than progressive.

What is more, it would be a mistake to see the sorts of changes
introduced into the characters of George and Richard merely as

manipulations to bring them in line with Crabbe's own beliefs. Rather, these changes are the result of what happens in the rest of the poem, where Crabbe shows that George and Richard have been thinking about their motives for some time, and thus have become acquainted with the sorts of influences operating on character. Although in his first conception of the poem, the brothers were fairly static in their dispositions, Crabbe soon came to see that the device of storytelling demanded that the brothers tell something of their own lives as well as the lives of others. As a result, actions which at any one time are mysteriously and unpredictably associated with inner states of mind and outward circumstances become explicable in terms of patterns of behaviour. In this way George and Richard are given a degree of freedom, because over a period of time they can observe their beliefs under the pressure of new experience and in the light of their own self-awareness. In extending the bewildering existential instant of time into duration, Crabbe reveals the hidden patterns of behaviour—a factor that was usually missing in his earlier satiric sketches.

This lack of change was particularly noticeable in *The Village* where it seemed impossible to improve the terrible living conditions because all the inhabitants were victims, and no one was able to rise above his fallen nature. It will be recalled that there Crabbe had introduced Robert Manners as a type of pastoral solution. In *Tales of the Hall* Crabbe still occasionally portrays individuals totally without self-knowledge and therefore incapable of change, but now these portrayals serve as foils to the characters who do change. Book X offers a particularly good example, for here Jacques and Maria find their happiness threatened by their parents' blind political hatred. In this case, political beliefs become irrational tools to create a specious self-identity and to bludgeon others into submission. But in his characterization of Richard and George, Crabbe ensures that the political opposites permit resolution once the individuals realize that their beliefs result as much from emotion as from reason.

In part of course Crabbe builds into the poem his own solution by showing George and Richard—conservative and liberal—

reaching an understanding, but an understanding that ignores the entire radical point of view. In purely aesthetic terms, this need not be a flaw, for every artist must select and omit. Yet one can still ask whether the poem gives a faithful picture of the times, and since Crabbe's resolution between the brothers leaves out the radical point of view, it might seem to be flawed. However, this question turns out to be bogus when examined closely, for the artist, especially the artist working with characters, can never be expected to give *the* picture of the time, only *a* picture. For instance, one of the reasons for Jane Austen's success in creating such a believable picture of rural England at the turn of the century is that her fictional perspective and its implied values are exactly right for the section of the community which she describes. About the problems of the very poor and the very rich she says nothing directly. Thus within the confines of her social world Jane Austen can describe how self-awareness, sensitivity, and knowledge of convention almost always lead to the correct social and personal choice. But when the order inherent in Jane Austen's world disappears, as is the case in the novels of Scott and the Brontës, who deal with a much wider spectrum of life, then Jane Austen's resolution is no longer possible, since the personal solution can be at odds with the requirements for social success. In Crabbe's case his portrayal of England is partly through the two brothers George and Richard, and their resolution is convincing, because it is in terms of their needs and requirements. But in the course of their storytelling, the brothers introduce many other characters, and the question arises as to how the brothers' solution can apply to these people. Yet Crabbe makes no attempt to give their answer a general application. Rather, he insists on each character solving, or not solving, his particular problems in terms of his own personal and social expectations. What the brothers' response suggests is that others can also succeed in solving their difficulties.

It is surprising to find how many similarities *Tales of the Hall* has to Wordsworth's *Excursion*, but in *The Excursion* the many stories about the lower classes told by the Wanderer and the Pastor all support their own philosophies of life. Where *Tales of the Hall* is stronger is that George, Richard, and Jacques tell stories of individuals who seek, but are not always able to find, a satisfactory way of life. The Maid finds love after a life of turmoil, but Ruth is forced to commit suicide. And as has been seen, Robert and James kill one another. While *The Excursion* soon begins to pall, because every situation is manipulated to teach the same doctrine, *Tales of the Hall* offers a wide diversity of stories, and becomes truly polycentric.

Indeed, Crabbe even introduces the subject of revolution into the story of William Bailey. As a self-educated farmhand who has taught himself both to read and to write, William is the type who might easily be swayed by radical ideas. Heartbroken at the news of Fanny's seduction, William leaves his farm to wander the country. Proud, self-taught, a member of the lower class, William seems the logical person to turn Radical.

During his wanderings William first meets many of the poor who teach him something of their problems—"And from the sick, the poor, the halt, the blind, / He learn'd the sorrows of his suffering kind" (XIX. 529–30). And this appears a good introduction for his subsequent meeting with some Radicals who, dissatisfied with their lot in life, blame the unjust state of society for their miserable existence:

> There were who spoke in terms of high disdain
> Of their contending against power in vain;
> Suffering from tyranny of law long borne;
> And life's best spirits in contentions worn.
> Happy in this, th' oppressors soon will die,
> Each with the vex'd and suffering man to lie—
> And thus consoled exclaim, "And is not sorrow dry?"
>
> (XIX. 546–52)

The passage is slightly ambiguous, since the reader is unsure whether or not Crabbe agrees that the law tyrannized people. But even if these Radicals were oppressed, the humour implicit in the last line—"And is not sorrow dry?"—dissolves the social criticism in irony. In an instant the dissatisfied vagrants are reduced from serious Radicals to idlers and cadgers.

Although William listens sympathetically to the oppressed, he rejects any suggestion that violence would help to change the social order. Any talk of revolutionary violence is labelled vice:

> But vice offended: when he met with those
> Who could a deed of violence propose,
> And cry, "Should they what we desire possess?
> Should they deprive us, and their laws oppress?"
> William would answer, "Ours is not redress."—
> "Would you oppression, then, for ever feel?"—
> "'Tis not my choice; but yet I must not steal."—
> "So, first they cheat us, and then make their laws
> To guard their treasures and to back their cause:
> What call you then, my friend, the rights of man?"—
> "To get his bread," said William, "if he can;
> And if he cannot, he must then depend
> Upon a Being he may make his friend."—
> "Make!" they replied; and conference had end.
>
> (XIX. 553–66)

The Radicals' proposal that William should join them in violent protest is not an idle one, and can be seen as a serious threat when viewed against the Luddite uprisings of 1812–13, and the East Anglia bread riots of 1816. The way in which William brusquely dismisses suggestions of violence, however, indicates that Crabbe had little sympathy with rioters and incendiaries.

Even though Crabbe does not give the Radicals a good hearing, he does not reject and abuse them as did the Tory periodicals of the time. William, it is true, refuses to join them. But then, they also refuse to join William. The argument comes to a head over the basic issues of the rights of man.[76] When William contends that the unemployed have no other recourse but to pray to God for help, the Radicals refuse to listen. A snort of defiance is all William receives when he tells them to turn to God. The argument ends with William's orthodox but unfeeling observation that the Radicals should attempt to make God their friend, the implication being that there will be no human intercession.

The curious feature of this passage is that the dialogue between William and the Radicals by no means settles any questions. The reader is left with the feeling that the Radicals deserve a better answer than William was able to give. This is not to claim that Crabbe supports the Radicals' call to violence, for obviously he does not; but on the other hand, the manner of presentation of the incident leaves William's reply in favour of passive obedience wholly inadequate. [77] Although William, and presumably Crabbe also, wants to label the violent proposals of the poor as "vice," clearly this will not do as an answer to all their proposals. But William has obviously little more than his commonplace with which to defend himself.

While it is apparent that Crabbe has not given the radical point of view enough of an airing to make the poem an adequate account of radicalism, it should be clear by now why Crabbe characterizes the Radical as he does. Crabbe saw Radicals in much the same terms as he saw zealous Christians: as individuals who had undergone a conversion to some larger belief in which their individuality was subsumed. Such people attempt to apply the abstract principles of their newfound faith to all problems in the world around them. For the religious zealot this conversion implies salvation through adherence to the letter of God's law; for the Radical, earthly utopia through violent overthrow of the established order. Since in both cases such people are unable to see clearly either their own motives or the details of the problem before them, they cannot act judiciously. For Crabbe to have presented a great number of Radicals in this context would have meant presenting satiric pasteboard figures; as has already been observed, in *Tales of the Hall* Crabbe has moved beyond such two-dimensional characterization.

At the same time, Crabbe's omission of a serious treatment of hard-line Radicals does not necessarily mean that the poem contains no radical implications. In his emphasis on the need for individuals to make private assessments of their own needs and desires in relation to the world around them, Crabbe's portrayals of the primacy of the individual's perceptions reflect the most radical element of democratic institutions. Moreover, in his presentation of lower-class people, Crabbe shows how much they have to offer the upper classes. In fact, throughout the poem it is the lower-class people who generally manage to achieve a full life, and who therefore have something to offer the upper classes. For instance, William Bailey and Frances enjoy a happy marriage. And of course it is Richard who makes the ideal marriage, not George. Moreover, the lower classes have the experience to instruct the upper classes: Farmer Ellis instructs Sir Owen Dale; Ruth's mother condemns the press gangs; and the gamekeepers teach the squire that men are more valuable than partridges and hares. Crabbe seems to have felt that knowledge, wealth, and refinement could easily dull an individual's authentic responses to life. Lady Barbara and her brother are "Above the vulgar, as we judged, in mind, / Below in peace, more sad as more refined" (XVI. 539–40). Of course, this does not mean that Crabbe gives all the positive values to the lower classes. For instance, George can say that Jacques will "oversee our creed," and Richard does not object to this proposal. But in other areas, Crabbe shows clearly that there exists a great need for the poor to educate their masters, an ideal that was soon to become central to the thinking of many Victorians. At a time when the upper classes were being exhorted to help the poor, Crabbe sets out, supposedly to show yet another example of this charity, only to reveal unexpectedly that often it is the poor who can aid the rich.

This reversal is especially true in the case of George and Richard: even though by the end of his life George has learned a great deal about his own irrationality, the way in which the power of fancy is usually stronger than reason, he finds that until the time he meets Richard, he "look'd not to have found, / A care, an interest in the world around" (XXII. 247–48). Until this point Crabbe had been showing George's growing self-knowledge almost as an end in itself.

But with the introduction of Richard, Crabbe indicates that, for George, clarity of perception is a necessary but not a sufficient end. As Jacques comments so pointedly:

> although alone to be
> Is freedom; so are men in deserts free. (x. 52–53)

What George learns about himself does not solve his problems; it allows him to perceive them more accurately. Yet this habit of paying attention to things as they are in the world around him is in fact an attitude that might easily be described by the clichéd word "loving." And when George meets Richard, a person who has also learned to see clearly, his mental and moral discipline creates the conditions under which "love" develops.

Crabbe might be thought to be illogical in his presentation of George and Richard's growing affection for one another, since he had previously shown that man's chief motivation came from selfish desires. Yet Crabbe has it both ways, since he admits that George's need of Richard's love is selfish. The reason that Crabbe does not violate his own principle is because George, although motivated by selfishness, has the ability to see Richard as a person in his own right, and is therefore able to leave Richard his entire freedom. Wanting to be a friend and not a patron, George does not attempt to make Richard accept his own view of what is right and true. The reason why many of the other characters fail in their search for love and friendship is that they attempt to force their friends to serve their own needs. Finch, for instance, cannot value Augusta for her own merits, but attempts to transform her into the intellectual that he first "saw" her as being.

Yet the brothers do not achieve this clear-sighted perception of one another immediately, and it is only in the course of time—by means of telling stories about their past and about the lives of others—that they come slowly to see each other without the veil of fantasy. Moreover, all of the stories concern this central theme. For instance, George tells the ghost stories of "The Cathedral Walk"—concerning the search for absolutes by means of the supernatural—to illustrate a time in his own life when he, as the victim of impulse, was searching for such absolutes. Again, when Richard receives a letter from his wife at home, this causes George to worry about the lack of love in his own life. The two brothers then "pursue the subject, half in play, / Half earnest, till the sadness wore away" (XIX. 5-6). By focusing their attention on the problem of seeing clearly, they gradually come to clarity of vision.

Furthermore, Crabbe insists that this is the only basis for strong emotions. When Richard says that Belwood, although rash in his marriage, nevertheless was passionately attached to his wife in the beginning, George retorts that "in men so weak / You may in vain the strong affections seek" (XV. 54-55). What George means is that Belwood's love was weak because he was unaware that he was pursuing the girl entirely out of "self-indulgence"; therefore, his "love" was not strong enough to meet even the slightest check. Belwood cannot, George suggests, bear very much reality, and therefore he cannot love. The story reveals that love is not the seizing and using of other people, but the recognition of "otherness," an ability that comes only when an individual has achieved a degree of detachment. In *Tales of the Hall*, the telling of the stories and the scrutinizing of other individuals is the exercising of a moral discipline which frees the individual from selfishly imposing his will on others and the world at large.

Since the political and social attitudes are extensions of personal concerns, what applies to the personal also applies to the political and social. Those who have no detachment, who are blind to the way in which their emotions are controlling their attitudes, tend towards extremism, while persons such as George and Richard who have become aware of themselves can coexist in their differences. Thus at the end of the poem George can say:

> Then thou and I, an independent two,
> May have our parties, and defend them too;
> Thy liberal notions, and my loyal fears,
> Will give us subjects for our future years.   (XXII. 412-15)

In Crabbe's view the most important requirement for a healthy country was not a particular program of social reform, but rather men of goodwill who would respect the opinions of others and allow their own beliefs to be scrutinized so that the least prejudiced solution could be reached. Of course such a response does not solve any problems in political science; one can still ask on what basis certain people are chosen as "men of goodwill" and others excluded. Moreover, the question remains as to who will choose. One might also ask if Crabbe's answer is not as much conditioned by hidden motives as that of the conservative and the revolutionary. Crabbe, I suspect, would be the first person to accept this objection; but on the other hand, he is not offering a *solution* to problems, but a *method* which could yield solutions.

More important still, he does not advance the method in terms of logical argument, but by giving the reader a "feel" for the ordinary rhythms of events and happenings in the everyday world. In Mrs. Haddakin's phrase, Crabbe has the uncanny ability of "'possessing' the reader's consciousness"[78] to reveal afresh the profound in the ordinary. In *Tales of the Hall* Crabbe achieves this possession of the reader's consciousness by means of a narrative structure that permits the brothers to arrive at a reconciliation by means of their stories, many of which describe the impossibility of such reconciliation for other people. Thus at one and the same time Crabbe is able to give a sense of people living out their solitary lives in many parts of the social spectrum, but also to show through the overview supplied by George and Richard how actually these "solitary" people are very much a part of a loosely linked society in which economic forces, social customs, and personal habits are all powerfully at work giving individuals their sense of solitude.

Crabbe also goes one step beyond to show the possibility of replacing this sense of solitude with something more positive. "Happiness" does not really do justice to what Crabbe has in mind, since usually it is associated with the satisfaction of present needs. The word Crabbe most often chooses in its place is "repose." *Tales of the Hall* ends with Crabbe's blessing—"Health, reader, and repose!" Book IX also ends with "repose," although this time with an edge of irony. And in Book X, after four attempts at courtship, the rector Jacques finally finds peace and "repose" from his frustrated sexual desires (X. 741). Sir Owen Dale also comments that "these female foes, / Or good or ill, will murder our repose" (XII. 850–51). In Crabbe's usage "repose" does not mean a state of passivity, since for Robert the poacher, "danger only could repose produce" (XXI. 157). Repose occurs when the individual is freed from following blindly the needs and desires thrown up by society, and can discover his own human aspirations. That these aspirations are irrational and yet not a-social in the best sense of social, Crabbe illustrates in his presentation of the two brothers who explore tentatively their responses to one another in an ever-growing relationship which is profoundly social.

Clearly then at this point, terms such as "social critic" and "moralist" do not adequately describe Crabbe's handling of his "fictions," for now Crabbe, the poet, links the elements of the personal and social in the creation of the poem that expresses his own faith, his own vision. It should also be apparent that the word "social" has now widened considerably; society is no longer an abstract quantity but individuals living in close proximity and acting out their desires in relationships with one another. To give a sense of this creation of the social out of the personal and vice versa, Crabbe required an art form in which individuals could be seen acting out such relationships. And to indicate the complexity of the interconnections, Crabbe has the brothers act out their relationship in terms of art, in telling the stories of their own lives and the lives of others. George and Richard end by doing what Crabbe himself does in *Tales of the Hall*; that is to say, they exist in complexity by narrating the various possible forms that men's lives can assume. This artistic contemplation frees them to pursue their own individually chosen, authentic social actions. Yet since so many of the other characters in *Tales of the Hall* fail in this endeavour, the brothers' success becomes not so much an answer as a testament to Crabbe's faith in mankind and in the soundness of the nation, a tempered optimism which he defended in the face of seemingly overwhelming evidence to the contrary.

CONCLUSION

Everyone who has attempted to write about Crabbe's poetry has commented on the difficulty of capturing his tone, and the consequent need to quote lengthy passages so as not to misrepresent. Francis Jeffrey, for instance, remarked that "the pattern of Crabbe's Arabesque is so large, that there is no getting a fair specimen of it without taking in a good space."[1] Since I also have found this to be true, and since much space in this study has been devoted to detailed accounts of the poems, it will be helpful to summarize briefly the main conclusions.

Clearly it is no accident that commentators have found it necessary to quote from Crabbe at such length; he builds into his poetry conflicting questions which then clash or are reconciled within the poem's dramatic structure. Unless the poems are quoted at length or discussed in detail, important considerations are often omitted. This is also the reason why Crabbe, who on the surface seems to be a straightforward poet, has seemed so difficult for many readers. His desire to represent faithfully the world as he perceived it led him to encompass complexities and contradictions without reducing them to a false unity.

In his descriptions of social conditions Crabbe was writing, not to prove or disprove a social or political theory, but because he wished to close the gap between true and false ways of seeing the country.[2] As Crabbe saw it, many eighteenth-century poets had accepted the premise that the universe was providentially ordered, and consequently had propagated a bucolic myth which ignored actual conditions and portrayed England as a "family" united by warm sentiment. In Gainsborough's pictures, for instance, even the beggars are happy. Crabbe's background, his temperament, and his training as an apothecary—what he termed "hard affliction's school"[3]

—all led him to oppose such a premise, and to create a poetry that began, not with an assumption about God's order, but with the minutiae of day-to-day experience. In many of his poems, he inserted footnotes to remind his readers that the descriptions deserved the status of observations, not hypotheses or mental constructs.

Like many eighteenth-century thinkers, such as Locke and Hume, Crabbe was determined to begin his explorations of the world with what was evident to his senses. Thus, in his early poem, "Midnight," Crabbe stated that a poet of humble birth like himself, "Hallows a Clod, and spurns Immensity" (line 128). Yet this loving attention to detail, this hallowing of the clod, did not create either a spiritualized conception of the temporal world or a utopia. In the first book of *The Village*, his close scrutiny of the harsh lives of the East Anglian villagers resulted in a portrait of man that resembled Hobbes's "state of nature" or Adam's life after the fall. Beginning with this empirical view of the world, which indicated that all men were "victims" of natural and social forces, there seemed no simple way of introducing a redemptive ethic. Hume, it will be recalled, had begun the *Treatise* with the intention of supplying a picture of human nature that would serve as a basis for ethics, but instead, the *Treatise* revealed that ethics could have no such basis.

Crabbe himself was clearly puzzled about the lack of answers to the philosophic problems of the day. In an early verse letter to "Mira," he "jingles" the complaint that his study of philosophy and science has destroyed his poetic gift:

> Of substance I've thought, and the varied disputes
> On the nature of man and the notions of brutes;
> Of systems confuted, and systems explain'd;
> Of science disputed, and tenets maintain'd.
> These, and such speculations on these kind of things,
> Have robb'd my poor Muse of her plume and her wings;
> Consumed the phlogiston you used to admire,
> The spirit extracted, extinguish'd the fire;
> Let out all the ether, so pure and refined,
> And left but a mere *caput mortuum* behind.[4]

This close linking of "the nature of man" with the "notions of brutes," so evident in the writing of the period,[5] is a subject that pervades Crabbe's later poetry. He indicates that man's nature is similar to that of the brutes in that he is conditioned by surroundings, and yet dissimilar in that man has freedom to make his own choices: in other words Crabbe wanted to provide the earthly man of flesh and blood with independence, and therefore significance. In *The Village*, Robert Manners is introduced by means of a transcendent leap to provide the example of freedom that the early parts of the poem had seemed to deny. In "The Hall of Justice" the two halves of the dichotomy are kept in balance by a sleight-of-hand adjustment of the poem's form. The later poems evidence an ever more subtle use of narrative form to contain the contradictions.

In Crabbe's own life, this awareness of the complexity of social problems, the necessity of adjusting the rights of the individual to the prescriptions of social edicts, is evident. For one thing, he admitted his incompetence to decide the great issues of the day. Even on such a major issue as parliamentary reform, his mind was uncommitted.[6] Crabbe was not uninterested in these subjects, but his ability to see both sides of a question often left him with the feeling that the country lacked the means and resources (as it did) to overcome the problems with which it was faced. On the subject of working men's combinations, he wrote to Miss Hoare:

> I am sorry for the want of Sufficient Work for the Willing
> and Industrious, and like you, I lament the use, and still
> more the increase, of Machinery; yet what can be done?
> Other Countries not so burdened with debt as we are
> contend with us: they also make Cloth and Birmingham
> Wares, and we are told that to lay aside our Inventions
> is to give up our Trade. God knows what will be the
> result of such Dilemmas, where on one side, the Masters
> feel the necessity of employing Agents who do not eat
> or drink, and on the other the men who are hungry and
> thirsty, threaten, and no wonder, their Rival the
> machines with utter Destruction. Who can truly say,

> if I were a master I would give up Machinery, if I were a
> workman I would starve in quiet? I leave the melancholy
> subject. A way will be found, though my Wisdom is at a
> a loss where to look for it. The Mule would not be
> tollerated in this Neighbourhood, and yet it is a sad thing
> to check and baffle Ingenuity, though a worse to do this
> by Hunger joined with a will to labour.[7]

As a result of this ambivalence, Crabbe's poetry often reveals a curious mixture of conservative principle—he wished in theory to uphold social standards—and liberal practice—he always devotes loving care to his portraits of the individual's struggle for freedom of expression. This tension, especially apparent in a poem such as *The Borough*, can be seen equally well in "Edward Shore" (Tale XI), "The Patron" (Tale V), "David Morris," and "The Insanity of Ambitious Love."[8]

The ambivalent handling of social questions in Crabbe's poetry has been a stumbling block to many readers. Nor can Crabbe be said to have resolved the problem successfully in all his poems; often he leans to one side or the other. Yet many times he manages to dissolve the problems by incorporating the conflict within the structure of his poems, advancing "sidelong" in a "crooked race." As the course of this argument has shown, and as *Tales of the Hall* substantiates, Crabbe's problem was to create a dramatic structure which could express the various sides of his own ambivalence of feeling. One can see this dramatic structure developing in the poems that follow *The Village*. "The Parish Register" and *The Borough* tend to break down the abstraction, society, and to show "society" as composed of men and women living out their day-to-day lives. The point is not that these individuals act rationally or ethically; on the contrary, a truthful portrayal of the obscure springs of man's motivation is one of Crabbe's hallmarks. Yet, in showing individuals living together and thereby creating a society, he could also show the way in which individuals who were unable to understand themselves were likewise incapable of seeing the ways in which their own lack of vision, in aggregate, created social problems. Thus Crabbe maintains a balance between the inner and the outer worlds: while both are complex, they yield objective truths to the persistent enquirer.

In *Tales of the Hall*, Crabbe's consummate artistic achievement, the emphasis on individuals is taken one step further when he introduces a number of narrators. By this means he could first show individuals learning about the degree to which their perceptions have been coloured by all kinds of conditioning factors, and then proceed to show the same individuals accepting this as a basic limitation. Unlike Wordsworth, Crabbe rarely shows the individual delighting in his recognition of the play of natural law, but the acceptance of the world does, in Crabbe's case, provide the mechanism which frees the individual to see the world around him—not coloured by his fantasies and his selfish desires, but as it is. Such a discipline can well be called "moral" since it allows the individual to act, not simply on his own account, but taking into consideration the many outside circumstances. It is by this means that Crabbe introduces a redemptive ethic. Indeed, Crabbe's account of ethical decision-making is not so far removed from Kant's. It certainly gives a firm basis for locating the kinds of changes necessary for social reform, not in particular issues, but in a recognition of the way social problems are closely connected with faulty perception.

Moreover, in *Tales of the Hall*, Crabbe shows the brothers achieving this rigorous but loving attention to detail by means of art, for it is by telling stories that they learn to perceive attentively one another and the world at large. Indeed, this is one of the functions of art, to provide a lens through which the world can be seen clearly and perhaps even "impersonally." So it is in *Tales of the Hall* that Crabbe is able to combine his empirical view of man's imperfectibility with a sense of morality by creating in his poetry the artistic machinery to accommodate his vision of the richness and complexity of the external world, and to show the brothers themselves achieving a resolution of their differences by means of their art of storytelling.

Notes

Chapter 1

1. See "Towards Defining an Age of Sensibility," *ELH*, XXIII (June 1956), 144–52.
2. *To the Palace of Wisdom,* Anchor ed. (New York, 1965), p. 387.
3. See Arthur Cronquist, "Taxonomic Principles," in *The Evolution and Classification of Flowering Plants* (Boston, 1968), pp. 3–47.
4. *Poems by George Crabbe*, ed. Adolphus W. Ward, I, 47 (ll. 12–13). Unless otherwise stated, all further quotations from Crabbe's poems are from this edition (hereafter cited as *Poems*).
5. Mark Akenside, *The Pleasures of Imagination*, new ed. (London, 1806), p. 20 (I. 174–83).
6. Quoted from Boswell's *Life of Johnson*, ed. G. B. Hill, rev. L. F. Powell (Oxford, 1934), IV, 175–76, n4.
7. For instance, see Scott of Amwell's letter to James Beattie, August 1783, quoted in *The Poetical Works of the Rev. George Crabbe*, ed. George Crabbe Jr., II, 99, n2 (hereafter cited as *Poetical Works*). Crabbe's son also emphasized the "classical" qualities of *The Village*. See *The Life of George Crabbe*, by his Son, p. 121 (vol. I of *Poetical Works*, hereafter cited as *Life*).
8. Johnson's accepted emendation is:

> On Mincio's banks, in Caesar's bounteous reign,
> If Tityrus found the Golden Age again,
> Must sleepy bards the flattering dream prolong,
> Mechanic echoes of the Mantuan song?
> From Truth and Nature shall we widely stray,
> Where Virgil, not where Fancy, leads the way?

As can be seen, Johnson retained Crabbe's fifth line in his emendation.
9. For an account of Crabbe's debt to the mock-pastoral tradition, see Varley Howe Lang, *Crabbe and the Eighteenth Century*.
10. See "A Discourse on Pastoral Poetry," in *The Poems of Alexander Pope*, ed. John Butt (London, 1963), p. 120.
11. See especially Richard Jago's *Edge-Hill* (London, 1767) and William Shenstone's *Rural Elegance* (London, 1750).

12. *Spectator*, no. 430, 14 July, 1712, ed. Donald F. Bond (Clarendon Press: Oxford, 1965), IV, 11.

13. *The Wanderer: A Vision* Canto V. 127–32, in *The Poetical Works of Richard Savage*, ed. Clarence Tracy (Cambridge, 1962), pp. 140–41.

14. See James McPhee, "Humanitarianism in English Poetry from Thomson to Wordsworth," Ph.D. thesis (University of Edinburgh, 1962), pp. 129–73.

15. [John Armstrong], *Of Benevolence: An Epistle to Eumenes* (London, 1751), pp. 5–7.

16. William Empson has suggested that the pastoral art form "is important for a nation with a strong class-system" because it "makes the classes feel part of a larger unity or simply at home with each other." See *Some Versions of Pastoral* (London, 1935), p. 199.

17. See P. H. Davis and V. H. Heywood, *Principles of Angiosperm Taxonomy* (New York, 1963), pp. 15–30.

18. See John Arthos, *The Language of Natural Description in Eighteenth Century Poetry* (Ann Arbor, 1949).

19. Lilian Haddakin, *The Poetry of Crabbe*, p. 134.

20. René Huchon, *George Crabbe and his Times 1754–1832*, p. 168.

21. James Thomson, "A Poem Sacred to the Memory of Sir Isaac Newton," ll. 39–42, in *The Works of James Thomson* (London, 1762), I, 210–11.

22. Ibid., l. 56.

23. It is interesting to note that Crabbe's botanical interests led him to collect grasses and coarse plants. He was relatively uninterested in the "beautiful flowers." See *Life*, chap. VII, pp. 164–65.

24. R. W. Harris, *Political Ideas 1760–1792* (London, 1963), p. 151.

25. Although Montesquieu in his *Esprit des Lois* (1748) relates government, law, and social conduct to physical and economic environment, in England one finds few references to a full-scale theory of environmental influence until the end of the century when it was popularized by such writers as Robert Owen. David Hume, for instance, in his essay "Of "National Characters" rejects altogether the idea of physical causes having any great influence on national character. See, however, Robert Wallace's *A Dissertation on the Numbers of Mankind* (1753) for a qualification of the Humean position.

26. See Letter II of *A free Inquiry into the Nature and Origin of Evil*, where Jenyns says: "Poverty or the want of riches is generally compensated by ... a greater share of health, and a more exquisite relish of the smallest enjoyments than those who possess them are usually blessed with." *The Works of Soame Jenyns* (Dublin, 1791), II, 38.

27. *Poetical Works*, II, 79, n3.

28. Arthur Sale, "The Development of Crabbe's Narrative Art," p. 482.

29. Robert Dodsley, *Agriculture*, Canto I. 337–40.
30. Rev. Joseph Townsend, *A Dissertation on the Poor Laws*, 2nd ed. (London, 1787), p. 7.
31. For an explanation of this pernicious system see J. L. and Barbara Hammond, *The Village Labourer 1760–1832* (London, 1919), pp. 164ff.
32. *Poems*, I, 136, n1.
33. Richard Burn, *The Justice of the Peace*, 23rd ed. (London, 1820), IV, 172.
34. Dorothy Marshall, *The English Poor in the Eighteenth Century* (London, 1926), p. 250.
35. *Edinburgh Review*, XII (1808), 131.
36. Both Wordsworth and Scott claimed to know the passage by heart. See *Poetical Works*, II, 83, n1.
37. See Huchon, pp. 63–64.
38. Crabbe may have received adverse criticism about these lines, for in later editions he added the following footnote: "Some apology is due for the insertion of a circumstance by no means common: that it has been a subject for complaint in any place is a sufficient reason for its being reckoned among the evils which may happen to the poor, and which must happen to them exclusively; nevertheless, it is just to remark, that such neglect is very rare in any part of the kingdom, and in many parts is totally unknown." *Poems*, I, 136, n2.
39. Huchon, p. 168.
40. Oliver Sigworth, *Nature's Sternest Painter*, p. 34.
41. Marshall, *English Poor in the Eighteenth Century*, p. 249.
42. Compare Cowper's account in *Truth* (1782) of the "ancient prude" watching the "am'rous couple in their play" while behind her walks her foot-boy, "a shiv'ring urchin" without proper clothes to keep him warm (ll. 131–48).
43. At first this society was called the Proclamation Society, after the famous Royal Proclamation against Vice in 1787. See J. L. and Barbara Hammond, *Village Labourer*, p. 222, and Muriel Jaeger, *Before Victoria*, 2nd ed. (London, 1967), p. 24.
44. Ian Gregor, "The Last Augustan," p. 40.
45. *Cyder* II. 18–20 in *The Poems of John Philips*, ed. M. G. Lloyd Thomas (Oxford, 1927), pp. 68–69.
46. See *Life*, chap. IV, pp. 89–97, and Huchon, p. 114. Crabbe himself was temperamentally aristocratic. His son notes that Crabbe "had seen the submission paid to the opinions of Johnson and Burke; and he always readily followed the lead of any one whom he thought skilled on the topic in question." *Life*, chap. IX, p. 236.
47. Nathaniel Wraxall, *The Historical and Posthumous Memoirs of Sir Nathaniel Wraxall*, ed. Henry B. Wheatley (London, 1884), V, 33.

Chapter 2

1. *Life*, chap. vii, p. 167.
2. *Poems*, I, 98.
3. Daniel Defoe, *The History of . . . Colonel Jack* (1722), Shakespeare Head ed. (Oxford, 1927), I, vii.
4. Daniel Defoe, *The Fortunate Mistress* (1724), Shakespeare Head ed., I, 28–29. For further information, see Maximillian E. Novak, *Defoe and the Nature of Man* (London, 1963), pp. 87–88.
5. Richard Savage, "Of Public Spirit in Regard to Public Works," second version (1737), in *The Poetical Works of Richard Savage*, ed. Clarence Tracy (Cambridge, 1962), p. 230, ll. 195–96.
6. Francis Jeffrey, review of *Poems, Edinburgh Review*, XII (1808), 149.
7. This anomaly was not corrected until 1836.
8. Sydney Smith, "Counsel for Prisoners," in *The Works of the Rev. Sydney Smith* (London, 1845), II, 225. This essay first appeared in *The Edinburgh Review* (1826).
9. John Locke, *The Second Treatise of Government* (1690), ed. J. W. Gough (Oxford, 1956), p. 69 (chap. XI, sec. 135).
10. *Life*, chap. IV, pp. 90–92.
11. *History of Colonel Jack*, I, 6.
12. John Locke, 3rd ed. enlarged (London, 1695), p. 2.
13. *A New View of Society*, Everyman ed. (London, 1966), pp. 71–72.
14. *A Serious Address to the People of Great Britain, In which certain consequences of the Present Rebellion are fully demonstrated* (London, 1745), p. 9.
15. An important idea throughout the eighteenth century. See Locke, *Second Treatise of Government*, p. 69.
16. James Grahame, "The Sabbath," in *Poems by James Grahame* (Edinburgh, 1807), I, 17–18.
17. The Evangelicals played an important role in this missionary work, but probably the publication of scholarly works such as James Hoyland's *A Historical Survey of the Customs, Habits, & Present State of the Gipsies* (York, 1816), based on the studies of H. M. G. Grellmen, helped to awaken interest as well.
18. James Crabb, *The Gipsies' Advocate; or, Observations on the Origin, Character, Manners, and Habits of the English Gipsies* (London, 1831), p. vii. Crabb worked with the gypsies in the New Forest and promoted Southampton education charities.
19. Ibid., p. 42.
20. Ibid., p. 43.

Chapter 3

1. William Paley, *Reasons for Contentment, Addressed to the Labouring Part of the British Public* (1793), in *Sermons and Tracts by the late Rev. William Paley* (London, 1815), pp. 187–88.
2. W. K. Thomas, "George Crabbe: Not Quite the Sternest," p. 167. See also W. K. Thomas, "Crabbe's Workhouse," pp. 149–61.
3. Preface to *The Borough* in *Poems*, I, 268.
4. Fanny Burney's portrait of Mr. Briggs in *Cecilia* (1782) is no doubt something of a caricature of merchant vulgarity, but that such a portrait could be drawn at all shows in what low esteem merchants were held.
5. Herbert J. Davis, "Swift's Use of Irony," in *The Uses of Irony*, William Andrews Clark Memorial Library (University of California, 1966), p. 44.
6. Oliver Sigworth, *Nature's Sternest Painter*, p. 94.
7. Francis Jeffrey, review of *The Borough, Edinburgh Review*, XVI (1810), 52.
8. *Poems*, I, 268.
9. Crabbe felt that the character of the borough's mayor was so odd that it merited an explanation in his preface. *Poems*, I, 274.
10. That many eighteenth-century fictional heroes—Tom Jones, William Booth, Jonathan Wild, Peregrine Pickle, Humphry Clinker, Dr. Primrose and his son George—spend time in prisons does not contradict this statement. Fielding, Smollett, and Goldsmith placed their heroes in jail to illustrate how the naturally good man often falls foul of conventional morality.
11. See *Life*, chap. IV, p. 92; chap. VII, p. 208.
12. To Miss Elizabeth Charter, *c.* October 1819, in *The Romance of an Elderly Poet*, ed. A. M. Broadley and Walter Jerrold, p. 241.
13. *Poems*, I, 279–80. See also *Life*, chap. VIII, p. 197, for a further comment.
14. *Edinburgh Review*, XVI (1810), 42.
15. Ibid., p. 43.
16. *Evelina* (1778). Benbow may well have been modelled on a friend of the Tovells. At least the description that Crabbe's son gives of this man agrees well with Crabbe's portrait of Benbow. See *Life*, chap. VI, pp. 145–46. It is unlikely that Crabbe had in mind William Benbow (1784–?), the famous Radical from Manchester.
17. "The Parish Register," II. 390–430. One often finds amongst Crabbe's contemporaries a wavering of attitude about the benefits and drawbacks associated with the change in village life as a result of changing agricultural methods. For example, Arthur Young decried the farmers' imitation of their superiors' way of life. *Annals of Agriculture*, XVII (1792), 152–53. But he also praised the new comforts brought by prosperity. *General View of the Agriculture of the County of Essex* (London, 1807), I, 123–24.

18. *New Monthly Magazine*, V (1816), 500.
19. D. H. Burden, "Crabbe and the Augustan Tradition," p. 87.
20. See E. P. Thompson, *The Making of the English Working Class* (London, 1965), pp. 418–23.
21. Edwin Chadwick's Poor Law Commission of the early 1830s.
22. "Thomas Day" in *DNB*.
23. This idea of designating a number of directors to look after the affairs of the almshouse was widely followed in the workhouses as well. Thus Crabbe's almshouse is representative of the type of control imposed on a great many institutions for the poor.
24. To Mary Leadbeater, 1 Dec. 1816, in *Life*, chap. IX, p. 232.
25. *Sir Charles Grandison* (1754).
26. To George Crabbe Jr., 26 Dec. 1833, in *Life*, chap. IX, p. 278.
27. Compare Samuel Bamford's statement: "That the gentry, or what were called the higher classes were too proud, or too indifferent to examine minutely into the abodes of poverty and distress, and that many of them were interested in returning a false or partial statement of things." *An Account of the Arrest and Imprisonment of Samuel Bamford . . . Written by Himself*, in *The Autobiography of Samuel Bamford*, ed. W. H. Chaloner (London, 1967), I, 332.
28. *Life*, chap. VI, p. 130.
29. It will be recalled that Henry Fielding, one of the great humanitarians of the eighteenth century, utterly dismissed the vagabonds as beneath his notice.
30. Robert Southey, *Sir Thomas More: or, Colloquies on the Progress and Prospects of Society* (London, 1829), Colloquy III, 1, 46. Crabbe's son felt it necessary to apologize for recounting that part of Crabbe's life in which he lived obscurely in the country. See *Life*, chap. VI, pp. 131–32.
31. See especially Georg Lukács, *Realism in Our Time*, trans. John and Necke Mander (New York, 1971).
32. Iris Murdoch, *The Sovereignty of Good* (London, 1970).
33. For a discussion of this point, see Philip Pinkus, "The Satiric Novels of Thomas Love Peacock," *Kansas Quarterly*, I, no. 3 (Summer 1969), 64–76.
34. Henry Crabb Robinson noted the ludicrous and costly nature of this parish litigation: "I spent several hours at the Clerkenwell Sessions. A case came before the court ludicrous from the minuteness required in the examination. Was the pauper settled in Parish A or B? The house he occupied was in both parishes, and models both of the house and the bed in which the pauper slept were laid before the court, that it might ascertain how much of his body lay in each parish. The court held the pauper to be settled where his head (being the nobler part) lay, though

one of his legs at least, and great part of his body, lay out of that parish."
Entry for 7 Dec. 1815, *Diary, Reminiscences, and Correspondence of
Henry Crabb Robinson,* ed. Thomas Sadler, 2nd ed. (London, 1869), I, 506.

35. Sidney and Beatrice Webb, *English Poor Law History, Part 1: The Old
Poor Law,* in *English Local Government,* reprint ed. (London, 1963),
VII, 347.

36. See, for instance, the elaborate arrangements Moll Flanders makes to
convince the parish of Bath that she will be able to care for the child
she is to have there. *Moll Flanders,* Shakespeare Head ed., I, 122.

37. This improvement in the road system was partly due to the recognition
of its importance after the Jacobite invasion of 1745. See Paul Mantoux,
The Industrial Revolution in the Eighteenth Century, rev. ed. (London,
1961), p. 116.

38. In the year ending 25 March, 1834, "the sums expended in England and
Wales in suits of law, removal of paupers, etc." amounted to
£258,604.1s. See *Ninth Annual Report of the Poor Law Commissioners*
(1843), p. 34. Also J. L. and Barbara Hammond, *The Village Labourer
1760–1832* (London, 1919), p. 215.

39. To George Crabbe Jr., n.d., in *Life,* chap. X, p. 301.

40. G. E. Mingay, *English Landed Society in the Eighteenth Century*
(London, 1963), p. 221.

41. In fact Crabbe does not draw any distinction between the three classes of
medical practitioners of this period: the physician, a member of the
College of Surgeons and educated at Oxford, Cambridge, or Trinity
College, Dublin; the licensed doctor, trained on the continent or at one of
the Scottish universities; and the apothecary. See D. Marshall,
English People in the Eighteenth Century (London, 1956), p. 53.

42. Friedrich Engels reported that brandy and even opium were still being
given to children as late as 1844. *The Condition of the Working Class in
England,* trans. W. O. Henderson *et al* (Oxford, 1958), p. 114.

43. *English Landed Society in the Eighteenth Century,* p. 221.

44. *Life,* chap. VII, p. 161. His son mentions that he began taking opium as a
medicine "on one of his early journeys into Suffolk" (i.e. *c.* 1790).

45. *Poems,* I, 277. As a guide to later readers, Crabbe's son gave this
explanation in *Poetical Works,* III, 283, n1.

46. *Poetical Works,* III, 291, n1.

47. Sidney and Beatrice Webb, *English Poor Law History, Part 1,* p. 146.

48. In his account of Isaac Ashford in "The Parish Register" Crabbe gave a
description of yet another type of workhouse. There he presented a parish
in which the overseers "contracted" the care of the poor to private
individuals. These "contractors" agreed to supply the necessities of life
to the poor at so much per head.

49. All such statements are of course only broad generalizations. Even in those parishes where the policy was to send all paupers to the workhouse, no doubt one would still find the exceptional case of a widow or orphan allowed to remain on a weekly dole.

50. Sidney and Beatrice Webb, *English Poor Law History, Part 1*, p. 136.

51. *General View of the Agriculture of the County of Suffolk* (London, 1794), p. 92.

52. Sidney and Beatrice Webb, *English Poor Law History, Part 1*, p. 126.

53. Ibid., p. 129.

54. George Rose, *Observations on the Poor Laws, and on the Management of the Poor in Great Britain* ... (London, 1805), pp. 34–36.

55. At New Lanark, Robert Owen had a system whereby, "those now employed at the establishment contribute to a fund which supports them when too ill to work, or superannuated. ... After they have spent nearly half a century in unremitting industry, they should, if possible, enjoy a comfortable independence." See *A New View of Society*, Everyman ed., p. 59.

56. Leslie Stephen, *Hours in a Library*, II, 51.

57. *English Poor Law History, Part 1*, p. 139.

58. Under the new Poor Law of 1834, the aim was to standardize treatment of the poor throughout the United Kingdom.

59. Howard Mills, ed., *George Crabbe: Tales, 1812 and Other Selected Poems*, p. xxx.

60. *Poetical Works*, IV, 39, n1.

61. *Edinburgh Annual Register* (1801), pp. 35–36.

62. M. Dorothy George, *London Life in the XVIIIth Century* (London, 1925), p. 225.

63. Richard Burn, *The History of the Poor Laws* (London, 1764), p. 212.

64. *London Life in the XVIIIth Century*, p. 226.

65. The seventeenth-century ballad "The cryes of the Dead" tells the story of how Richard Price, a weaver, murdered three of his apprentices. See *A Pepysian Garland*, ed. H. E. Rollins (Cambridge, 1922), pp. 222–28.

66. "The disappearance of an apprentice was too common a thing to provoke suspicion." George, *London Life in the XVIIIth Century*, p. 230.

67. Interestingly enough, in 1816, six years after the publication of *The Borough*, an important act was passed, which greatly discouraged apprentice labour.

68. Thomas Paine, *Rights of Man: Part the Second* (London, 1792), p. vii.

Chapter 4

1. Lilian Haddakin, *Poetry of Crabbe,* p. 46.
2. One of the most influential statements on this brand of realism is Virginia Woolf's "Mr. Bennett and Mrs. Brown."
3. Edmund Burke, *An Appeal from the New to the Old Whigs* (1791), in *The Works of Edmund Burke,* Bohn's Library ed. (London, 1901–1906), III, 78.
4. These poems are to be found in *New Poems by George Crabbe,* ed. Arthur Pollard. "The Insanity of Ambitious Love" was completed in 1816, "David Morris" probably much later. See Pollard's introduction to *New Poems.*
5. Preface to *Poems,* in *Poems,* I, 98.
6. The poem is complete in a first draft at least. At the end of the MS, Crabbe has written in cipher: "LINES 380 FINIS. Nov. 28. 1816."
7. At this time many English poets, including Byron, Shelley, Keats, and Wordsworth, were influenced by Dante through the translation of Henry Cary. See Ian Jack, *English Literature 1815–1832* (Oxford, 1963), pp. 378–82. In *Nightmare Abbey* (chap. VI) Peacock also comments on the new interest in Dante.
8. Crabbe was by no means unaware of the new urban and industrial areas, as many critics from the time of Hazlitt have attempted to suggest. Indeed, one of his friends was Dr. Cartwright, the inventor of the power loom. Crabbe's son gives an interesting account of a visit his parents made to Dr. Cartwright's factory (*Life,* chap. VI, p. 136), and this visit may well have been the inspiration for "The Insanity of Ambitious Love."
9. A similar type of ending, although with more justification, occurs in Tale XXI of *Tales* where the father of the "learned boy" refutes his son's new principles of free thought by burning his books and beating him into submission.
10. In Burke's writings (especially *Letters on a Regicide Peace*), one can see much the same feeling of helplessness before the vast social and political changes encompassed in the French Revolution.
11. See *Life,* chap. IX, pp. 255–56; and Crabbe to Mary Leadbeater, 3 Feb. 1826, in *The Leadbeater Papers* (London, 1862), II, 400. Crabbe often remarks that Trowbridge, his last parish, was a busy manufacturing centre.
12. See *Observations on the Effect of the Manufacturing System* (1815).
13. René Huchon, *George Crabbe,* p. 332.
14. Robert L. Chamberlain, *George Crabbe,* p. 125.
15. Compare the number of "good" families in Jane Austen's novels who are either in trade themselves of have connections with trade.

16. Benjamin Disraeli gives just such an account in *Sybil; Or the Two Nations* (London, 1845), I, 311 (bk. II, chap. XVI).
17. In 1810 the Earl of Harrowby pointed out that many non-resident incumbents "of livings of £50, £60, or £70 a year, put into their own pockets a portion of this wretched pittance, and left much less than the wages of a day-labourer for the subsistence of their curates." William Cobbett, *Parliamentary Debates*, XVII, 765.
18. William Wilberforce, *A Practical View of the Prevailing Religious System of Professed Christians*, 2nd ed. (London, 1797), p. 405.
19. *Life*, chap. I, p. 19.
20. See Crabbe's Journal for 21 July 1817. Quoted in *Life*, chap. IX, p. 253.
21. For Crabbe's comments on his wife and their marriage see *Life*, chap. VIII, p. 211, and *Romance of an Elderly Poet*, ed. A. M. Broadley and Walter Jerrold, p. 80. See also A. Hayter, *Opium and the Romantic Imagination*, p. 185.
22. In *Tales of the Hall*, Crabbe refers to man as "A worm of other class" (XIII. 16); it is clear from the passage that Crabbe recognized that the Mosaic account of creation was inaccurate.
23. To Miss Elizabeth Charter, 18 July 1816, in *Romance of an Elderly Poet*, p. 139.
24. To George Crabbe Jr., 4 Feb. 1831, in F. M. Link, ed., "Three Crabbe Letters," pp. 205–206.
25. Ibid.
26. Crabbe believed that religion would profit if theologians would stop accepting everything in the Bible as divinely inspired. He said to his son: "I believe that we do not differ much in our Ideas of the Inspiration of the Scriptures, if plenery & intire Inspiration be meant and I think that the Defenders of Christianity & the Authority of the old and new Testaments would rather gain than loose, by relaxing somewhat from the high Ground which they take in debating on this Matter." Ibid., p. 205.

Chapter 5

1. Howard Mills, ed., *George Crabbe: Tales, 1812 and Other Selected Poems*, p. xix.
2. J. L. and Barbara Hammond, *The Village Labourer 1760–1832*, p. 194; Chester Kirby, "English Game Law Reform," in *Essays in Modern English History in Honour of Wilbur Cortez Abbott* (Cambridge, Mass., 1941), p. 367.

3. In a footnote to "Smugglers and Poachers" Crabbe's son says, "The subject of 'Smugglers and Poachers' was suggested to Mr. Crabbe by Sir Samuel Romilly, on the 10th of September, 1818," *Poetical Works,* VII, 274. This particular piece of information must be treated with some reservation since there is no further corroboration. Romilly arrived at Cowes, in the Isle of Wight, on 3 September and stayed until the end of the month. If Crabbe's son is correct, then Romilly must have made his suggestion to Crabbe by letter. No such letter is extant. The letter of course may be lost, but since Crabbe's son was notoriously inaccurate with dates (he says Romilly died on 30 October, when actually he died on 2 November), possibly Romilly suggested the story at an earlier date.

4. In his *Memoirs,* Romilly records for Tuesday, 23 June: "A very pleasant dinner with Crabbe (whom I had never before seen)." *Memoirs of the Life of Sir Samuel Romilly* (London, 1840), III, 362.

5. Ibid., III, 275.

6. *Poetical Works,* VII, 275.

7. Kirby, "English Game Law Reform," p. 369.

8. Chester Kirby, "The English Game Law System," *American Historical Review,* XXXVIII (New York, 1933), 250.

9. The following works contain detailed commentary on the game laws: J. L. and Barbara Hammond, *The Village Labourer 1760–1832,* pp. 186–99; Chester Kirby, "English Game Law Reform," in *Essays in Modern English History in Honour of Wilbur Cortez Abbott* (Cambridge, Mass., 1941), pp. 345–80; Chester Kirby, "The English Game Law System," *American Historical Review,* XXXVIII (1933), 240–62; Charles Chenevix Trench, *The Poacher and the Squire* (London, 1967). The three *Reports* of the Select Committees (1816, 1823, 1828) contain invaluable evidence, although they must be used cautiously since in many cases the manner of questioning was designed to support the preconceived ideas of the committee members. Harriet Martineau's *Forest and Game-Law Tales* (London, 1845–46) offers an excellent summary of the problems caused by the game laws. Although Miss Martineau's game-law tales have little artistic merit they are among the best "literary" social documentaries to be found.

10. [Sydney Smith], review of *Three Letters on the Game Laws, Edinburgh Review,* XXXI, (1818–19), 295. Colonel Wood's Select Committee of 1816 had reported: "Your Committee conceive, that in the present state of society, there is little probability that the Laws above referred to [the game laws] can continue adequate to the object for which they were originally enacted." See p. 3 of *Report.*

11. Sir William Blackstone, *Commentaries on the Laws of England,* II (1765–69), 411–19.

12. Sir William Elford, *A Few Cursory Remarks on the Obnoxious Parts of the Game Laws*, 2nd ed., in *The Pamphleteer*, x (London, 1817), 21. I can find no copy of the 1st edition. The advertisement to the 2nd edition states that the pamphlet was first published "between twenty and thirty years ago."

13. This important act is 22–23 Car. II. c. 25.

14. For some examples, see William Marshall, *The Rural Economy of Norfolk,* 2nd ed. (London, 1795), I, 175. The first edition was published in 1787.

15. *Report from the Select Committee on the Laws Relating to Game* (1823), pp. 3–4.

16. This increase in the amount of game eaten by the wealthy people of the city is only one instance of the way in which the middle and lower classes were adopting the eating habits of their superiors. The increase in the consumption of tea and sugar by the lower classes throughout the eighteenth century is perhaps the best known instance of this trend.

17. *Report from the Select Committee* (1823), p. 4.

18. A. J. Peacock, *Bread or Blood* (London, 1965), p. 38.

19. *Report from the Select Committee* (1828), p. 78.

20. 39–40 Geo. III. c. 50. In Crabbe's county, Wiltshire, in the period from 17 May 1816, to June 1817, sixty-nine people were confined in houses of correction for offences against the game laws. See *Returns . . . of the Number of Persons . . . in Confinement in the different Gaols in England and Wales, for Offences against the Game Laws* (1817), p. 13.

21. 42 Geo. III. c. 107. Trench notes, "In the first sixty years of the eighteenth century there were only six acts directed against ordinary poaching of small game; in the next fifty-six years there were thirty-three such acts, most of them tightening up the law and increasing the penalties." *The Poacher and the Squire*, p. 124.

22. The Select Committees on the game laws discovered that the poachers were often gamekeepers and wealthy farmers. Some poulterers in Leadenhall market were supplied regularly with game by the owners of estates.

23. See the account of conditions of the labouring poor in *The Times,* 18 Dec. 1830.

24. Richard Burn, "Game," in *The Justice of the Peace* (1820), II, 530.

25. *Thoughts on the Expediency of Legalizing the Sale of Game* (London, 1823), p. 20. The author of this pamphlet is the same man who wrote *Three Letters on the Game Laws*. He was probably a country gentleman of Norfolk.

26. Burn, "Game," pp. 531–32. However, this provision was repealed by 48 Geo. III. c. 93.

27. This paternalistic attitude to the poor is found in a particularly repugnant form in Rev. Legh Richmond's *Dairyman's Daughter* (1809), with a reputed circulation of two million copies.

28. Potter Macqueen, *Thoughts and Suggestions on the present Condition of the Country*. Quoted from *The Times*, 18 Dec. 1830.

29. *The Prelude* I. 306–14, 1850 version, ed. E. de Selincourt (Oxford, 1926), p. 19.

30. "David Morris," l. 252, in *New Poems by George Crabbe*, ed. Arthur Pollard, p. 132.

31. *Report from the Select Committee* (1828), p. 91.

32. *Report from the Select Committee* (1823), p. 4.

33. Such generalizations positively invite debate. Nor is their verification by any means simple, since the supporting evidence—statements by working-class men and women—has not survived (nor could it be expected to survive). However, E. P. Thompson has shown that to some extent "there have always persisted popular attitudes towards crime, amounting at times to an unwritten code, quite distinct from the laws of the land." He concludes: "Rarely have the two codes been more sharply distinguished from each other than in the second half of the 18th century." *The Making of the English Working Class*, pp. 59–60.

34. Edward Christian, *A Treatise on the Game Laws* (London, 1817), p. 293.

35. Blackstone, *Commentaries*, II, 417.

36. Letter II, in *The Pamphleteer*, XI (1818), 351. The pagination is incorrect at this point and reads "451."

37. *Edinburgh Review*, XXXI (1818–19), 305.

38. Review of *Tales of the Hall*, *Christian Observer*, XVIII (1819), 665.

39. To J. Hatchard, 11 Nov. 1819, in *Romance of an Elderly Poet*, p. 243.

40. Note how easily the terms "smuggler" and "poacher" are intermixed in this argument.

41. D. H. Burden, "Crabbe and the Augustan Tradition," p. 90.

42. The poem first appeared in the volume of *The Edinburgh Annual Register* for the year 1809, published in 1811. See vol. II, pt. II, 591–95.

43. Scott to James Ballantyne, 23 Oct. 1810, in *The Letters of Sir Walter Scott*, ed. H. J. C. Grierson, I (1932–37), 412. Scott was not altogether correct in saying that Crabbe had never described a poacher. Crabbe included a sketch of the "rustic infidel" who "poach'd the wood, and on the warren snared" in "The Parish Register" I. 787–823.

44. René Huchon, *George Crabbe*, p. 434, n2.

45. Lockhart claims that this statement is to be found in Crabbe's son's biography. See J. G. Lockhart, *The Life of Sir Walter Scott* (Edinburgh, 1902), III, 288. However, Crabbe's biography contains no such statement.

46. Sir Walter Scott, *The Poetical Works of Sir Walter Scott,* ed. J. Logie Robertson (London, 1894), p. 712. The lines are unnumbered.

47. *Rights of Man,* 3rd ed. (London, 1791), pp. 61–62.

48. Lord Mountmorres told Fanny Burney that he thought the game laws would bring the French Revolution to England. See *Diary and Letters of Madame D'Arblay* (London, 1843), V, 76 (pt. II, for 1789).

49. Crabbe described the poacher in "The Parish Register" as one who called "the wants of rogues the rights of man" (I. 815).

50. The Game Law Act of 1671.

51. See Burn, "Game," p. 531.

52. *Edinburgh Review,* XXXI (1818–19), 301.

53. For confirmation of this point, see *Report from the Select Committee* (1828), pp. 90–91.

54. 43 Geo. III. c. 58. By this act ten new capital felonies were created.

55. Minor offences against the game laws were summarily judged by the local magistrates; serious offences were held over until the quarterly assizes. See Kirby, "The English Game Law System," p. 251.

56. *Report from the Select Committee* (1828), pp. 75–78.

57. Kirby, "English Game Law System," pp. 250–52.

58. Huchon, p. 462.

59. See Romilly's comments on the effect of prisons. *Memoirs,* III, 345, and *Observations on the Criminal Law of England* (London, 1810).

60. William Bryan Cooke explained how "the feeling of the common people appeared to be in favour of the murderer, and against the keeper." See the *Report from the Select Committee* (1828), p. 75.

61. E. P. Thompson, *The Making of the English Working Class,* pp. 82–83. Vicesimus Knox commented: "The employment of spies and informers is a virtual declaration of hostilities against the people. It argues a want of confidence in them. It argues a fear and jealousy of them. It argues a desire to destroy them by ambuscade. It is, in civil government, what stratagems are in a state of war." See *The Spirit of Despotism* (London, 1821), p. 34.

62. See Kirby, "English Game Law System," pp. 245–46. In 1796 Pitt proposed in the House that gamekeepers should be formed into a section of the militia. See William Cobbett's *Parliamentary History* (London, 1818), XXXII, 1211.

63. See *Report from the Select Committee* (1828), pp. 81–83.

64. G. R. Hibbard, "Crabbe and Shakespeare," pp. 92–93.

65. Crabbe to Hatchard, in *Romance of an Elderly Poet,* p. 243.

Chapter 6

1. That the word "moralist" is somewhat vague, I realize, but it is being used in Basil Willey's sense in *The English Moralists*, and as applied to such writers as Samuel Johnson, George Eliot, and Matthew Arnold, as one who instructs man in his ethical duties.
2. David Hume, *A Treatise of Human Nature*, ed. T. H. Green and T. H. Grose (London, 1874), II, 195 (bk. II, pt. III, sec. iii).
3. One of the jokes circulating at the time of publication of *Tales of the Hall* was the extent to which it dealt with love. Jeffrey commented: "It is rather remarkable, too, that Mr C. seems to become more amorous as he grows older,—the interest of almost all the stories in this collection turning on the tender passion." *Edinburgh Review*, XXXII (1819), 126.
4. Compare Crabbe's treatment of the motives of those who help to finance the building of the hospital in *The Borough*, Letter XVII.
5. Jane Austen, *Emma*, in *The Novels of Jane Austen*, ed. R. W. Chapman, p. 83 (vol. I, chap. X). Emma is well aware that her feeling of compassion for the poor will vanish relatively quickly.
6. John Moore, *Mordaunt*, ed. W. L. Renwick (London, 1965), pp. 312-13 (Letter 64).
7. Robert and Samuel Wilberforce, *The Life of William Wilberforce* (London, 1839), I, 238.
8. If one compares Miss Burney's treatment of the same topic in *Cecilia*, one can appreciate Crabbe's development of a difficult subject. When Cecilia is disappointed in her expectations of London life, she turns to help the poor. But Miss Burney does not appreciate the irony implicit in this decision. She attempts to portray Cecilia's good works as being motivated *only* by altruism. See *Cecilia*, 4th ed. (London, 1784), I, 88.
9. Robert and Samuel Wilberforce, *Life of Wilberforce*, I, 238.
10. This story has obvious similarities to "The Patron" (Tale V, *Tales*) and "David Morris."
11. *Life*, chap. IX, pp. 221, 260-61.
12. To George Crabbe Jr., *c.* 1834, in *Life*, chap. X, p. 301.
13. To Miss Elizabeth Charter, 9 Nov. 1824, in *Romance of an Elderly Poet*, *p.* 273.
14. To Miss Elizabeth Charter, *c.* 25 Nov. 1815, ibid., p. 116.
15. Although the Romantics emphasized the workings of the unconscious, the idea was by no means new with them. Pope had said: "Oft in the Passions' wild rotation tost, / Our spring of action to ourselves is lost" (*Moral Essays*, I. 41-42). And Johnson commented: "Consider the state of mankind, and inquire how few can be supposed to act upon any

occasions, whether small or great, with all the reasons of action present to their minds" (*Rasselas,* chap. XXIX).

16. In the late eighteenth century, moral philosophers placed great emphasis upon the role of man's habits in determining his actions. James Beattie noted: "Something, no doubt, depends on the peculiar constitution of different minds; and something too perhaps on the structure and temperament of different bodies: but in fashioning the character, and in giving impulse and direction to genius, the influence of habit is certainly very great." *Elements of Moral Science* (Edinburgh, 1790), I, 227–28.

17. Since most of the characters in *Tales of the Hall* are not in danger of falling into poverty, no urgent economic reason exists for late marriage.

18. Concerned for the sanctity of marriage, Maria Edgeworth permits one of her characters to argue for a standard of marriage which cuts across human values. She says, "Nothing could tend more to prevent the ill conduct of women in high life, than the certainty that men who, from their fortune, birth, and character, might be deemed the most desirable matches, would shun alliances with the *daughters* of women of tainted reputation" (my italics). *Patronage*, 2nd ed. (London, 1814), I, 131.

19. Robert L. Chamberlain, *George Crabbe*, p. 116.

20. Many people believed in ghosts. In 1778 Dr. Johnson said, "It is wonderful that five thousand years have now elapsed since the creation of the world, and still it is undecided whether or not there has ever been an instance of the spirit of any person appearing after death. All argument is against it; but all belief is for it." *Life of Johnson*, III, 230. Boswell's own fear of ghosts was notorious. See *Boswell's London Journal*, ed. F. A. Pottle (New York, 1950), p. 214.

21. Although it seems obvious by the end of the poem that Crabbe does not believe in Lady Barbara's ghost, the reviewer for *The British Critic* certainly seems to have believed Crabbe meant to portray a real ghost. *British Critic*, n.s., XII (1819), 298.

22. To Mary Leadbeater, 26 March 1824, in *The Leadbeater Papers* (London, 1862), II, 385.

23. *An Essay on Man* I, 189–90, ed. Maynard Mack, Twickenham edition (London, 1950), p. 38.

24. Compare the character of Scythrop (modelled on Shelley) in *Nightmare Abbey:* "In the congenial solitude of Nightmare Abbey, the distempered ideas of metaphysical romance and romantic metaphysics had ample time and space to germinate into a fertile crop of chimeras, which rapidly shot up into vigorous and abundant vegetation." *The Novels of Thomas Love Peacock,* ed. David Garnett (London, 1963), p. 362.

25. Percy Bysshe Shelley, *The Defence of Poetry,* in Percy Reprints (Blackwell: Oxford, 1923), p. 33.

26. *Defence of Poetry*, p. 27.

27. Writing to Boswell about melancholy (11 Sept. 1777), Johnson said, "That distrust which intrudes so often on your mind is a mode of melancholy, which, if it be the business of a wise man to be happy, it is foolish to indulge; and if it be a duty to preserve our faculties entire for their proper use, it is criminal." Boswell's *Life of Johnson*, ed. G. B. Hill and L. F. Powell (Clarendon Press: Oxford, 1934–65), III, 135.

28. "The Human Abstract," in *Songs of Innocence and Experience* (1789–94), in *The Complete Writings of William Blake*, ed. G. Keynes (London, 1966), p. 217.

29. *Life*, chap. IX, pp. 219–20.

30. Ibid., p. 260.

31. *Blackwood's Edinburgh Magazine*, V (July 1819), 473.

32. Sir F. M. Eden, *The State of the Poor*, I, 404.

33. *Poems by George Crabbe*, "Variants Section," III, 527.

34. Soame Jenyns is an excellent example. He remarked: "Superior beings may probably form to themselves, or receive from their Creator, government without tyranny or corruption, and religions without delusions or absurdities; but man cannot: God indeed may remove him into so exalted a society; but whilst he continues to be man, he must be subject to innumerable evils; amongst which those I call political and religious are far from being the least." *A Free Inquiry into the Nature and Origin of Evil*, in *The Works of Soame Jenyns*, II, 87–88 (Letter V).

35. Once again Crabbe is pointing out that much of the distress in England is caused, not by the malevolence of the wealthy, but by their lack of real concern for the lower orders. As Vicesimus Knox commented, "Indifference is scarcely less culpable than corruption." *The Spirit of Despotism* (London, 1821), p. 9.

36. In *The Borough*, the innkeeper comments: "The instant you enter my door you're my lord" (in prefatory poem to Letter XI).

37. *Monthly Review*, XC (November 1819), 237.

38. Not only for alehouse keepers, but perhaps for the gentry as well. George would have married Rosabella in spite of her many liaisons had she been able to reform her life as had Frances.

39. *Edinburgh Review*, XXXII (1819), 145.

40. John Wilson's comment in *Blackwood's Edinburgh Magazine*, V (July 1819), 472.

41. An ordained minister, John became Crabbe's curate.

42. To Miss Elizabeth Charter, 26 March 1819, in *Romance of an Elderly Poet*, p. 230.

43. 23 Aug. 1815. Ibid., p. 103.

44. See *Romance of an Elderly Poet*, pp. 42–47.

45. Miss Hoare told Crabbe's son that Johnson gave Crabbe the following advice at their second meeting in London: "Never fear putting the strongest and best things you can think of into the mouth of your speaker, whatever may be his condition." See *Life,* chap. IV, p. 100.
46. In Tale I of *Tales,* Crabbe employs a similar technique when he contrasts the Tory, Justice Bolt, with the Radical, Hammond.
47. *Life,* chap. VII, pp. 175–76.
48. For Trowbridge, Aldborough, and the University of Cambridge. See Huchon, p. 454, n2.
49. Lockhart to John Wilson Croker, 26 Jan. 1835, in Myron F. Brightfield, *John Wilson Croker* (London, 1940), p. 265, n118.
50. To George Crabbe Jr., 28 June 1826, in René Huchon, *George Crabbe,* p. 455, n2. Significantly enough, the election was unopposed.
51. To Miss Elizabeth Charter, 11 Feb. 1817, in *Romance of an Elderly Poet,* pp. 154–55.
52. To George Crabbe Jr., 4 Feb. 1831, in F. M. Link, ed., "Three Crabbe Letters," p. 206.
53. *Life,* chap. X, pp. 311–13.
54. To George Crabbe Jr., n.d., in Huchon, p. 456.
55. *The Age of Reform 1815–1870,* Oxford History of England series (Oxford, 1938), p. 77.
56. Compare Croker's statement in a letter of late November or early December 1831 to Lord Hertford: "I find that those who some months ago derided my alarms are now at least as much frightened as I am." See *The Croker Papers,* ed. Louis Jennings (London, 1884), II, 140.
57. The second bill had passed the Commons in September 1831, after a session of three months; it was defeated in the House of Lords on 8 Oct. 1831, after a debate of five days. The rejection of the bill precipitated riots in Nottingham, Derby, and Bristol.
58. To George Crabbe Jr., 24 Oct. 1831, in *Life,* chap. X, pp. 310–11.
59. Huchon, p. 456.
60. Once Crabbe made up his mind to support a particular person in politics, nothing would dissuade him. Bowles tells how "a riotous, tumultuous, and most appalling mob" besieged Crabbe's house when they learned he was planning to give his vote to an unpopular candidate: "In the face of the furious assemblage, he came out calmly, told them they might kill him if they chose, but, whilst alive, nothing should prevent his giving a vote at the election, according to his promise and principles, and set off, undisturbed and unhurt, to vote for Mr. Benett." *Life,* chap. IX, pp. 220–21.
61. MS sermon on "Epistle to the Hebrews" 2nd and 3rd Verse, in the John Murray Collection. Several other sermons contain similar emendations.

62. Crabbe made a practice of noting the date and place every time he preached his sermons. The first entry is for 22 February 1829, Trowbridge, and the last is 21 April 1833, preached at Hadescoe Toft. As Crabbe died 3 February 1832, it is clear that his son George took over the sermons. I suggest that it was George and not John who used Crabbe's sermons after his death because the sermons carry the note that they were preached at Pucklechurch, George's vicarage until 1834.

63. *Romance of an Elderly Poet*, pp. 214–15.

64. To George Crabbe Jr., 7 May 1827, in Huchon, p. 455.

65. Johnson gives the following definition in his *Dictionary*: "Tory. (A cant term, derived, I suppose, from an Irish word signifying a savage.) One who adheres to the ancient constitution of the state, and the apostolical hierarchy of the church of England, opposed to a whig."

66. *Life*, chap. IX, pp. 221–22, n1.

67. *Edinburgh Review*, XXXII (1819), 126.

68. This change of opinion about the Dissenters can be seen in the opinions he expressed in his new church at Trowbridge. At Muston he had preached against the Dissenters; at Trowbridge, he accepted them warmly. See *Life*, chap. IX, pp. 221–22.

69. Crabbe "hailed the beginning of the French Revolution." *Life*, chap. VII, p. 174.

70. 6 April 1780.

71. *Poems*, II, 487–88.

72. Ibid., p. 488.

73. Ibid.

74. It is often difficult to be certain when irony is intended in discussions of social or political reform at this period. Arguments that a person of today would think conclusive reasons for effecting change were often used in the late eighteenth and early nineteenth centuries to show the impossibility of change. For instance Soame Jenyns opens his *Thoughts on a Parliamentary Reform* by saying, "The great object of a parliamentary reform I take to be this, to procure a parliament totally independent on the crown and its ministers; in which no member shall be intimidated by power, seduced by hopes, or corrupted by interest." But the modern reader is sadly mistaken if he thinks Soame Jenyns to be in favour of such a reform. See *Thoughts on a Parliamentary Reform*, 2nd ed. (London, 1784), pp. 1–2.

75. Crabbe's son quotes the letter in *Life*, chap. VII, p. 178. But he does not say to whom the letter was written, nor does he give its date.

76. Crabbe is making an obvious reference to Tom Paine's *Rights of Man* (1791), the influence of which can hardly be overestimated at this period. See E. P. Thompson, *The Making of the English Working Class*, pp. 87–114.

77. That Crabbe refused to condemn the Radicals can be seen again in Tale I of *Tales* where he presents the Radical Hammond who called "loudly for reform" and "hail'd the prospect of the storm" (*Tales* I. 237–38). Crabbe presents Hammond as a salutary example to the reactionary Justice Bolt who believes England's government is perfect and that her church leaves nothing "to mend or to restore" (*Tales* I. 405). While Crabbe does not agree with the Radicals in their call to revolution, he is prepared to acknowledge that they serve a purpose in counteracting the much more powerful forces of reaction.
78. Lilian Haddakin, *Poetry of Crabbe*, p. 167.

Conclusion

1. Francis Jeffrey, *Edinburgh Review*, XXXII (1819), 140. For a similar comment see Lilian Haddakin, *Poetry of Crabbe*, p. 14.
2. See Raymond Williams, "Pastoral and Counter Pastoral," in *Critical Quarterly*, X (1968), 277–78.
3. *Poems*, I, 66.
4. Ibid.
5. See, for instance, William Smellie's *The Philosophy of Natural History* (Edinburgh, 1790–99).
6. See above, p. 223.
7. To Miss Hoare, 27 Jan. 1829, in *Romance of an Elderly Poet*, p. 293.
8. For these last two poems, see *New Poems by George Crabbe*, ed. Arthur Pollard.

Select bibliography

Editions of George Crabbe's Poetry

Poems by George Crabbe, ed. Adolphus W. Ward. 3 vols. London, 1905–1907.
The Poetical Works of the Rev. George Crabbe, ed. George Crabbe Jr. 8 vols.
London, 1834. Vol. I contains the *Life*.
New Poems by George Crabbe, ed. Arthur Pollard. Liverpool University
Press, 1960.

Other works of George Crabbe

BROADLEY, A. M. and JERROLD, WALTER, ed. *The Romance of an Elderly Poet*.
London, 1913.
BRUMBAUGH, THOMAS B., ed. "George Crabbe: An Unpublished Sermon,"
Notes and Queries, n.s., VIII (1961), 20–21.
BULBOUGH, GEOFFREY, ed. "A Letter of Crabbe to Scott," *Times Literary
Supplement*, 22 Sept. 1932, p. 666.
[CRABBE, GEORGE]. "Biographical Account of the Rev. George Crabbe,
L.L.B.," *New Monthly Magazine*, IV (1815), 511–17. Crabbe published
this account of his life anonymously.
DAVENPORT, WILLIAM H., ed. "An Uncollected Poem by George Crabbe,"
Notes and Queries, CLXXV (1938), 471.
FORSTER, E. M., ed. "Crabbe on Smugglers; an Unpublished Letter,"
Spectator, CXLVIII (20 Feb. 1932), 245.
HASTINGS, JOHN D., ed. *Posthumous Sermons by the Rev. George Crabbe*.
London, 1850.
LINK, F. M., ed. "Three Crabbe Letters," *English Language Notes*, II (1965),
200–206.

POLLARD, ARTHUR, ed. "Two New Letters of Crabbe," *Review of English Studies*, n.s., II (October 1951), 375–77.

WECTER, DIXON, ed. "Four Letters from George Crabbe to Edmund Burke," *Review of English Studies*, XIV (July 1938), 298.

Critical Studies of George Crabbe

AINGER, ALFRED. *Crabbe*. English Men of Letters series. London, 1903.

BATDORF, FRANKLIN P. "The Background of Crabbe's Village," *Notes and Queries*, CXCIV (1949), 477–78.

BRETT, R. L. *George Crabbe*. British Council "Writers and their Work" series. London, 1956.

BREWER, A. M. "Crabbe and Eighteenth Century Pastoral." Ph.D. thesis. University of Nottingham, 1951.

BREWSTER, ELIZABETH. "George Crabbe and William Wordsworth." *University of Toronto Quarterly*, XLII (Winter 1973), 142–55.

———. "Two Friends: George Crabbe and Sir Walter Scott," *Queen's Quarterly*, LXXVIII (1971), 602–13.

BROMAN, WALTER. "Factors in Crabbe's Eminence in the Early Nineteenth Century," *Modern Philology*, LI (August 1953), 42–49.

BROWN, WALLACE CABLE. *The Triumph of Form*. Chapel Hill, 1948. Chap. VII.

BURDEN, D. H. "Crabbe and the Augustan Tradition," in *Essays and Poems Presented to Lord David Cecil*, ed. W. W. Robson. London, 1970. Pp. 77–92.

CHAMBERLAIN, ROBERT L. *George Crabbe*. Twayne Series. New York, 1965.

———. "Unpublished Poetry of Crabbe from the Murray MS. Collection: With an Introductory Essay on Crabbe." Ph.D. thesis. Syracuse University, 1950.

CHILD, HAROLD. "George Crabbe," in *The Cambridge History of English Literature*, ed. A. W. Ward and A. R. Waller. New ed. Cambridge, 1932. XI, 140–152.

CRUTTWELL, PATRICK. "The Last Augustan," *Hudson Review*, VII (1954), 533–54.

DIFFEY, CAROLE T. "Journey to Experience: Crabbe's 'Silford Hall'." *Durham University Journal*, n.s., XXX (1969), 129–34.

EVANS, J. H. *The Poems of George Crabbe: A Literary & Historical Study*. London, 1933.

FORSTER, E. M. "George Crabbe and Peter Grimes," *Two Cheers for Democracy*. London, 1951.

———. Introduction to *The Life of George Crabbe*. World's Classics ed. London, 1932.

GALLON, D. N. "Silford Hall or the Happy Day," *Modern Language Review*, LXI (1966), 384–94.

GREGOR, IAN. "The Last Augustan," *Dublin Review*, CLXXIX (First Quarter 1955), 37–50.

HADDAKIN, LILIAN. *The Poetry of Crabbe*. London, 1955.

HAYTER, ALETHEA. *Opium and the Romantic Imagination*. London, 1968.

HAZLITT, WILLIAM. *The Spirit of the Age*. London, 1825.

HEATH-STUBBS, J. "Crabbe and the Eighteenth Century," *Penguin New Writing*, XXV (1945), 129–45.

HIBBARD, G. R. "Crabbe and Shakespeare," in *Renaissance and Modern Essays*, ed. G. R. Hibbard. London, 1966.

HUCHON, RENÉ. *George Crabbe and his Times 1754–1832*, trans. Frederick Clarke. London, 1907.

HUMPHREYS, A. L. *Piccadilly Bookmen: Memorials of the House of Hatchard*. London, 1893.

JEFFREY, FRANCIS. Review articles in *Edinburgh Review*, XII (1808), 131–51; XVI (1810), 30–55; XX (1812), 277–305; XXXII (1819), 118–48.

KEBBEL, T. E. *Life of George Crabbe*. London, 1888.

LANG, VARLEY HOWE. *Crabbe and the Eighteenth Century*. Baltimore, 1938.

LEAVIS, F. R. *Revaluation*. London, 1936.

LUCAS, F. L. Introduction to *George Crabbe: An Anthology*. Cambridge, 1933.

MILLS, HOWARD, ed. Introduction to *George Crabbe: Tales, 1812 and Other Selected Poems*. Cambridge, 1967.

MORE, PAUL ELMER. *Shelburne Essays*. 2nd series. New York and London, 1905.

POLLARD, ARTHUR. "A Study of Crabbe's Thought on Christian Duty and Doctrine; And its Place in His Poetry." Ph.D. thesis. Oxford, 1952.

———. ed. *Crabbe: The Critical Heritage*. London, 1972.

POUND, EZRA. "The Rev. G. Crabbe," *The Literary Essays of Ezra Pound*. London, 1954.

SAINTSBURY, GEORGE. "George Crabbe," in *The Collected Essays and Papers of George Saintsbury*. London, 1923. I, 1–25.

SALE, ARTHUR. "The Development of Crabbe's Narrative Art," *Cambridge Journal*, V (May 1952), 480–92.

———. Introduction to *The Village*. London, 1950.

SIGWORTH, OLIVER F. *Nature's Sternest Painter*. Tucson, 1965.

STEPHEN, LESLIE. "Crabbe's Poetry," *Hours in a Library*. 2nd series.
New ed. London, 1892.
THOMAS, W. K. "Crabbe's Borough: the Process of Montage,"
University of Toronto Quarterly, XXXVI (1967) 181–92.
———. "Crabbe's Workhouse," *Huntingdon Library Quarterly*, XXXII
(1969), 149–61.
———. "Crabbe's View of the Poor," *Revue de l'Université d'Ottawa*, XXXVI
(1966), 453–85.
———. "George Crabbe: Not Quite the Sternest," *Studies in Romanticism*,
VII (Spring 1968), 166–75.
TOLIVER, HAROLD E. *Pastoral Forms and Attitudes*. Berkeley, Calif., 1971.
WHITEHEAD, FRANK, ed. *George Crabbe: Selections from His Poetry*.
London, 1955.
WILLIAMS, RAYMOND. "Pastoral and Counter Pastoral," *Critical Quarterly*,
X (1967), 277–90.
WINN, NORMAN FIELD. "The Treatment of Humble Life in the Poetry of
George Crabbe and William Wordsworth." Ph.D. thesis.
University of Washington, 1955.

A list of eighteenth and nineteenth-century reviews of Crabbe's poetry
is given in Huchon, pp. 523–28.

Index